Making Use of PHP

D1473225

Making Use of PHP

Ashok Appu

Wiley Publishing, Inc.

Publisher: Robert Ipsen
Editor: Ben Ryan
Developmental Editor: Kathryn A. Malm
Managing Editor: Pamela Hanley
New Media Editor: Brian Snapp
Text Design & Composition: J. Wiley Composition Services

Designations used by companies to distinguish their products are often claimed as trademarks. In all instances where Wiley Publishing, Inc., is aware of a claim, the product names appear in initial capital or ALL CAPITAL LETTERS. Readers, however, should contact the appropriate companies for more complete information regarding trademarks and registration.

This book is printed on acid-free paper. ∞

Copyright © 2002 by NIIT (USA) Inc. All rights reserved.

Published by Wiley Publishing, Inc.

Published simultaneously in Canada.

No part of this publication may be reproduced, stored in a retrieval system or transmitted in any form or by any means, electronic, mechanical, photocopying, recording, scanning or otherwise, except as permitted under Sections 107 or 108 of the 1976 United States Copyright Act, without either the prior written permission of the Publisher, or authorization through payment of the appropriate per-copy fee to the Copyright Clearance Center, 222 Rosewood Drive, Danvers, MA 01923, (978) 750-8400, fax (978) 750-4744. Requests to the Publisher for permission should be addressed to the Permissions Department, John Wiley & Sons, Inc., 605 Third Avenue, New York, NY 10158-0012, (212) 850-6011, fax (212) 850-6008, E-Mail: PERMREQ @ WILEY.COM.

This publication is designed to provide accurate and authoritative information in regard to the subject matter covered. It is sold with the understanding that the publisher is not engaged in professional services. If professional advice or other expert assistance is required, the services of a competent professional person should be sought.

Library of Congress Cataloging-in-Publication Data:

ISBN: 0-471-21973-8

Wiley also publishes its books in a variety of electronic formats. Some content that appears in print may not be available in electronic books.

Printed in the United States of America.

10   9   8   7   6   5   4   3   2   1

Contents

Introduction

In today's information world, many individuals, organizations, and enterprises want to bring applications to the Web. In this environment, PHP (Hypertext Preprocessor) is one of the scripting languages that has emerged as a world leader. PHP is a server-side scripting language that is platform independent. It is used to write dynamically generated Web pages quickly. It can also be used to create database-driven Web sites for e-commerce, community portals, and other Web-based applications. Today, PHP is probably the most widely used non-Microsoft scripting language. PHP can be deployed over Windows platforms running IIS and SQL and over Linux platforms running Apache Web server and MySQL. Endorsements for PHP include the following from Nathan Wallace.

*Nathan Wallace has spent the last two years running Synop, a PHP development company. He built and maintains the PHP Knowledge Base as part of http://www.faqts.com. After 18 months of development and refinement, Synop is in the release process for a number of large PHP applications. See also URL: http://conferences.oreillynet.com/cs/os2001/view/e_spkr/700.

Low cost, greater flexibility, high stability, and ease of development — PHP is fast emerging as the right choice for personal or commercial use on a small or large scale!

One of the great things about PHP is that it requires almost no specific training for a programmer to pick it up and start doing interesting things. In fact, the language is so simple that most of the training really needs to go into more general Web programming concepts such as form handling, request sequences and code structure.

The tremendous growth of e-business has resulted in a demand for fast and reliable Web applications. The only way for companies to be successful in e-business is to have experts who can create such Web applications. This book bridges the ever-increasing gap between the market demand and the availability of such expertise. The first step to becoming an expert is to get an in-depth knowledge of the scripting language, PHP, which is exactly what this book offers. It begins with the basics of scripting and seamlessly moves on to the intricacies. Along with the conceptual information, this book also provides extensive practical exercises that allow the reader to gain valuable real-life exposure to creating different types of applications.

The aim of this book is to make learning an enjoyable and energizing experience.

How This Book Is Organized

This book moves away from the traditional content-based approach and uses the problem-solving approach to deliver the concepts of PHP. Problems used in the book are presented against the backdrop of real-life scenarios. Each problem is followed by a task list that helps to solve the given problem while explaining the concepts and their implementation. This practical approach will help readers understand the application of the language and its usage in various scenarios.

Chapter 1 introduces the essential Internet concepts that a reader should be aware of before proceeding to other chapters. This chapter provides an introduction to frequently used Internet terminology and also gives a brief introduction to types of scripting languages.

Chapter 2 is a getting-started guide that discusses the basics of PHP. This chapter steps through the procedure used to install and configure PHP on Linux and Windows platform. Then, it covers basic concepts of HTML as a refresher. Finally, it discusses the basic syntax of PHP and how to execute PHP scripts on the command prompt and how to view the output of PHP scripts in the browser.

Chapter 3 introduces the programming basics of PHP. The chapter covers concepts such as data types and operators that are used in PHP.

Chapter 4 covers concepts related to control structures. The chapter begins with an introduction to control structures, then discusses the conditional statements, and finally discusses loops and how they are used in PHP.

Chapter 5 introduces the concept of functions. It discusses the types of functions and the difference between user-defined and built-in functions and then discusses the concept of creating a user-defined function.

Chapter 6 introduces the concept of arrays. It begins with an introduction to arrays and moves on to creating enumerated and associative arrays. Then, it discusses the concept of looping through arrays and how arrays can be manipulated in PHP.

Chapter 7 introduces the concept of classes. The chapter begins with an introduction to object-oriented programming and how it is implemented with PHP. Then, it discusses the basics of classes and objects and covers the concepts of creating and using classes and objects in PHP.

Chapter 8 covers the concept of form parsing using PHP. This chapter discusses how data entered in an HTML form can be directed to a PHP script for calculation.

Chapter 9 introduces the concept of using and manipulating files and their content with PHP. It introduces several built-in file-related functions in PHP that can be used to perform file-related tasks.

Chapter 10 gives an introduction to database concepts and discusses how they are used with Web applications. It also discusses the basic syntax that is used to perform tasks on the database server.

Chapter 11 gives a detailed explanation of how built-in functions are used in PHP for database interactivity. It discusses how to write PHP code to automate database interactions and explains how user input accepted in an HTML form can be stored and retrieved from a database.

Chapter 12 discusses database authentication. It introduces the basic concept of authentication and moves on to how passwords are stored, retrieved, and checked when a user is authenticated. The chapter also introduces built-in functions that are used to securely store passwords in the database.

Chapter 13 discusses the concept of cookies and how they are implemented using PHP. It also discusses the built-in functions that are used to set cookies on the client-side and then read them.

Chapter 14 discusses sessions. The chapter begins with an introduction to how sessions are used on the server side to maintain the state of dynamic Web applications and then discusses the various session-related built-in functions that are used in PHP.

Chapter 15 discusses the concept of email and how it can be sent using PHP. It also discusses the built-in mail() function that is used to send mail using PHP.

Who Should Read This Book

This book is a guide for readers who have basic knowledge of programming. It is also of great help to the following people:

- Software engineers
- Web application developers
- Information application developers

Tools You Will Need

For performing the tasks in this book, you will need a Pentium 200-MHz computer with a minimum of 64 MB of RAM (128 MB of RAM is recommended). You will also need the following software:

- Operating system: Linux 7.2 or Windows 2000 Server
- Web server: Apache 1.3.20 (on Linux) and IIS 5.0 (on Windows)
- Netscape Navigator 4.78 (On Linux)
- RDBMS: MySQL 3.23.41
- PHP 4.0.6

What's on the CD-ROM, Disk, and Web Site

The following is available on the site www.wiley/compbooks/appu.com:

- PHP 4.0.6
- All the code snippets used in the book.

Scenario

All problem statements in this book are based on the scenario of the Mega Music Mart, an online CD store. The following section elaborates on the setup of the Mega Music Mart.

Mega Music Mart: The Complete Music Shop

Mega Music Mart is a renowned music store in the United States of America. It has shopping stores located in almost every city of the United States. Recently, Craig Osbourne, the CEO of Mega Music Mart, has decided to increase operations and invest in an online shopping store that will allow users from anywhere in the world to buy CDs from Mega Music Mart. After several discussions with his marketing and sales teams, he has decided to introduce another department that will create, deploy, and maintain the site. This department will primarily consist of developers who write the code for the site and a system administrator who will maintain the operating system and the database server. Craig has appointed Steve Wilkinson as the head of the development team. Steve's responsibilities include coordinating with development team and at the same time strategizing for improvement initiatives for the site. The system administrator, Rick Mustaine, is responsible for the proper functioning of the site and for ensuring site availability at all times. Rick works hand-in-hand with the development team to check whether the code is developed in a way that it doesn't adversely affect the security of the Web site and also is optimized in a way that the least possible system memory is used.

Site Architecture

Though there were several options, the development team and Rick decided that the site would be deployed on Apache Web server on a Red Hat Linux 7.2 platform. The backend server will be MySQL and it will be used to store site-related data. The members of the development team have suggested to use PHP to create the site. The following will be the structure of the site:

- The site will implement a shopping cart that will accept valid global credit cards for payment for the CDs bought online.
- In order to purchase CDs, each user will need to create a login in the site. After a user creates a login, all personal details pertaining to that user will be stored in a table in the database. This information will be used from time to time and will also be updated as and when a user purchases CDs.

The music CDs will be categorized on the basis of the following genre:

- Rock
- Heavy Metal
- Rap
- Jazz
- Pop

Features of the Site

The user interface will primarily contain the following:

- There will be a home page that will contain news updates related to the music front and links to other music site. The home page will also contain a link to the sign up page where new users can choose a login ID and password.
- The login details of a user will be stored in a database.
- The user will be able to browse music CDs on the basis of the genre.
- The user will also be able to search for Music CDs by the artist name or CD title.
- A feedback section on the Web site will be included that will allow users to provide feedback based on their past experiences with the site.

Future Plans

As a part of the future plans, Craig along with his marketing team has decided to implement the following:

Improve the CD collection by adding CDs in the following music categories:

- Grunge
- Trance
- Classical
- Fusion
- Country

- Introduce a new range of clothing that would include sweatshirts, headbands, jackets, and carry bags with the Mega Music Mart Logo. These would also be available for purchase online.

- Create a section for song lyrics where lyrics of various songs by various artists will be available in text files and will be freely downloadable.

- Introduce a section for upcoming rock bands. This section will contain unreleased versions of songs by various upcoming rock bands. The songs will be available in MP3 format and will be available for free download for registered users.

Internet Basics

OBJECTIVES:

In this lesson, you will learn to:
- ✓ Identify the features of the Internet
- ✓ Identify the terminology used in connection with the Internet
- ✓ Discuss cross-browser compatibility
- ✓ Distinguish between client- and server-side scripting languages

Getting Started

Ever since the advent of computers, researchers have indulged in a continuous quest to bring the world closer through computers. This effort gave rise to the Internet. It is through the Internet that today millions of people communicate and share information, regardless of their location. This chapter will focus on the basics of the Internet and also shed light upon how the Internet works.

Introducing the Internet

The Internet can be defined as a network of globally connected computers that is decentralized by design. This definition can be broken down into three parts. Let's understand each part of the definition in isolation.

Is a network.   A network is a collection of computers. The Internet can also be referred to as a network because it is a collection of millions of computers.

Globally connected computers.   This means that you can be connected to the Internet, regardless of your location. The Internet has brought people in the world closer by connecting computers located in the remotest of locations.

Decentralized design.   The Internet has a decentralized design. That is, there is no centralized body that controls the way in which the Internet functions. The Internet does provide online services that are centrally administered, but as a whole, it would not be incorrect to say that the Internet has a decentralized design. Each computer connected to the Internet is called a *host*. The operator/user of a particular host can choose from the millions of available Internet services and can also make services available through the Internet.

Internet Terminology

To understand how the Internet works, it is a good idea to first be familiar with the terms that are commonly used in connection with the Internet. These terms are discussed in the following subsections.

Client

A client is any computer on the network that requests services from another computer on the network. To be able to request services and access the resources present on some other computer on the network, the client should have adequate access permissions.

Server

A server is a computer that receives requests from client computers, processes these requests, and sends the output to the respective client computers that had placed the requests. The range of services that a server can offer a client is based on the permissions possessed by the client. The server computer defines these permissions.

Client-Server Network

Client-server network is one of the most basic common architectures that is used for computer connectivity. In this type of network, several client computers are connected to the server and also to each other. Client computers request services from the server computer, and the server accepts or rejects these requests. The server computer is also responsible for storing relevant information that is frequently used by the client

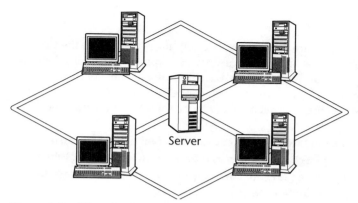

Figure 1.1   Client-Server Network.

most suited for a setup that has a large number of clients. Figure 1.1 illustrates how client computers are connected to the server.

In the Internet scenario, each user, typically a client, connects to a Web site that is hosted on a server. The user then requests services from this server, and depending on the permissions possessed by the user, the server processes these requests.

Web Server

A Web server is a computer that is dedicated to provide Web services to clients on the Internet. Web services are often provided through Web sites that are hosted on a Web server that is accessed by a client. However, before the clients can access the site, it is preferable to register the domain name at a Domain Name Service.

Browser

To access the content of a Web site, users must have a browser that can help them locate a Web site on the Internet and then view the content of a Web page. Users can also use the browser to download and upload files on the Internet. A few popular browsers that are used worldwide are Internet Explorer, Netscape Navigator, and Opera. To access a Web site, a user needs to specify an address that helps the browser track a particular Web site.

URL

A unique resource locator (URL) is a link that is used to access a Web site on the Internet. A URL is unique to each site, and is typically based on the nature of the site. Without specifying a valid URL, users cannot access a particular site. For example, to access the official Web site for PHP, the user will need to specify the URL www.php.net.

ISP

Internet service providers (ISPs) are companies that help users connect to the Internet for a monthly fee. In return, they provide a username, a password, and telephone number. The username and the password are used to authenticate the user on the Internet. The telephone number is used to establish connection with the dial-up server of the ISP. However, to access the Internet a user (client computer) requires a modem.

TIP In addition to providing Internet services to individual users, ISPs also provide Internet services to large companies in return for an annual fee. When such a company subscribes to an ISP, the company provides Internet access to all the computers on the corporate network.

Modem

To access the Internet, a user requires a hardware device called a modem. The word *modem* originated from the words *modulator* and *demodulator*. A modem transmits data over telephone lines as analog signals and then converts them digital signals that can be interpreted by a computer.

Web Page

Any page that is hosted on the Internet is a Web page. A Web page is viewed by using a browser. The basic framework of Web pages can be designed using a language called *HyperText Markup Language (HTML)*.

Web Development

Web development is the process of creating Web pages for a Web site that will be hosted on the Internet. You can use a combination of HTML and other scripting languages to develop interactive Web pages.

NOTE Scripting languages are discussed later in the chapter under the heading *Scripting Languages*.

Site Hosting

To enable people to access your site, you need to host it. You can either host the site on your own Web server or you can buy space from a Web site–hosting company. In either case, you need a registered domain name. Besides providing space, site-hosting companies also register your domain name. If you don't have adequate funds to host your own site, buying space from a known Web-hosting company would be an intelligent choice.

TIP It is advisable to register your domain name with well-known search engines such as Google, Lycos, and Exite. This makes your site more popular and easily accessible to users.

Access Methods

Access methods refer to the means of accessing sites on the Internet. There are two access methods that you can use to access the Internet. Let's discuss them.

Dial-up Connection

A dial-up connection is the access method that uses telephone lines to connect to the Internet. It is the most common way that individuals who use home computers connect to the Internet. To connect to the Internet by using dial up, the user needs to specify a username, a password, and a telephone number. After the connection is established, the user can start browsing sites on the Internet. Figure 1.2 illustrates a dial-up connection.

Leased Lines

Another popular method of accessing sites on the Internet is through leased lines. These lines maintain a dedicated connection with the Internet. Unlike dial-up connections, a user need not connect to the Internet using a modem. Leased lines are faster than dial-up connections because they can handle higher data transmission speed. Figure 1.3 depicts a corporate network connected to the Internet by using a leased line.

Bandwidth

Bandwidth refers to the rate of data transfer over the Internet. The higher the bandwidth, the higher the connection speed. Bandwidth is measured in *kilobits per second (Kbps)* or *megabits per second (Mbps)*. A modem supports bandwidth up to 56 Kbps, whereas leased lines such as a digital subscriber line (DSL) support up to 8 Mbps.

TIP Another upcoming technology that may replace slow network connectivity is the cable modem. By using cable modems, even household PC users can get rid of the hassle of dialing up every time they connect to the Internet. Cable modems are known to support bandwidths up to 52 Mbps.

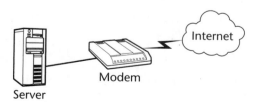

Figure 1.2 Dial-up connection.

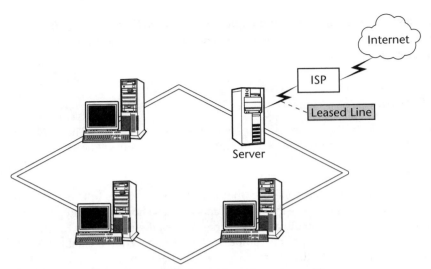

Figure 1.3   Connecting to the Internet by using a leased line.

Cross-Browser Compatibility

As discussed earlier, several browsers are available for accessing the Internet. The choice of browser entirely depends on the preference of the user. Although this increases the availability of options for the users, it also gives way to problems. When Web pages are developed, if they are tested using a single browser, the developer will be unaware of how the Web page will appear when viewed using a different browser. In some cases, a Web page that is displayed perfectly on Internet Explorer might not be displayed properly on Netscape Navigator. This leads to browser incompatibility, which might occur because of the following:

Browser version.   Sometimes, you might test your Web site by using the latest version of a browser. However, if your users aren't using the same version, they might not be able to view the contents of a Web page properly. You may have visited sites that display a warning indicating that the Web site is best viewed with IE 5 or higher. This suggests that the Web site might not appear as intended if the user is using an earlier version of Internet Explorer than version 5.

HTML tags.   Certain HTML tags are specific to particular browsers and don't appear properly when viewed using other browsers.

Fonts.   Certain fonts are specific to particular browsers and don't appear properly when viewed using other browsers.

To avoid incompatibility issues, you should:

- Test your Web site on different browsers during the development and after the development phase.

- Ensure that the important information present on your site is best viewed without version or browser dependencies.

- Avoid using HTML tags that are not supported by certain browsers.
- Avoid using fonts that are not supported by certain browsers.

Protocols

Protocols are a set of rules that are followed on a network to facilitate communication between two different computers on a network or different networks. *HyperText Transfer Protocol (HTTP)* is used for communication on the Internet. When you specify a site address, it starts with http, this indicates that HTTP protocol is used to connect to the Internet.

Scripting Languages

With the evolution of the Internet and increasing competition, the need to develop more interactive Web pages arose. Users were no longer interested in viewing the same old noninteractive Web pages that were created using HTML. But it was challenging and required a lot of time and expertise to make Web pages more interactive using languages such as C++.

Developers started looking for an alternative that would help them develop more interactive Web pages in a shorter time and with ease. This led to the introduction of scripting languages, programming languages that can be embedded within HTML tags to make Web pages more attractive and interactive. Over the past couple of years, several scripting languages have been introduced.

Using scripting languages, you can achieve the following functionality:

- You can dynamically modify the content of a Web page at the time when the page is downloaded.
- Scripts can accompany forms and can be used to process input or information provided by a user for checking the validity of the information.
- Scripts can be triggered by events. That is, you can use scripts to respond and react to events such as form submission, mouse action, and selection.
- Scripts can be used to check authenticity. For example, a script can check whether the username and password specified by a user during logon are valid or not.
- Scripts can be used to create graphical user interface elements. Linking the script to form controls called buttons can do this.

There are two types of scripting languages, *client-side* and *server-side*.

Client-Side Scripting

Client-side scripting languages execute on a client computer. This means that a script executes when a page is downloaded on a client computer or when a link is activated. Client-side scripting was introduced so that the server did not have to handle the entire processing load. There are several advantages of using client-side scripting languages.

Reduces the load on a server.   Client-side scripting languages result in a script being executed on the client machine, thereby reducing the load on the server. Imagine a situation where thousands of users are connected to the server and are trying to log on simultaneously. A server-side script that checks whether the username entered by a user contains any special characters will have to be verified by the server every time a user enters a username or password, overloading the server. Such a situation can be avoided by using client-side scripting so that usernames and passwords are verified on the user's machine.

Reduces network traffic.   When a script is executed on the client side, the network traffic is also reduced to a large extent.

There are certain limitations to using client-side scripting:

- The scope of client-side scripting is limited. You cannot use client-side scripting languages to perform complex tasks such as interacting with a database server or accessing local files and directories.
- The client-side scripting code that you use is visible to users.

A few examples of client-side scripting languages are:

JavaScript.   JavaScript is a popular scripting language that was developed by Netscape. JavaScript was developed using Java as the base language. It can be embedded within HTML and is an open source language that doesn't require a license.

VBScript.   VBScript stands for Visual Basic Scripting Edition. This is another popular scripting language and was developed by Microsoft. VBScript is based on the Visual Basic programming language.

Jscript.   JScript is Microsoft's version of JavaScript. It is very similar to JavaScript.

Server-Side Scripting

Server-side scripting is just the opposite of client-side scripting. All the scripts are executed on the server side. It is used to perform more complex tasks that require a lot of processing power. The advantages of server-side scripting are:

- When you use server-side scripting, all processing takes place before a Web page is sent to the browser. As a result, the code remains hidden from users.
- Server-side scripting is browser independent. That is, the browser used does not have any impact on the processing of code because all the processing takes place on the server.

A few disadvantages of using server-side scripting are:

- To use server-side scripting you might require a high-configuration server.
- Running complex tasks on the server side might require a lot of processing speed and also possibly slow down the Web site.

TIP You should design your Web site in such a way that you take the best possible advantage of both client- and server-side scripting languages. This will help you protect your code and ensure that you derive the maximum performance from the server.

A few examples of server-side scripting languages are:

PHP. HyperText Pre Processor (PHP) is an open source server-side scripting language. PHP scripts can be embedded within HTML to create dynamic Web pages.

Perl. Perl stands for Practical Extraction and Report Language. Larry Wall developed Perl for writing CGI scripts.

JSP. Java Server Pages (JSP) was developed by Sun Microsystems. JSP is a powerful server-side scripting language.

Python. Python is an interpreted object-oriented programming language. It was developed by Guido Van Rossum. Although Python is not a dedicated scripting language, it can be used for server-side scripting.

Summary

In this chapter, you learned about Internet basics. Next, you were introduced to the terminology that is used in connection with the Internet. Finally, you learned about client- and server-side scripting languages.

Basics of PHP

In this lesson, you will learn to:

- Define PHP
- Discuss the history and evolution of PHP
- Discuss the generic features of PHP
- Identify the new features in PHP 4
- Install and configure PHP on a Linux platform
- Install and configure PHP on a Windows platform
- Recall the basics of HTML
- Write the first PHP code
- Embed PHP code in HTML
- Parse PHP code
- Execute PHP code from the command prompt
- Escape PHP code
- Comment PHP code

Getting Started

Since the advent of the Internet, developers have been working toward improving the functionality offered by their Web sites. Over the last decade, there has been a tremendous surge in the popularity of Web-based applications and e-commerce, leading to competition on the Web. Hosting a Web site on the Internet is not a big deal today. What distinguishes popular sites from unpopular ones is their level of functionality and visual appeal. Gone are the days when entire sites were created using HTML. Now we need more interactive and dynamic Web pages. This need resulted in the advent of scripting languages. PHP may be only one of the many scripting languages present today, but it is definitely the first choice of millions of Web developers around the world.

In the previous chapter, you were introduced to few of the popular server- and client-side scripting languages. In this chapter, you will realize why PHP is a popular scripting language. The chapter is divided into three topics. The first covers the history and evolution of PHP as a scripting language, the second discusses the steps for installing PHP on Linux and Windows servers, and the third topic covers the absolute basics of programming with PHP.

Introducing PHP

PHP is one of the fastest-growing scripting languages. Due to its useful features and easy-to-understand syntax, PHP is very popular in the world of Web development. Following is an excerpt of an article posted at Netcraft's site at the URL www.netcraft. com/survey/index-200101.html.

> *Also making notable progress is the scripting language PHP. Earlier this month Zend announced the availability of the first commercial products to support use of PHP, including significant performance improvements through script caching. The PHP module is compiled into the Apache server on over 5 million web sites, or approaching 40% of all Apache sites. Although PHP will only be in use on a fraction of these sites currently, it is regarded as easier to program than perl or jsp, and has created a broad developer community in a relatively short space of time. PHP, together with MySQL and Apache, has become the de facto way of developing web applications in the Linux environment, in a similar way to the IIS/ASP/SQL-Server combination in the Microsoft world.*

This excerpt indicates the pace at which PHP has gained popularity. Initially, PHP was just a set of macros used by developers to maintain personal home pages. Later on, PHP evolved as a complete object-oriented language.

Basic Features of PHP

Although PHP is known for its various advanced features, it is a good idea to first become familiar with the basic features of PHP, which can be summed up as follows:

- Is a server-side scripting language
- Capable of handling database-driven e-commerce Web sites
- Easier to write than any other scripting language
- Improved with every release
- Can be embedded within HTML to create dynamic and interactive Web pages.
- Can be used to create images
- Is used to read and write files
- Is used for sending emails

History and Evolution of PHP

PHP was first released in 1994 by Rasmus Lerdof. At the time, PHP was being used as a set of Web publishing macros and nothing else, and many people didn't know about its existence. But soon the first version of PHP was released. It became available to developers in early 1995. By this time, quite a few developers had started perceiving PHP as a useful tool that could be used to maintain home pages. At this time, PHP consisted of special macros and a dozen of other utilities that made it the obvious choice for developers. Developers were now able to use PHP to add important functionality, such as guest books and counters, to their Web pages.

PHP/FI

The next version of PHP was called PHP/FI (FI stands for form interpreter), and it included the following new features:

- PHP could interpret HTML form data in a piece of code.
- Database interactivity was built in.

PHP/FI was more powerful than the previous version of PHP and soon attracted the attention of several developers, who started working together to find ways to improve this software.

PHP 3

The next version of PHP, PHP 3, was created when two developers, Zeev Suraski and Andi Gutmans got together to create a new *parser* for PHP. A parser is one of the core programs used to convert the source to a form that the compiler or interpreter can understand. The compiler then dissects this code and converts it to object code. It is as important as an engine is for a car. A considerable number of new features were added to PHP 3. After PHP 3 was released, it became an instant hit and many experienced developers started using it to develop Web applications.

Soon the combination of PHP 3, Apache, and MySQL was considered the best possible option for Web development. Apart from extraordinary performance, this combination was considered ideal because all technologies were open source and available at no cost. As a result, licensing issues were also no longer a problem. In addition to this, Apache is the most popular Web server in use today across the world.

TIP **PHP has several built-in Apache- and MySQL-specific functions, which, if used intelligently, can result in a powerful combination.**

The compatibility story doesn't end here. Apache and MySQL are ideal software programs that can be used with PHP, but PHP also works with other software. PHP has been tried and tested on other Web servers such as *Internet Information Server (IIS)* and *Personal Web Server (PWS)*. There are no reported complaints about compatibility of different database servers with PHP, and it works perfectly with database servers such as MS SQL Server, Oracle, Informix, and mSQL.

Web development was not just about writing hard-coded HTML pages anymore. It was now more complex, and support for database interactivity was significant. Web applications were developed in such a way that data was sent and retrieved by multiple senders and recipients at the same time. This was when PHP 4 was released.

PHP 4

PHP 4 is the latest version of PHP. There are more than a few reasons why developers feel that PHP 4 is the right choice for the current scenario. Some of the most important reasons are:

- PHP 4 can be downloaded from PHP's official Web site without charge.
- Other software used with PHP such as Apache and MySQL is also available at no cost.

TIP **According to a survey conducted by www.securityspace.com, PHP is the most popular scripting language to use as a module to Apache. In October 2001, there were an estimated 1,107,914 users of PHP as compared with 328,856 users of Perl, 473,053 users of open SSI, and 1873 users of mod_python. This survey indicates that 44.80% of users worldwide are using PHP instead of other scripting languages that can be used as a module to Apache.**

- Although it is correct to say that PHP is open source, it is wrong to assume that there is not enough support available for developers who choose PHP for Web development. Several developers have tried and tested applications using PHP. The advice of these developers is available at no cost on the Internet.
- The Internet also offers a number of support documents that can be downloaded at no cost.

- In addition to this, there are several free mailing lists that developers can join. They can then query the mailing lists about problems they are facing.

- All bugs that are detected in PHP are immediately rectified. A dedicated team of expert developers addresses these bugs.

- PHP helps developers decrease the development time taken to complete a script because all HTML code is separated from PHP code.

- PHP is comparable with Active Server Pages (ASP) when it comes to performance, and it is as popular on Linux platforms as ASP is popular on Windows platforms. Certain features of PHP make it a better choice than ASP because to some extent PHP is platform independent. It can also be used effectively on Windows platforms.

TIP PHP is also doing well on other platforms such as Windows. The PHP IIS module is considered to be extremely stable. This module also provides support for COM objects.

Another reason that PHP is better than ASP is that PHP code can be compiled to detect errors in the code. The compiler points out mistakes, which the developer can then rectify. There is no compiler available with ASP that compiles ASP code.

Portability is another very important feature of PHP. The ability of PHP to work with any combination of software makes it portable. It also works with almost any combination of operating system, Web server, and database server.

As discussed earlier, several additional features were incorporated in PHP 4 over and above the existing features of PHP 3. The following were introduced with the release of PHP 4:

- Support for the boolean data type.

- The foreach statement.

- Backward compatibility with PHP 3, which means that all the programs created using PHP 3 are guaranteed to run on PHP 4.

- COM/DCOM support, which is available only for Windows.

- Introduction of new functions and additional functionality added to certain existing functions.

- Supports ftp, which was not supported in PHP 3.

- The "= = =" operator, which checks that two values are equal and whether the data types of these values are same.

- Makes more efficient use of existing memory.

- Introduction of enhanced features that extend the functionality of object-oriented programming.

- Better ways to create classes and objects.

- Runtime binding of functions, which allows a developer to call a function even before it is declared.

- Built-in support for Java and XML.

- The PHP highlighter, which enables a developer to view the source code instead of a complete script and provides a faster and better look at the source.

- Support for variable assignment by reference, which helps the developer link two variables in such a way that the value of one becomes dependent on the value of the other variable. This means that whenever a value is assigned to one of the variables, the other variable's value is also updated accordingly.

- A php.ini file that is simple to understand and configure.

- GET, POST methods that support multidimensional arrays.

- Simpler nesting of objects in arrays and of arrays in objects.

- Elimination of all syntax limitations that existed in PHP 3.

- Enhanced support for Web servers, made possible by including *Server API (SAPI)*.

- Supports full encryption using the mcrypt library and also hash encryption, using Triple DES, MD5, Blowfish, and SHA1 encryption algorithms, among others.

- Includes a Perl Compatible Regular Expressions (PCRE) library.

- Can reference variables using quotes and variable expansion using double quotes.

Installing and Configuring PHP

One of the strongest benefits of using PHP is its portability. You just think of a software combination and PHP can be configured on it. When you decide to use PHP for Web development, you will have several software combinations to choose from, and several Web servers and database servers are also supported by PHP. This section will give you the skills required to install and configure PHP on both Windows and Linux platforms.

NOTE Although the steps for Windows installation will be dealt with in detail, this book will primarily focus on using PHP on a Linux platform as a module to Apache.

Installing PHP on a Windows Box

When installing PHP on a Windows platform, you can work with several combinations. You can choose to use Apache and MySQL with Windows or elect to use the conventional IIS and Microsoft SQL Server 2000 combination. Following are the steps needed to configure PHP on Windows 2000 Advanced Server; they also include configuring an IIS Web server so that PHP files can be executed and opened in Internet Explorer:

1. Download the file *php406-installer.exe* from www.php.net.
2. Double-click the file *php406-installer.exe* to start installing PHP. The Welcome screen of the installer Wizard appears (Figure 2.1). Click Next to proceed.
3. In the License Agreement screen, click the I Agree button to proceed (Figure 2.2).

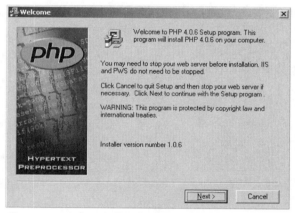

Figure 2.1   The Welcome screen.

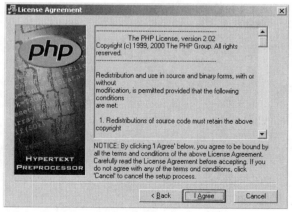

Figure 2.2   The License Agreement screen.

4. In the Installation Type screen select Advanced and then click Next to continue (Figure 2.3).

5. In the Choose Destination Location screen, click Next (Figure 2.4).

6. In the Choose Upload Temporary Directory screen, click Next (Figure 2.5).

7. In the Choose Session Save Directory screen, click Next (Figure 2.6).

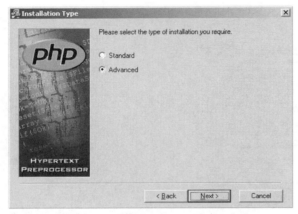

Figure 2.3 The Installation Type screen.

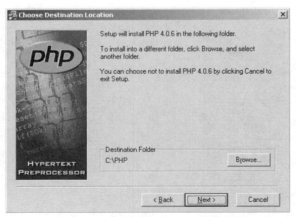

Figure 2.4 The Choose Destination Location screen.

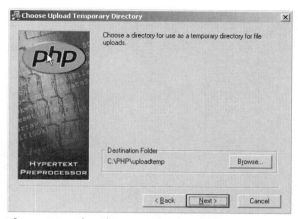

Figure 2.5 The Choose Upload Temporary Directory screen.

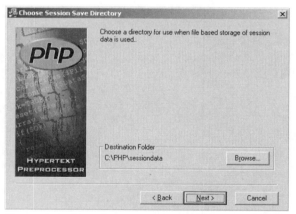

Figure 2.6 The Choose Session Save Directory screen.

8. In the Mail Configuration screen specify the SMTP server address and your e-mail address. These fields are optional and can be skipped.

9. In the Error Reporting Level screen, verify that Display all errors warnings and notices is selected, and click Next (Figure 2.7).

10. In the Server Type screen select Microsoft IIS 4 or higher, and click Next (Figure 2.8).

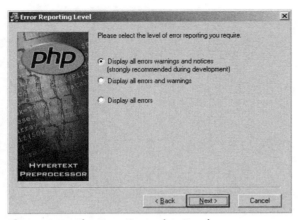

Figure 2.7   The Error Reporting Level screen.

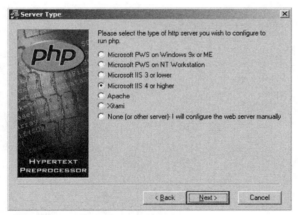

Figure 2.8   The Server Type screen.

11. In the File Extensions screen, verify that the option .php is checked, and click Next to proceed (Figure 2.9).

12. In the Start Installation screen, click Next (Figure 2.10).

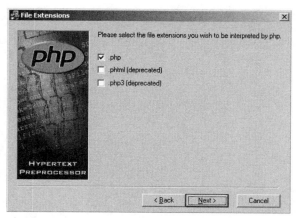

Figure 2.9   The File Extensions screen.

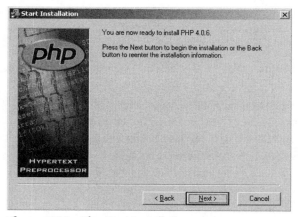

Figure 2.10   The Start Installation screen.

13. In the IIS ScriptMap Node Selection screen, check the Default Web Site option (Figure 2.11).

NOTE A prompt may ask whether or not you want to retain the earlier version of php.ini file. Click No to proceed.

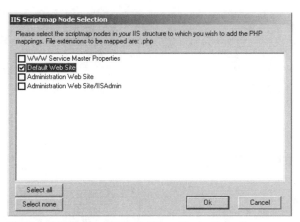

Figure 2.11   The IIS ScriptMap Node Selection screen.

After you perform these steps, the Installation Complete screen appears, indicating that the installation was successful.

Now that you have successfully configured IIS to work with PHP, let's see if IIS is functioning properly and the PHP code is getting executed.

1. Create a file with a .php extension.

NOTE The preceding steps can be used to install version PHP 4.0.6. These steps will not work for an earlier version of PHP because the Windows installer version of PHP was released with PHP 4.0.6. If you want to install an earlier version of PHP, follow the instructions given in the next section.

2. This file should contain the code `<?phpinfo();?>`.
3. Save the file as *test.php in c:\Inetpub\wwwroot.*
4. Open Internet Explorer.
5. In the Address box specify the address as http://localhost/test.php and press enter. Figure 2.12 illustrates the output of the file test.php.

Installing an Earlier Version of PHP 4

In you want to install an earlier version of PHP 4, use the following steps:

NOTE These steps have been verified with respect to version 4.0.4pl1.

1. Download the file *php-4.0.4pl1-Win32.zip* from www.php.net.

2. Double-click the file *php-4.0.4pl1-Win32.zip*. Extract and save the PHP installation files to C:\PHP 4.

3. Copy the php.ini file that comes bundled with the PHP distribution to the c:\WINNT folder. If you don't have the php.ini file, you can copy the php.ini-dist file to the WINNT folder and later rename this file to php.ini.

4. Copy the file *php4ts.dll* to the c:\WINNT\system32 folder. Then copy the file msvcrt.dll from c:\PHP4\dlls to c:\WINNT\system32. This is mandatory because PHP 4 relies on external DLL files for execution.

NOTE After following these steps, you will be able to execute PHP programs from the command prompt in Windows. However, you will need to specify a .php extension to the PHP files that you create. You will also need to copy these files to the PHP directory and then execute them.

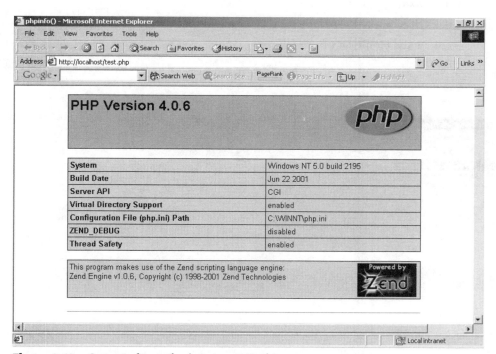

Figure 2.12 Output of test.php in Internet Explorer.

Configuring IIS 4.0 to Work with PHP

For versions of PHP that were released prior to 4.0.6, unless you configure IIS to work with PHP, you will not be able to view the output of PHP programs in the browser. The following are the steps that you need to follow to configure IIS for PHP:

1. Choose Start, Programs, Administrative Tools, and then Internet Services Manager to open the Internet Information Services window (Figure 2.13).

2. In the left pane, expand the computer name.

3. In the left pane, right-click the Default Web Site option and choose Properties from the shortcut menu.

4. In the Default Web Site Properties dialog box, select the ISAPI Filters tab (Figure 2.14).

5. Click the Add button, located above the Remove button, to open the Filter Properties dialog box (Figure 2.15).

6. Specify the filter name as PHP.

7. Click the Browse button and navigate to the location of the php4isapi.dll file. (This file is located in the sapi folder, which is in the c:\PHP folder.)

8. Click Open.

9. Click OK to apply the settings and close the Filter Properties dialog box.

10. Activate the Home Directory tab.

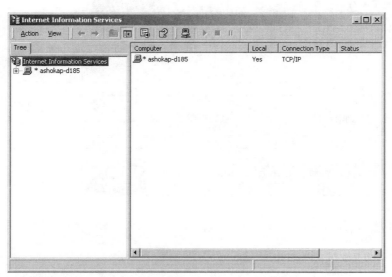

Figure 2.13   The Internet Information Services window.

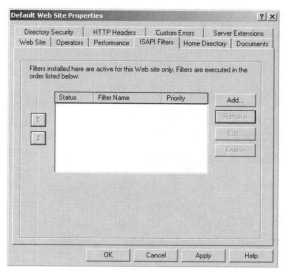

Figure 2.14 The ISAPI Filters tab.

Figure 2.15 The Filter Properties dialog box.

11. Under Application Settings, click the Configuration button to open the Application Configuration dialog box.

12. Verify that the App Mappings tab is activated.

13. Under Application Mappings, click the Add button to open the Add/Edit Application Extension Mapping dialog box.

14. Click Browse and navigate to the location of the php4isapi.dll file. Click Open.

15. In the Extension box, specify the extension as .php.

16. Verify that the Script engine box is checked, as shown in Figure 2.16.

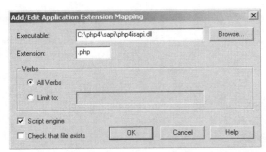

Figure 2.16 The Add/Edit Application Extension Mapping dialog box.

17. Click OK.

18. Click OK to close the Application Configuration dialog box.

19. Click OK to close the Default Web Site Properties dialog box and close the Internet Information Services window.

20. Open the Run dialog box. Type cmd to access the command prompt window.

21. Type the command net stop iisadmin to stop all IIS-related services. A message will appear that asks if you want to stop World Wide Publishing Service and Simple Mail Transfer Protocol. Type y and proceed.

22. Type the command net start iisadmin to restart IIS.

23. Type net start w3svc to start World Wide Web Publishing Service.

TIP To test whether everything was configured properly, follow the same steps that you followed to verify your installation of the latest version of PHP.

Installing PHP on a Linux Box

Although PHP is compatible with a variety of software combinations, it works best with Apache and MySQL on a Linux platform. This section will guide you through the steps that are required to configure PHP to work with Apache and MySQL on your Linux box.

The Custom-Everything Option

While installing Red Hat Linux, you are provided with a choice of the type of installation you prefer. One of the different options available is the Custom-Everything option. This is the installation method that we have chosen for this book.

If you are not worried about the space occupied by the software, this option is the most convenient to use because it installs Apache, MySQL, and PHP. After you complete your installation using this option, you can start programming with PHP without configuring anything else. However, you will need to be careful about a few things, such as:

1. The httpd service should be running. If it is not, type the command `ntsysv` and enable the httpd service.

2. Then type the following command to start the httpd service:

   `#/etc/rc.d/init.d/httpd start`

If you did not install PHP while installing Red Hat Linux, you may want to install it separately. There are two ways by which you can install PHP:

- Compiling from source as an Apache module.
- Installing PHP by using Red Hat Package manager (RPM).

NOTE Both these installation types assume that you have Red Hat Linux 7.2 installed with the version of Apache that comes bundled with it.

Compiling from Source as a Apache Module

Another way you can configure PHP is by compiling from source as an Apache module. The steps of installation are:

1. Download the file php-4.0.6.tar.gz from www.php.net.

2. Uncompress the tar file by typing:

   `#tar zxvf php-4.0.6.tar.gz`

   This will create a folder named php-4.0.6 and the contents of the tar file will be automatically copied to this folder.

3. Move to the directory php-4.0.6 with this command:

   `#cd php-4.0.6`

4. Configure PHP with MySQL by typing:

   `#./configure –with-mysql –with-apxs`

5. Compile the PHP distribution files by typing:

   `#make`

6. To transfer all files to the appropriate location with the appropriate permissions, type:

   `#make install`

7. Verify that the following three files are present in the /etc/httpd/conf/httpd. conf file and are not commented:

```
LoadModule php4_module libexec/libphp4.so
AddModule mod_php4.c
AddType application/x-httpd-php .php
```

8. Copy the `php.ini-dist` file to /usr/local/lib directory.

9. Restart httpd by typing:

```
#/etc/rc.d/init.d/httpd restart
```

You can follow these steps to ensure that PHP was configured properly.

1. Create a file named `verify.php` in the /var/www/html directory of the root user.

2. Type the following code in this file:

```
<?phpinfo();?>
```

3. Open Netscape Navigator and type the following URL:

```
http://localhost/verify.php
```

If you have configured PHP by following the steps properly, you will see the output shown in Figure 2.17.

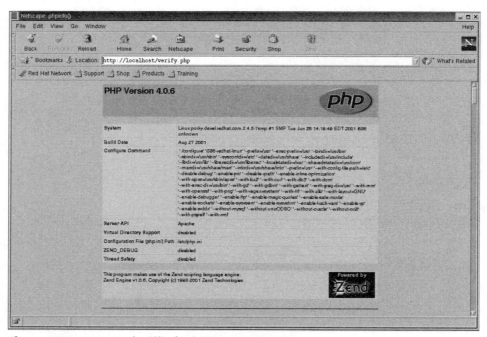

Figure 2.17   Output of verify.php in Netscape Navigator.

NOTE After installing PHP, you will be able to view the output of PHP files in the browser. But you may not be able to run PHP from the command prompt. Installing the RPM file for PHP on your Linux machine can solve this problem.

RPM Installation

PHP can also be installed using Red Hat Package Manager. Use this method if you are not experienced enough to handle complicated installations that involve compiling. Although this method is the simplest out of the three, it has certain drawbacks, which are:

- When you use RPM installation, you cannot specify compile options while installing PHP. This is because RPM has precompiled binaries.
- After you perform an RPM installation of PHP, you cannot perform any kind of postinstall configuration.

To perform an RPM installation for PHP, use the following command:

```
$rpm -ivh php-4.0.6-7.i386.rpm
```

TIP You can download the RPM files for the latest packages from www.rpmfind.com. You can also get the RPM file used for PHP installation from the Red Hat Linux CD.

Understanding PHP Basics

Now that you know how to install and configure PHP, it is time to get accustomed to coding with PHP. This section will equip you with all the basic skills that you should master before you proceed to other chapters of this book; it will cover the following topics:

- Revising HTML
- Understanding how PHP code is parsed
- Understanding a simple PHP program
- Embedding PHP in HTML
- Executing PHP from the command prompt
- Encountering a parse error
- Executing PHP and viewing the output in the browser
- Escaping PHP code
- Commenting PHP code

Revising HTML

Before you actually begin writing programs in PHP, it is a good idea to reexamine the basics of HTML. This will help you embed PHP code in HTML in a more effective way. You can use HTML along with PHP to create attractive and dynamic Web pages. Here are a few pointers to HTML to refresh your memory:

- HyperText Markup Language (HTML) is the most common markup language and has been used extensively to create Web pages. HTML was derived from Standard Generalized Markup Language (SGML). However, HTML is much simpler than SGML as far as usage is concerned.

- Markup languages, such as HTML, use *labels*. These labels are used to specify text or images. These labels are called *tags*.

- These tags are used to contain specific *elements* of HTML. Elements, the heart of any HTML document, are logical blocks that determine how text or an image will appear when displayed on a Web page.

- To use these elements, you need to specify them within opening and closing tags. An opening tag marks the beginning of an element, and a closing tag marks the end of an element.

- Each HTML document will always contain the <HTML> </HTML> element, which indicates that the text in the document is hypertext.

- Each element has certain characteristics called *attributes* of the elements. For example, the attributes of the element <TABLE> are ALIGN, WIDTH, BORDER, CELLSPACING, and CELLPADDING. Each of these attributes can be specified within the TABLE element.

Consider the following HTML code:

```
<HTML>
<HEAD>
<TITLE>Introducing HTML</TITLE>
</HEAD>
<BODY>
    <FONT COLOR="BLUE">
    <H1><CENTER>A Brief Introduction to HTML</CENTER></H1>
    </FONT>
    <FONT SIZE=3>
    <P>
    <I><CENTER>"HyperText Markup Language (HTML) is a popular markup
language that is used worldwide to create Web pages."</CENTER></I>
    </P>
    </FONT>
<TABLE BORDER=1 ALIGN=CENTER>
<TD><B><CENTER>HTML
```

```
Elements</CENTER></B></TD><TD><B><CENTER>Explanation</CENTER></B></TD>
<TR><TD>A</TD><TD>This element represents the anchor. The anchor is either
a hypertext link or the destination of the link.</TD></TR>
<TR><TD>B</TD><TD>This element stands for Bold. It is used to make the
text appear bold.</TD></TR>
<TR><TD>BODY</TD><TD>This element contains the body text of the HTML
document.</TD></TR>
<TR><TD>BR</TD><TD>This element indicates the end of a line.</TD></TR>
<TR><TD>CAPTION</TD><TD>This element is used to specify a caption for
the table.</TD></TR>
<TR><TD>CENTER</TD><TD>This element indicates that the text should be
center-aligned.</TD></TR>
<TR><TD>COL</TD><TD>This element is used to specify the characteristics of
a table column.</TD></TR>
<TR><TD>FONT</TD><TD>This element is used to alter the font size and color
of the text.</TD></TR>
<TR><TD>FORM</TD><TD>This element defines the characteristics of a
interactive form.</TD></TR>
<TR><TD>FRAME</TD><TD>This element is used to specify a rectangular space
or frame.</TD></TR>
<TR><TD>FRAMESET</TD><TD>This element contains frames that are used to
divide a window into rectangular subspaces.</TD></TR>
<TR><TD>H1-H6</TD><TD>These elements are used to specify the heading
levels for content. The H1 element being the first heading and H6 the
last.</TD></TR>
<TR><TD>HEAD</TD><TD>This element is used to specify the header
information of the document.</TD></TR>
<TR><TD>HTML</TD><TD>This element contains the entire HTML
document.</TD></TR>
<TR><TD>IMG</TD><TD>This element is used to specify an inline
image.</TD></TR>
<TR><TD>INPUT</TD><TD>This element defines a form control that is used by
the user to enter input.</TD></TR>
<TR><TD>LABEL</TD><TD>This element is used to associate a label with a
form control.</TD></TR>
<TR><TD>P</TD><TD>This element is used to define a paragraph.</TD></TR>
<TR><TD>TABLE</TD><TD>This element is used to define a table that
consists of data represented in rows and columns.</TD></TR>
<TR><TD>TD</TD><TD>This element is used to specify the data that would be
present in a cell.</TD></TR>
<TR><TD>TITLE</TD><TD>This element is used to specify the title for the
document.</TD></TR>
<TR><TD>TR</TD><TD>This element is used to specify the TD and TH
elements.</TD></TR>
</TABLE>
</BODY>
</HTML>
```

The output of the preceding code is shown in Figure 2.18.

In the preceding code, the following elements were used:

HTML.   Contains the entire HTML document; it marks the beginning and end of an HTML document.

HEAD.   Specifies the header information of the document.

TITLE.   Specifies the title for the document.

BODY.   Contains the body text of the HTML document.

FONT.   Alters the font size and color of text.

H1.   Contains that part of the text within the HTML document that needs to appear as Heading 1 on a Web page.

P.   Defines a paragraph.

TABLE.   Defines a table that consists of data represented in rows and columns.

TD.   Specifies the data that will be present in a cell.

TR.   Specifies TD and TH elements.

CENTER.   Indicates that the text should be centrally aligned.

B.   Used to make the text bold.

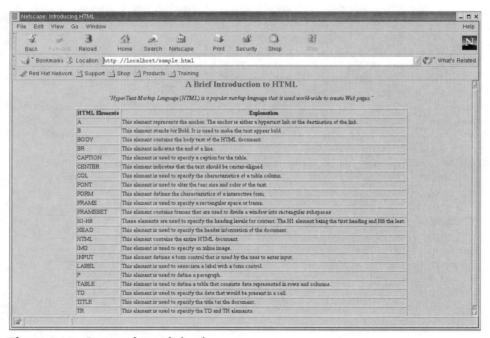

Figure 2.18   Output of sample.html.

The preceding code also consists of attributes that are used with elements. The attributes are:

- The COLOR attribute is used with the FONT element to specify that the Heading 1 should appear in blue.

- The SIZE attribute is used with the FONT element to specify that the size of the text should be 3.

- The BORDER attribute is used with the TABLE element to specify the thickness of the table border.

- The ALIGN attribute is used with the TABLE element to specify that the table should be centrally aligned.

Understanding How PHP Code Is Parsed

Consider that you have a file that contains both HTML and PHP code. Whenever you view the file on a Web page, the PHP code in the file will be executed and will remain hidden from the user. In contrast, the HTML code in the file remains visible to the user. If you have wondered how PHP is separated from HTML even though they coexist, the answer is simple: PHP code is parsed. The process of parsing begins when a Web browser requests a Web page with a .php extension, and it proceeds as follows:

- As soon as a Web server encounters any such request, it forwards this request to the PHP parser.

- The PHP parser searches for the .php file and then scans that file for PHP code.

- As soon as the parser encounters PHP code, it executes it and replaces the original code with the output.

- The result, or output, of the code is sent back to the Web server.

- The Web server sends this output to the Web browser.

- The Web browser then displays the output on the user's screen.

Although the steps are detailed, they take place within seconds. The actual speed at which the code is executed and the output is displayed depends on the configuration of the server that you are using.

Understanding Simple PHP Code

It's time to begin writing PHP code. The following simple code sample shows how PHP programs are written:

```
<?php
echo "Welcome to the world of music";
?>
```

Let's examine this code line by line:

- The first line consists of the opening tag, `<?php`. Each program in PHP should have an opening tag.

- The second line consists of the `echo` statement. In this program, the echo statement is used to display the message "Welcome to the world of music." Notice that the message is in double quotes. The second line ends with a semicolon, which depicts the end of the line. Each code line in PHP should end with a semicolon.

- The third line consists of the closing tag, `?>`. The closing tag marks the end of the PHP code and is mandatory.

NOTE The importance of using opening and closing tags is discussed in the next section.

Embedding PHP in HTML

By now you know that the PHP parser scans PHP files and then separates PHP code from HTML. To distinguish PHP code from HTML code, it is essential that you use PHP start and end tags. There are three ways of specifying them, as shown in Table 2.1. You can use any of them.

The following code uses each of these tags:

```
//Code Sample 1
<?
echo "Hello World!", "\n";
?>
//Code Sample 2
<?php
echo "Welcome to Mega Music Mart.", "\n";
?>
//Code Sample 3
<script language = "php">
echo "The best online music store.", "\n";
</script>
```

In this code:

- Code Sample 1 illustrates the usage of the `<?` and `?>` opening and closing tags.

- Code Sample 2 illustrates the usage of the `<?php` and `?>` opening closing tags.

- Code Sample 3 illustrates the usage of the `<script language = "php">` opening tag and the `</script>` closing tag.

- The `echo` statement is used to print the message that appears within double quotes.

Table 2.1 Start and End Tags in PHP

START TAGS	END TAGS
<?	?>
<?php	?>
<script language = "php">	</script>

The output of the code is:

```
X-Powered-By: PHP/4.0.6
Content-type: text/html
Hello World!
Welcome to Mega Music Mart.
The best online music store.
```

Executing PHP from the Command Prompt

PHP code can be executed in a browser as well as from the command prompt. You might want to check your PHP code before embedding it in HTML. The command prompt is useful in such situations. A developer can quickly check whether the code is working or not from it. However, HTML tags are not recognized on the command prompt.

The steps for executing PHP code from the command prompt are as follows:

1. Create a text file named testing.php.

NOTE All PHP programs should have a .php extension. Otherwise, the parser will not be able to search for the file.

2. Write the following PHP code in the text file:

```
<?php
echo "Hello World";
?>
```

3. Execute the code from the command prompt by issuing the following command:

```
$php testing.php
```

NOTE Every time you want to execute the PHP code, you need to precede the filename with the letters *php*. Moreover, if you are executing the code in the Windows command prompt, you will need to copy the file to the PHP folder to execute it.

The output of the code appears is:

```
X-Powered-By: PHP/4.0.6
Content-type: text/html
Hello World
```

Encountering a Parse Error

A parse error is encountered when the code has syntax errors in it. For example, each line of PHP code should end with a semicolon. If you don't specify one, you get parse error, and the code will not be executed. Similarly, you might encounter a parse error when you forget to use double quotes. In addition to these possibilities, there are several others that might result in a parse error. You will know more about these errors in this section. The PHP parser tells you the exact line on which it encounters a parse error. Developers find this a useful feature because they can correct their mistakes without verifying the entire code.

Consider a code sample where double quotes are not specified at the end of a line:

```
<?php
echo "Hello World;
?>
```

The output of this code is:

```
X-Powered-By: PHP/4.0.6
Content-type: text/html
<br>
<b>Parse error</b>:  parse error in <b>parse.php</b> on line
<b>5</b><br>
```

It is evident from the output that the PHP code was not executed. This parse error can be rectified by using closing double quotes after the word *World*.

Executing PHP and Viewing the Output in the Browser

It is essential that you know how to execute PHP code and display the output in a browser when developing Web applications using PHP. While displaying the output in a browser, you can also use HTML code in your PHP file because the browser will display the result of the HTML code as well.

If you have successfully installed and configured PHP according to the steps detailed under *Installing and Configuring PHP*, executing PHP from Linux and Windows platforms should not be a problem. However, you need to check the following settings before attempting to execute PHP and view the output in the browser (additional instructions follow for Red Hat Linux and Windows 2000). For Linux:

- Verify that PHP is installed properly.
- Verify that Apache service is running.

- Verify that the settings in the httpd.conf file that is located in the /etc/httpd/ conf directory are correct.

- Verify that the file whose output you want to view is present in the /var/ www/html directory.

For Windows:

- Verify that PHP is installed and configured properly.

- Verify that the IIS Web server is configured properly.

- Verify that the files that you intend to execute are present in the c:\WINNT\Inetpub\wwwroot directory.

After you check these settings, you should be able to run PHP code and view its output in the browser.

If you are using Red Hat Linux, you need to do the following to view the output on the browser:

1. Move to the directory /var/www/html.

2. Create a file named **onlinux**.php using the vi editor.

3. Type the following code in the file:

```
<HTML>
<HEAD>
<TITLE>Displaying the output on the browser</TITLE>
</HEAD>
<BODY>
<?php
echo "Hello World";
?>
</BODY>
</HTML>
```

4. Save and close the file.

5. Open Netscape Navigator.

6. In the Address box, type `http://localhost/filename` and press Enter.

If you are using PHP with Windows 2000, you need to perform the following steps to view the output in the browser:

1. Open Notepad.

2. Type the following code.

```
<HTML>
<HEAD>
<TITLE>Display the output in the Browser</TITLE>
</HEAD>
<BODY>
<?php
```

```
echo "Hello World";
?>
</BODY>
</HTML>
```

3. Save the file that contains the code in the c:\Intepub\wwwroot folder.

4. Open Internet Explorer.

5. In the Address box type `http://localhost/filename` and press Enter.

Escaping PHP Code

Escaping code is the process of overlooking instances of special characters in the code that would be interpreted as part of the code by the PHP parser. Consider the following code:

```
<?php
echo "Dave said, "I love music!"";
?>
```

The output of this code is:

```
X-Powered-By: PHP/4.0.6
Content-type: text/html
<br>
<b>Parse error</b>:  parse error, expecting `','' or `';'' in
<b>parse.php</b> on line <b>2</b><br>
```

This shows that the parser encountered an error because you used double quotes within double quotes, which confuses the parser, and the code is not executed. Therefore, you need to escape the additional double quotes. To do this, you can use an escape character before the character that needs to be escaped by the parser. An example is the backslash (\). After you use an escape character, the parser no longer interprets the additional double quotes as part of the syntax. Consider the following code:

```
<?php
echo "Dave said, \"I love music!\"";
?>
```

Because you have used backslashes, the output is now:

```
X-Powered-By: PHP/4.0.6
Content-type: text/html
Dave said, "I love music!"
```

Commenting PHP Code

Comments are an integral part of any program. They are statements that are not executed along with code. They help developers remember and recall why they have used a particular code block in a script. Comments are particularly useful when there are several developers working on the same code. The comments of one developer help the others understand the logic of the code, which saves time because other developers spend less time trying to interpret the code. There are four ways of specifying comments in your code:

<!- - Put comment here - ->   This is an HTML comment. Comments stated like this will be ignored by the browser and will not be interpreted.

//Put comment here   This kind of comment is commonly used within PHP code. The two front slashes segregate the comment from the rest of PHP code.

#Put comment here   The hash character can also be used to specify comments within PHP code. This is a shell-style comment.

/*Put comment here*/   This is a C-style comment; in C language comments are specified in this way.

PHP supports all of these ways of specifying comments and you can use them in your PHP code. The following example shows how comment statements are skipped in code:

```
<?php
echo "A list of Comments";
//This is one way of commenting code.
/*This is another.*/
#This is yet another.
?>
```

This code uses all of the comment methods that can be used in PHP. The output of the preceding code will ignore all lines that are commented and will appear as follows:

```
X-Powered-By: PHP/4.0.6
Content-type: text/html
A list of Comments
```

Summary

In this chapter, you learned about the history of PHP. You also learned about the general features of PHP and the new features of PHP 4. Then, you learned to install and configure PHP for both Windows and Linux platforms. Finally, you learned about the basics of PHP programming. You wrote the first PHP code and learned to execute it and display the output on the command prompt and in a browser. You also learned to escape PHP code and effectively use the comments in PHP programs.

Programming Basics

OBJECTIVES:

In this lesson, you will learn to:

- ✓ Identify a variable
- ✓ Declare a variable
- ✓ Identify the data types used in PHP
- ✓ Use data type juggling
- ✓ Identify constants
- ✓ Distinguish between a constant and a variable
- ✓ Discuss operators
- ✓ Use Arithmetic operators
- ✓ Use Assignment operators
- ✓ Use Comparison operators
- ✓ Use Increment and Decrement operators
- ✓ Use String operators
- ✓ Use Logical operators

Getting Started

In school, you used x and y to represent values in algebraic equations. These representations could consist of almost any value and as a result were not constant. On the contrary, pi had a constant value of 3.14. No matter what, this value could never change. PHP provides you with variables and constants for storing and manipulating data in programs.

PHP allocates memory to each variable and constant that you use in your program. As in algebra, the values of variables may change in a program, but the values of constants don't. You must assign unique names to variables and constants. If a name or a number is used to refer to an area in memory in which a value is stored, the number or name used is a variable.

Each variable that is used in a program must be declared; that is, the program must contain a statement specifying precisely what type of information the variable will contain. This applies to every variable used in a program, regardless of its type.

In this chapter, you will learn about basic programming concepts. In the section *Handling Data* you will be introduced to the concept of variables, data types, and constants. In the following section, *Introducing Operators*, you will learn how to use operators in PHP.

Introducing Variables

Variables are known to hold data that can change during the compilation or runtime of a program. You need to remember the following points regarding them:

- A variable can be declared using a dollar sign preceding the variable name.

- A variable name can start with an underscore or with a letter.

- Variables are case sensitive. Therefore, $Philip is not the same as $philip.

Naming Conventions

Similar to other programming languages such as C and C++, PHP follows a naming convention that should be used while declaring variables. Consider the following example:

```
$samplevariable = 6;//Understanding the naming convention used.
```

The example shows the naming convention used for variables in PHP:

The Dollar sign.   In PHP, each variable that you declare should begin with a dollar sign.

Variable name.   It is advisable to choose meaningful variable names. This helps developers understand why a variable was declared when the code is examined. For example, if you use the variable name $g for grade, you might misinterpret it for group at a later stage. Therefore, when you begin using PHP to develop applications, use meaningful variable names.

Operator.   The equal sign is an operator that assigns a value to a variable.

Data type (value assigned to a variable).   The number 6 is the value assigned to the variable $samplevariable.

Variables are assigned using values. These values can be of boolean, integer, float, or string type. Once declared, variables can be referenced in a script.

Handling Data

Every programming language has its own set of *data types* that help developers write programs. A data type is a classification of data. This could mean categorizing the type of data as an amount of money, time, or percentage. In PHP, the data types can be broadly classified as scalar and compound data types.

Scalar Data Type

Four types of data fall under the category of scalar data type: boolean, integer, float, and string.

Boolean

The boolean data type was introduced in version 4 of PHP. It can either be true or false. The numeric representation of the boolean data type is 1 for true and 0 for false. The following example uses this data type:

```php
<?php
$varbool = True; //Is a boolean type variable.
?>
```

Integer

An integer data type consists of numbers. These numbers can be negative or positive {....-2, -1, 0, 1, 2, 3....}. You can use the minus sign to depict negative numbers and the plus sign for positive numbers (if no sign is used, a positive number is assumed). The size of an integer in PHP solely depends on the operating system that you are using. Typically, the size of an integer can be up to 2 billion. In the following code, $varnum is an integer type variable with a value of 6:

```php
<?php
$varnum = 6; //Is an integer.
?>
```

Float

A float is a data type that is also used for storing numbers. Conventionally, floats are used to express only decimal numbers; you can use the integer data type for nondecimal numbers. Floats are also known as doubles or real numbers and have a precision of up to 14 decimal places. In the following code, $varflo is a float type variable and has a value of 1.921839237947:

```
<?php
$ varflo = 1.921839237947 // Is a float type variable
?>
```

String

A string can be best defined as a series of characters. In PHP, a character is nothing but a byte. There are 256 different types of characters that can be used in strings. There is no maximum limit specification in relation to strings in PHP; therefore, you need not worry about a very long string. There are two ways to specify a string, discussed in the following sections.

Single quoted

You can use single quotes to specify a simple string. However, when a string is enclosed in single quotes and it also contains some text enclosed in double quotes, you must use the backslash escape character to escape the single quote. In other words, when you don't want the parser to treat single quotes as syntax and display them as part of the output of the code, you need to use a backslash before the single quotes.

Let's consider a simple example to understand how single quotes are used to specify a string:

```
echo 'I love heavy metal';  //Will print the string on the screen.
```

When you execute the preceding code, the text I love heavy metal will appear on the screen. Now, let's take another example where the string you specify contains single quotes:

```
echo 'I'm a music freak';
```

In this case, the message I'm a music freak will be printed on the screen. Now, consider an example where double quotes are used within single quotes and single quote is present in the text enclosed in double quotes:

```
echo ' Philip replied: " I'm alright " '  //Will return an error.
```

When you try to execute this statement, an error message will appear on the screen. This is because when you use a single quote within double quotes, you need to escape the single quote with a backslash. In the following the statement is written correctly:

```
echo ' Philip replied: " I\'m alright " '
```

The output will be `Philip replied: I'm alright.` Consider another example:

```
echo ' The file is stored in C:\\Data '
```

Now the output will be `The file is stored in C:\Data.`

Another thing that you should remember when using single-quoted strings is that such strings don't support *variable expansion*: If you use the name of a variable within single quotes and try to print the value of the variable, the name of the variable will be printed instead of its value. Consider the following example:

```
<?php
$a = "World";
echo 'Hello $a';
?>
```

The output will be `Hello $a`.

Double quoted

A double-quoted string supports several other escape characters. Table 3.1 lists the escaped characters that are supported in double-quoted strings.

Compound Data Types

PHP consists of two compound types, arrays and objects

Arrays

By now you are familiar with the concept of variables, which are used to store a specific value. However, only one value can be assigned to a variable at a time. This is not the case with arrays, which are special types of variables that can store more than one value. Arrays are useful when you need to store related variable data under one variable name.

Table 3.1 Escaped Characters

SEQUENCE	MEANING
\n	New line
\r	Carriage
\t	Horizontal tab
\\	Backslash
\$	Dollar sign
\"	Double quote

An array can be declared in the following way:

```
$arr_name [key] = value
```

In this statement:

- arr_name is the name of the array.
- key is any string or a nonnegative integer. If you want to modify an array, it is best not to specify a key and to leave the square brackets empty.
- value is the data that is held in the array.

To understand the concept of arrays, consider the following code:

```
<?php
$arr_name[0] = "An";
$arr_name[1] ="array";
$arr_name[2] ="is in";
$arr_name[3] ="the";
$arr_name[4] ="making!";
echo "$arr_name[0] $arr_name[1] $arr_name[2] $arr_name[3]
$arr_name[4]","\n";    //The value assigned to each element
is printed in a single line.
?>
```

In PHP, if you don't specify the size of an array at the time of declaration, a value of 0 is assumed as the key for the first element of the array. The output of the preceding code will be:

```
X-Powered-By: PHP/4.0.6
Content-type: text/html
An array is in the making!
```

NOTE The concept of arrays is covered in detail in the chapter "Arrays."

Objects

Objects are the building blocks of a programming language. An object is an entity that can hold data and specify what needs to be done with the data. Most of the internal workings of an object are hidden from the code that uses them. Objects are a bundle of variables and functions that are derived from a class. To understand the concept of objects you should be familiar with the following terminology:

Object orientation.   The programming concept that revolves around objects. An object is an instance of a class.

Class.   A class is an entity that exhibits certain behavior and exposes certain attributes to retain state.

Properties. The characteristics of an object defined by the class to which it belongs.

Methods. Tasks that can be performed by objects on the data they contain.

NOTE Concepts pertaining to objects are covered in detail in the chapter "Classes."

Juggling Data Types

PHP doesn't require the developer to explicitly specify a data type for a variable at the time of declaration. In PHP, you need not worry about data type mismatches in an expression. Consider the following example:

```
$nextitemcode = 1+ "40 is the present item code";  //$nextitemcode is
now 41.
```

In most other languages, the preceding code will not be valid. In PHP, this statement is valid, and it also generates the expected output. This is because in PHP a variable doesn't have a fixed data type assigned to it and can store any data type. The result of an expression is calculated on the basis of the operator and not on the basis of the operands. Examine the following code for a better understanding of juggling data types:

```
<?php
$a = "Philip";
$a += 2 ;  //The += operator is used to add the initial value assigned
to the variable to the number specified.
echo "$a";   //The value of $a is now 2.
?>
```

In this example, $a contains a value that is of the string data type. In the next line, the += operator changes the initial variable assigned to $a to 2, as shown in the following output:

```
X-Powered-By: PHP/4.0.6
Content-type: text/html
2
```

Consider another example where the .= operator is used to concatenate strings:

```
<?php
$a = "Philip";
$a .= 2;   //The .= operator is used to concatenate two strings.
echo "$a";   //The value of $a is now Philip2.
?>
```

The `.=` operator tells PHP that the number 2 is a string even though it is not specified in single quotes or double quotes. As a result, it concatenates the initial value with the new value of `$a`, and the output is `Philip2`.

> **NOTE** The operators += and .= are discussed in the section *Introducing Operators*.

Constants

A *constant* is a name that identifies a simple value. By nature, a constant is the opposite of a variable because the value of a constant remains fixed and doesn't change when the script is executed. Constants have the following characteristics:

- A constant is case-sensitive by default.
- By convention, constants are expressed in uppercase letters.
- A constant can begin with either an underscore or with a letter, followed by any number of underscores, letters, or numbers.

There are several other differences between variables and constants:

- A constant name never begins with a dollar sign.
- After a constant is set, it is not possible to redefine or undefine it.
- A constant can contain only scalar data types: boolean, integer, float, and string.
- A constant can be accessed and used anywhere in a script regardless of variable scoping rules.

Defining Constants

A simple way to define a constant is by using the `define ()` function. After you define a constant, you can read its value anytime you want by simply using its name. To read a constant's value, you can use the `constant ()` function. To obtain a list of all defined constants, you can use the `get_defined_constants` function.

In the following code, a constant CONS is defined with the value `Welcome to the world of music`. Notice that constants are case sensitive, and the value assigned to the constant CONS doesn't appear when you try to print the value of the constant cons:

```php
<?php
define ("CONS", "Welcome to the world of music.");
echo CONS, "\n"; //Will display the output "Welcome to the world of
music".
echo cons, "\n";  //Will display the word "cons".
?>
```

In this code, the constant CONS is defined with the value "Welcome to the world of music". Because constants are case-sensitive, the value assigned to CONS doesn't appear when you try to print the value of the constant cons.

Introducing Operators

In the previous section you learned about variables, data types, and constants and how to declare them. However, to use or declare variables or constants you need operators. The following problem and its solution explain the use of operators.

Problem Statement

Mega Music Mart has 1,000 music CDs in its stock at the beginning of September and 250 new music CDs are added to the stock during the month. By the end of the month, Mega Music Mart has sold 500 music CDs. Dave has been asked to write code to calculate the number of CDs that remain in the store.

Task List

✔ **Identify the operators to be used**

✔ **Write the code**

✔ **Execute the code**

Identify the Operators to Be Used

Operators are an integral part of any programming language; they are symbols that represent a specific action. For example, the plus sign indicates that addition needs to be performed and is an operator used for addition. Using operators, you can perform a number of operations on a variable:

- Assign a value to a variable
- Change the value of a variable
- Compare two or more values
- Specify a condition

There are six basic operator categories:

- Arithmetic
- Assignment
- Comparison
- Increment/decrement
- String
- Logical

Arithmetic Operators

Arithmetic operators are used to perform elementary mathematical calculations and are used when the value of variable declared is integer type. Table 3.2 shows how operators are used.

Let us look at some examples for a better understanding of arithmetic operators:

```
//Addition
$a = 6;
$b = 3;
$c = $a  + $b ;    // The value of $c is now 9.
//Subtraction
$a = 8
$b = 2
$c = $a - $b ;     //The value of $c is now 6.
//Multiplication
$a = 6
$b = 2
$c = $a * $b ;     //The value of $c is now 12.
//Division
$a = 12;
$b = 6;
$c = $a / $b ;     //The value of $c is now 2.
//Modulus
$a = 16
$b = 2
$c = $a % $b ;     //The value of $c is now 0.
```

This is because 16 is perfectly divisible by 2 and doesn't result in a remainder.

Table 3.2   Arithmetic Operators

NAME	EXAMPLE	OUTPUT
Addition	$a + $b	The sum of $a and $b
Subtraction	$a - $b	The difference between $a and $b
Multiplication	$a * $b	The product of $a and $b
Division	$a /$b	The quotient of $a and $b
Modulus	$a % $b	The remainder after dividing $a and $b

Assignment Operators

Assignment operators are used to assign a specific value to a variable. They are also used to change the existing value of a variable by adding to or subtracting from the variable's current value. A few examples are =, +=, and .=.

TIP In PHP, = does not mean equal to; = = is used for this.

In PHP, you can use more than one assignment operator in a single statement, as in the following code:

```
$a = ($b=3) + ($c=1);
```

The variables $a, $b, and $c are now integer types and will hold the values 4, 3, and 1, respectively. Table 3.3 illustrates how different assignment operators can be used.

To understand the concept of assignment operators, let's take the example of Mega Music Mart, the online music store that wants to keep track of the stock at the end of each month.

Result

The assignments operators that Dave will need to use are:

- ■ = to assign a value to the variable totalcd.
- ■ += to add fresh stock of CD to the existing stock
- ■ −= to subtract the number of CDs sold from the total number of CDs

Table 3.3 Assignment Operators

OPERATOR	USAGE	OUTPUT
+=	$a += 6	Adds the original value assigned to the variable $a to 6. If the original value of $a was 9, the current value of $a will become 15.
−=	$a −= 6	Subtracts the number specified from the original value of $a. If the original value of $a was 9, the current value of $a will become 3.
.=	$a .= "Strings of the guitar"	Concatenates (adds) the new value specified with the original value of the variable.

Write the Code

The following illustrates how to write code to display the in-stock CDs at the end of the month of September.

```
<HTML>
<HEAD>
<TITLE>Calculate the number of CDs in stock</TITLE>
</HEAD>
<BODY>
<?php
$totalcd = 1000;
echo "<H1>Total number of Music CDs: $totalcd</H1>";
$totalcd += 250;
echo "<H1>Total number of CDs after adding fresh stock: $totalcd</H1>";
$totalcd -= 500;
echo "<H1>Stock at the end of the month (Post Sales): $totalcd</H1>";
?>
</BODY>
</HTML>
```

Execute the Code

To execute the code and view it on the browser, perform the following steps:

1. Save the text file with a .php extension in /var/www/html as **assign.php**.

2. Launch Netscape Navigator.

3. In the Address box type `http://localhost(servername)/assign.php`.

> **NOTE** If the name for your server is not localhost, substitute its name in the URL to execute the file in the browser. For example, if the name of your server is server1.mydomain.com, you will need to use the following URL to execute assign.php: http://server1/assign.php.

Figure 3.1 illustrates the output of the code.

Problem Statement

Mega Music Mart wants to calculate its profit or loss for September. It earned $6,000 dollars in the month had expenses of $4,000. The development team needs to write a code to do the calculation.

Task List

✔ **Identify the operators to be used**

✔ **Write the code**

✔ **Execute the code**

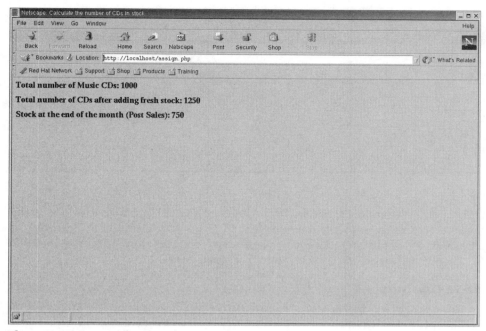

Figure 3.1 Output of assign.php.

Identify the Operators to Be Used

Comparison operators are used to compare two given values. Table 3.4 lists the various comparison operators.

Table 3.4 Comparison Operators

NAME	SYMBOL	EXAMPLE	DESCRIPTION
Equal to	= =	$a = =$b	The value of $a is equal to that $b.
Not equal to	! =	$a ! = $b	The value of $a is not equal to that of $b.
Less than	<	$a < $b	The value of $a is less than that of $b.
More than	>	$a > $b	The value of $a is greater than that of $b.

(continues)

Table 3.4 Comparison Operators *(Continued)*

NAME	SYMBOL	EXAMPLE	DESCRIPTION
Less than equal to	<=	$a <= $b	The value of $a is either less than or equal to that of $b.
Greater than equal to	>=	$a >= $b	The value of $a is either greater than or equal to that of $b.
Identical	= = =	$a===$b	The value of $a is equal to that of $b only when they are of the same data type.

Comparison operators check for the statement being either true or false. For example, when coding, if you write the statement $a = = $b, the result can either be true (a is equal to b) or false (a is not equal to b). Comparison operators are best used in coding when you also use if...else and while statements.

The `if` Construct

In most cases, you will need to use *control structures,* or *constructs,* in your code to use the operators effectively. Control structures are statements that check conditions, assign a value, create a loop within the code, or call a function.

The `if` construct is a conditional construct. It is used to check for a conditional statement and perform some action if the condition is true or false. The `if` conditional construct is followed by a logical expression in which data is compared and a decision is made based on the result of the comparison. The syntax of the `if` construct is as follows:

```
if $a + $b >5   //A conditional statement.
{
echo "The sum is greater than 5.";
}
```

The if construct has been used to check for a condition. Only when the sum of the variables $a and $b is more than 5 will the message The sum is greater than 5. appear. If the condition specified is false, no message will be printed. Notice that the action to be performed is enclosed within curly brackets.

The `else` Statement

The `else` statement is used to specify an action to be performed after a specific condition has been checked, and it is used with the `if` construct.

A condition can be either true or false. Therefore, you might want to perform an action in both cases. The `if` and the `else` construct can be used together to achieve this result. The following is an example where both `if` and `else` constructs have been used:

```
if $a + $b +$c = = 20
{
echo "The sum is equal to 20.";
}
```

```
else
{
echo "The sum is not equal to 20.";
}
```

The sum of $a, $b, and $c is checked. If the statement is true (the sum is equal to 20), the message The sum is equal to 20. is displayed; if the statement is false, the message specified with the else construct is displayed.

Let us now look at what Mega Music Mart wants to do.

Write the Code

The following is the code that Dave writes:

```
<HTML>
<HEAD>
<TITLE>Calculating Profit or Loss for Mega Music Mart</TITLE>
</HEAD>
<BODY>
<?php
$totalrevenue = 6000;
$totalcost = 4000;
$profit = $totalrevenue - $totalcost;
$loss = $totalcost - $totalrevenue;
if ($totalrevenue > $totalcost)  //The if statement has been used to
check for conditions.
{
echo "<H1>You have gained a profit of $profit dollars!</H1>";
}
if ($totalrevenue < $totalcost)
{
echo "<H1>You have incurred loss of $loss dollars</H1>";
}
if ($totalrevenue == $totalcost)
{
echo "<H1>You have neither gained profit nor incurred loss</H1>";
}
?>
</BODY>
</HTML>
```

Execute the Code

To execute the code and view it on the browser, perform the following steps:

1. Save the text file with a .php extension in /var/www/html as **compare.php**.

2. Open Netscape Navigator.

3. In the Address box type http://localhost/compare.php.

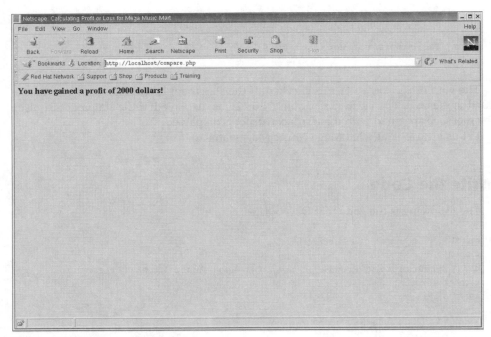

Figure 3.2   Output of compare.php.

Figure 3.2 illustrates the output of the code.

Problem Statement

Mega Music Mart wants to categorize the rock music CDs it has as Old Releases and New Releases. Write the code to check whether a CD was released before or after 2001.

Task List

✔ **Identify the operators to be used**

✔ **Write the code**

✔ **Execute the code**

Identify the Operators to be Used

In order to decide which operators will be used to accomplish the task, let's discuss the following operators:

- Incrementing and Decrementing operators
- String operators
- Logical operators

Incrementing and Decrementing Operators

In PHP, the concept of incrementing and decrementing operators is similar to that in the C language. There are two types of incrementing and decrementing operators, *postincrementing/decrementing operators* and *preincrementing/decrementing operators*. Postincrementing operators are placed after a variable name, and preincrementing/decrementing operators are placed before the name. Table 3.5 lists the different incrementing and decrementing operators and how they are used.

Consider the following code for a better understanding of incrementing and decrementing operators. This code shows how the postincrementing operator works:

```
//Postincrementing operator
<?php
$a = 5;
$b = $a++;
echo "$b", "\n";   //Returns the value 5.
echo "$a", "\n";   //Returns the value 6.
?>
```

A value of 5 is assigned to $a and a value of $a is assigned to $b. Because of the postincrementing ++ operator, in the output the value of $b is first 5 and then it becomes 6, as explained in the table.

Now consider an example of postdecrementing operator:

```
//Postdecrementing operator
<?php
$a = 5;
$b = $a--;
echo "$b", "\n";    //Returns the value 5.
echo "$a", "\n";   //Returns the value 4.
?>
```

Table 3.5   Incrementing and Decrementing Operators

NAME	EXAMPLE	RESULT
Postincrementing operator	$a++	Returns the value of $a and then adds 1 to the value
Postdecrementing operator	$a—	Returns the value of $a and then subtracts 1 from the value
Preincrementing operator	++$a	Adds 1 to the value of $a and then returns the new value
Predecrementing operator	—$a	Subtracts 1 from the value of $a and the returns the new value

A value of 5 is assigned to the variable $a and a value of $a is given to $b. In the output, because of the postdecrementing -- operator, the value of $b is first 5 and then becomes 4.

Now let's consider an example of preincrementing operator:

```
//Preincrementing operator
<?php
$a = 5;
$b = ++$a;
echo "$b", "\n";//Returns the value 6.
echo "$a", "\n";  //Returns the value 6.
?>
```

A value of 5 is assigned to the variable $a and a value of $a is assigned to $b. In the output the value of $b is 6 remains the same. This is because the preincrementing ++ operator adds 1 to the variable $a and then returns the new value of $a.

Consider an example of predecrementing operator:

```
//Predecrementing operator
<?php
$a = 5;
$b = --$a;
echo "$b", "\n";// Returns the value 4.
echo "$a", "\n";  //Returns the value 4.
?>
```

A value of 5 is assigned to the variable $a and a value of $a is assigned to $b. In the output the first value of $b is 4. Its value does not change because the operator subtracts 1 from the variable $a and then returns the new value when the value of the variable is called.

String Operators

When you start writing PHP code, you will realize the importance of string operators. PHP uses two kinds of string operators, *concatenation,* (.) and *concatenating assignment* (. =). The concatenation operator is used when you want to combine the left and right arguments between which the operator is placed. The concatenating assignment operator is a combination of the concatenation operator and the assignment operator.

The following is example of using the concatenation operator:

```
//Concatenation Operator
<?php
$a = "My name is";
$b = $a . " Philip!";//Now the variable $b contains "My name is
Philip!".
echo $b;
?>
```

The output of this code is:

```
X-Powered-By: PHP/4.0.6
Content-type: text/html
My name is Philip!
```

An example of the concatenating assignment operator is:

```php
//Concatenating Assignment operator
<?php
$a = "My name is";
$a .= " Philip!";    //Now the variable $a contains "My name is Philip!".
echo $a;
?>
```

The output of this code will be same of that of the earlier code, but in this code the concatenating assignment operator is used.

TIP **Either method can be used to concatenate strings.**

Logical Operators

Logical operators are used in PHP to determine the status of conditions. When you use if...else or while statements, logical operators execute code based on the status of a condition. In this section, we will discuss only two logical operators:

■ The and operator (&&) is used when a statement has two conditions to be checked. If both the conditions are true, the statement is true.

■ The or operator (||) is also used when a statement has two conditions to be checked. In this case if either of the two conditions is true, the statement is true.

Let us now take the example of Mega Music Mart and its needs to arrange its rock music CDs. The operators that the development team will use are =, <, = =, and &&. The following code checks whether the CD is an old release or a new release:

```
<HTML>
<HEAD>
<TITLE>Classifiaction of Rock CDs</TITLE>
<BODY>
<?php
$cdrelease = 2001;
$cdgenre = "Rock";
if (($cdrelease < 2001) && ($cdgenre == "Rock"))
{
echo "<H1>This is an old release.</H1>";
}
else
{
echo "<H1>This is a new release!!</H1>";
}
?>
</BODY>
</HTML>
```

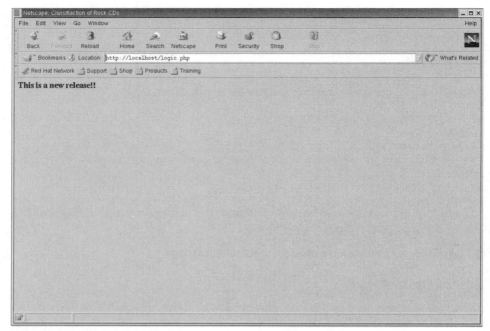

Figure 3.3   Output of logic.php.

The && operator has been used with the if statement to check for two conditions. The first condition checks the value of $cdrelease (year of release of the CD), and the second one checks whether the value of $cdgenre is Rock.

Execute the Code

To execute the code and view it in the browser, perform the following steps:

1. Save the text file with a .php extension in /var/www/html as **logic.php**.

2. Launch Netscape Navigator.

3. In the Address box, type http://localhost/logic.php.

Figure 3.3 illustrates the output of the code on a Web page.

Summary

In this chapter, you learned how to begin programming with PHP. The first portion covered concepts related to variables, data types, and constants. You learned how to declare variables and about the data types supported by PHP and both scalar and compound data types. Finally, you were introduced to constants. You also learned about operators and how to use different types of operators, such as arithmetic, assignment, comparison, incrementing/decrementing, and logical operators.

Control Structures

OBJECTIVES:

In this lesson, you will learn to:

- ✔ Identify control structures
- ✔ Distinguish between a condition and a statement
- ✔ Use conditional statements in your program
- ✔ Use looping statements in your program

Getting Started

In the previous chapter, you learned about variables, data types, and constants. Now it's time to learn how to use them effectively to change the flow of a program based on user interaction. This can be accomplished using control structures in your program.

This chapter is divided into three sections. The first gives an introduction to control structures, the second discusses the conditional constructs used in PHP, and the last one discusses the looping statements that are used in PHP.

Introduction to Control Structures

When you start writing programs in PHP, you will realize the importance of using control structures. They are used to control how a statement will be executed, adding useful functionality to the PHP code and making it more flexible.

Conditions and Statements

Control structures are usually based on conditions and therefore always have conditions associated with them. They check the status of these conditions, which can be either true or false. A statement can be used with a control structure to tell the program what to do depending on the result of the condition specified. Consider the following example to understand how a condition differs from a statement: If John promises that he won't neglect his studies, allow him to buy the guitar. This sentence can be broken into two parts, a condition and a statement. The first part of the sentence, If John promises that he won't neglect his studies, is a condition. The status of the condition will decide whether John will be allowed to buy the guitar or not. If the condition is true, John will be allowed to buy the guitar.

Features of Control Structures

Here are a few things that you can do using control structures in your program:

- Facilitate the execution of alternate blocks of code. That is, you will be able to guide the flow of a program depending on the result of a condition specified.

- Check for multiple conditions by using the appropriate combination of control structures.

- Selectively execute a piece of code depending on the value returned by another piece of code in a program.

- Repeatedly execute the same code.

TIP Curly brackets ({ }) are used to separate statements from the rest of a code block.

Using Conditional Statements

Problem Statement

Mega Music Mart has come up with a new marketing scheme that will offer a discount to its retailers based on the number of CDs sold. The price of a CD is $20. The details of the scheme are:

- If 10 CDs are purchased, the discount will be 10 percent.
- For more than 10 and less than or equal to 20 CDs, the discount will be 15 percent.
- For more than 20 and less than or equal to 30 CDs, the discount will be 20 percent.
- For more than 30 and less than or equal to 40 CDs, the discount will be 25 percent.

Task List

Sarah has been asked to write the code to calculate the discount on the basis of the number of CDs purchased by a retailer. To do this, she will need to:

✔ **Identify the conditional statements to be used**

✔ **Write the code**

✔ **Execute the code**

Identify the Conditional Statements to Be Used

As the name suggests, conditional statements are used to check for conditions and execute code on the basis of the value returned. This section discusses if, else, elseif, and switch conditional statements.

The *if* Statement

We discussed the if statement briefly in the previous chapter; this section contains a detailed explanation of it. The if statement is one of the most commonly used statements in PHP or any programming language; it has the following:

Allows conditional execution. The if statement can check for a particular condition and also perform a specific action depending on whether the condition is true or false.

Is capable of containing multiple code blocks. You can set more than one operation to be performed depending on the result of the condition specified in the PHP code.

Can also be nested within an existing if statement. You can use another if statement within an existing one to check another condition within an existing condition.

The following example shows how the if statement is used. The usage of most other control structures is the same.

```
if (put condition within parentheses)
{
//put code to be executed here
}
```

You can see that the condition is stated within parentheses. In addition, observe that the code to be executed is specified within curly brackets. Consider the following code:

```php
<?php
$hobby = "Music";
if ($hobby = "Music")
{
echo "You have an interesting hobby";
}
?>
```

The expression `if ($hobby = "Music")` is a condition. Only when this condition returns a true value will the next statement in the code be executed and printed. If the statement doesn't return a true value, the next statement in the code will be ignored. The variable `$hobby` has been assigned a string type value, `Music`. Therefore, the condition is true and the output is as follows:

```
X-Powered-By: PHP/4.0.6
Content-type: text/html
You have an interesting hobby
```

The `else` Statement

The `else` statement, as discussed in the previous chapter, is always used with the `if` statement. When you use the `if` statement, you can check for a condition and specify a statement to be executed when the condition is true. The `else` statement is used to specify a statement in case the result of the condition is false. The usage of the `else` statement is similar to that of the `if` statement. The `else` statement is also used to check an alternative block of code. Consider the following code:

```php
<?php
$hobby = "Dance";
if ($hobby != "Dance")
{
echo "Don't you like dancing?";
}
else
{
echo "You like dancing!";
}
?>
```

Here, `$hobby` contains a string type value, `Dance`. The `if` condition checks whether the value of the variable `$hobby` is not equal to `Dance`. If this statement is true, the message `"Don't you like dancing?"` will appear. The predetermined value of `$hobby` is `Dance`. Therefore, the condition is false. The `else` statement is specified to perform an action when the condition is false. As a result, the message `"You like dancing!"` is output.

The elseif Statement

The elseif statement, as the name suggests, is a combination of the else and if statements. You can check for multiple conditions by using the elseif statement. You can also have multiple elseif statements under an if statement. An elseif statement is executed only when the previous if statement returns a false value. The elseif statement can also be written as else if (two words). The output in both the cases will be the same. To understand the elseif statement, consider the following code:

```php
<?php
$ilike = "Dance";
if ($ilike = "Music")
{
echo "Do you like singing?";
}
elseif ($ilike = "Dance")
{
echo "Do you like dancing?";
}
else
{
echo "You like neither music nor dance";
}
?>
```

The variable ilike is a string type variable with the value "Dance". Therefore, when the first condition in the if statement is verified, the result is false. Then, the condition given with the elseif statement is checked. If the if statement was true, the elseif statement would not have been checked. In the preceding example, the else statement will be ignored because the elseif statement is true. Therefore, the output of the code on the command prompt will be:

```
X-Powered-By: PHP/4.0.6
Content-type: text/html
Do you like singing?
```

The switch Statement

The switch statement can be used in placement of the if statement. Similar to the if statement, the switch statement is also used to change the flow of a program depending on the evaluation of an expression. Although the if statement is also used to achieve the same result, there are certain differences between the if and switch statements:

- The elseif statement can be used with the if statement to evaluate multiple conditions and expressions. In contrast, switch evaluates only one expression at a time and executes the corresponding code specified for the expression.

- The result generated as part of the if statement returns a boolean value, which is either true or false, but in the case of switch, the result of a condition can be evaluated against any number of values.

Whenever you use the `switch` statement, you can use a corresponding `case` statement to derive a high level of functionality from the code. That is, using multiple cases, you can check the result of the `switch` statement and direct the code to perform different operations depending on the type of result generated. The following code shows how the `switch` statement can be used:

```php
<?php
$choice = "Rock";
switch ($choice)
    {
    case "Pop":
        print "I listen to Pop not Rock";
        break;
    case "Rap":
        print "I listen to Rap and not Rock";
        break;
    case "Jazz":
        print "I listen to Jazz not Rock";
        break;
    case "Rock":
        print "I listen to only Rock music";
        break;
    }
?>
```

In this code, notice that:

- Multiple `case` statements have been used with respect to the `switch` statement.
- Each `case` statement ends with a colon.
- A `break` statement is included in each `case` statement.

The preceding code checks for the string `"Rock"` in each `case` statement. The code keeps checking each case one after the other until it finds the case where the value of the variable `$choice` is `"Rock"`. Then the particular message is printed. If you had specified this case at the beginning of the code, other cases would not have been checked because of the `break` statements.

Ideally, you should use the `break` statement as part of the `case` statement to end the execution of a `switch` statement. In the preceding code each `switch` statement has a corresponding `case` statement, as well as a `break` statement.

The output of the preceding code is:

```
X-Powered-By: PHP/4.0.6
Content-type: text/html
I listen to only Rock music
```

NOTE The `break` statement is discussed with looping statements later in this chapter.

Result

The programming constructs that Sarah will need to use to write the program that calculates discounts for retailers based on the discount scheme are:

- The `if` conditional construct
- The `elseif` conditional construct

Write the Code

The code for the scenario is:

```
<HTML>
<HTML>
<HEAD>
<TITLE>Calculating Discount</TITLE>
</HEAD>
<BODY>
<H1><CENTER>Calculating Discount</CENTER></H1>
<?php
$price = 200;
$qty = 10;
echo "<H4>Original price is $price</H4>";
if ($qty =10)
 {
 $discount=10;
 }
 elseif ($qty <=20)
 {
 $discount=15;
 }
 elseif ($qty <=30)
 {
 $discount=20;
 }
 elseif($qty <=40)
 {
 $discount=25;
 }
echo "<H4>Discount is $discount percent</H4>";
echo "<H4>Price after discount is ", (($price * (100 - $discount)/100)),
"</H4>";@@@COMP: Break line as shown.@@@
?>
</BODY>
</HTML>
```

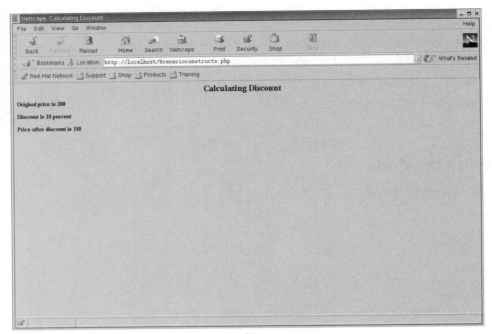

Figure 4.1   Output of Scenarioconstructs.php.

Execute the Code

To execute the code and view it in the browser, perform the following steps:

1. Save the text file in which you have written the code with a .php extension in /var/www/html as **Scenarioconstructs.php**.

2. Open Netscape Navigator.

3. In the Address box, type `http://localhost/Scenarioconstructs.php`.

Figure 4.1 illustrates the output of the code.

Using Loops in PHP

Problem Statement

Mega Music Mart has floated shares in the market. The marketing manager wants a report to be generated on the Web page that shows the dividend earned by shareholders based on the investment made. The marketing manager has asked the head of the development team to create a report and display it on the Web page. The following information has been provided:

- The price of a share is $20.
- The total number of shares is 20.
- The dividend rate is 10 percent on the cost of shares.

Task List

To create the Web page, the development team will need to:

✓ **Identify looping statements**

✓ **Write the code**

✓ **Execute the code**

Identify Looping Statements

Loops are an integral part of a programming language. Typically, the need to use loops in a program arises when you want to execute a piece of code repeatedly until a desired condition is achieved. There are many control structures that can be used to implement looping in a program.

The `while` Loop

The `while` loop is one of the simplest looping control structures in PHP. It behaves as it does in other programming languages, such as C. When you specify a condition and a code block along with the `while` loop, the code block is repeatedly executed until the condition becomes false.

> **TIP** Multiple statements can be nested and executed in a `while` loop.

To use the `while` loop, use the following syntax:

```
while (Put condition within parantheses)
{
//Put statement here
}
```

The following code illustrates the use of the `while` loop:

```
<?php
$a = 1;
while ($a <= 10)
{
echo $a++, "\n";
}
?>
```

The value of the variable $a has been declared as 1. Then, the value of $a is checked. The `while` loop continues to execute until the value of $a is less than or equal to 10.

The loop stops as soon as the value of $a is 10 and prints the numbers 1 to 10 on the screen. The output is:

```
X-Powered-By: PHP/4.0.6
Content-type: text/html
1
2
3
4
5
6
7
8
9
10
```

The do...while Loop

The do...while loop is just the opposite of the while loop. Unlike the while loop where the condition is checked repeatedly before the code is executed, in a do...while loop the specified code is executed at least once before the condition is checked. Typically, the do...while loop is used when you want to execute a code block at least once even if the result of the condition specified is false.

NOTE When you use the while loop, always remember to end the expression or the condition with a semicolon.

Consider the following code:

```
<?php
$a = 1;
do
{
echo $a, "\n";
$a++;
}
while ($a > 10);
?>
```

The value assigned to $a is 1. The do statement executes the code once and then checks for conditions in the while loop. When the while loop is encountered, the condition is proved false because the value $a is less than 10. As a result, the value 1 is printed on the screen.

The for Loop

The for loop is similar to the while loop and can achieve the same result. It is used to evaluate a set of conditional expressions at the beginning of each loop. The for loop is one of the most complex loops in PHP; with it you can accomplish three tasks in a single line: assign a variable, state a condition, and specify an incrementing variable. The usage of the for loop is as follows:

```
for (expr1, expr2, expr3)
{
//Put statement here
}
```

In this code sample, expr1 is a variable assignment, expr2 is the condition that needs to be checked, and expr3 is a variable increment. Notice that each expression specified in the for loop is separated using a semicolon. Although the code indicates that three expressions need to be specified, you need not specify all three expressions. If you leave the second expression empty, it results in an infinite loop.

The following code illustrates the use of the for loop:

```
<?php
for ($a = 1; $a <= 10; $a++)
{
echo "$a multiplied by 2 returns ".($a * 2), "\n";
}
?>
```

All three expressions have been specified with the for loop. In the first expression, the value of $a has been assigned as 1. In the second expression, a condition has been specified. Finally, in the third expression, the variable $a is incremented. The output of the preceding code will print the product of the value of $a and the number 2 until the value of $a has incremented to the number 10. The output of the code is:

```
X-Powered-By: PHP/4.0.6
Content-type: text/html
1 multiplied by 2 returns 2
2 multiplied by 2 returns 4
3 multiplied by 2 returns 6
4 multiplied by 2 returns 8
5 multiplied by 2 returns 10
6 multiplied by 2 returns 12
7 multiplied by 2 returns 14
8 multiplied by 2 returns 16
9 multiplied by 2 returns 18
10 multiplied by 2 returns 20
```

Breaking a Loop

Sometimes, you might want to break a loop before it completes execution. The break statement can do this. Consider the following code to understand why it might be essential to use the break statement within a loop:

```
<?php
for ($a = 1; $a <= 20; $a++)
{
```

```
$divide = 40/$a;
echo "The result of dividing 40 by $a is $divide", "\n";
}
?>
```

This code will divide the number 40 by the value of $a until the value of $a is less than or equal to 20. Then, the output is printed. However, in this case, the value of $a has been predetermined. In a real-life scenario, when you have a Web page and want the user to input the value of $a, problems might arise because you cannot control what the user enters. Imagine what would happen if a user entered the value of $a as -3. In this case, the number will be first divided by -3, -2, -1, and 0, before it is divided by 1. This is a problem because dividing any number by 0 can return a warning message.

To avoid such problems, you can use the break statement. In the preceding code, you can use the break statement in such a way that the number 40 is not divided by 0:

```
<?php
$a = -3;
for (; $a <= 20; $a++)
{
if ($a == 0)
break;
$divide = 40/$a;
echo "The result of dividing 40 by $a is $divide", "\n";
}
?>
```

It has been assumed that the user has entered the value -3. Therefore, to avoid dividing 40 by 0, a break statement is included in the code. The loop will immediately come to a halt when the break statement is encountered, and no warning messages will appear. The output of the code is:

```
X-Powered-By: PHP/4.0.6
Content-type: text/html
The result of dividing 40 by -3 is -13.333333333333
The result of dividing 40 by -2 is -20
The result of dividing 40 by -1 is -40
```

It is evident from the output that the loop was executed until the number 0 was encountered.

The continue Statement

The continue statement, unlike the break statement, doesn't break a loop. When you break a loop with the break statement, you cannot check for the same condition again. The continue statement just skips the specified iteration and doesn't cause the loop to end.

Examine the following code:

```
<?php
$a = -3;
for (; $a <= 20; $a++)
```

```
{
if ($a <= 0)
continue;
$divide = 40/$a;
echo "The result of dividing 40 by $a is $divide", "\n";
}
?>
```

The break statement has been replaced with the continue statement. Therefore, as soon as the value of $a is less than or equal to 0, that iteration is skipped and the loop starts all over again. The output of the code is:

```
X-Powered-By: PHP/4.0.6
Content-type: text/html
The result of dividing 40 by 1 is 40
The result of dividing 40 by 2 is 20
The result of dividing 40 by 3 is 13.333333333333
The result of dividing 40 by 4 is 10
The result of dividing 40 by 5 is 8
The result of dividing 40 by 6 is 6.6666666666667
The result of dividing 40 by 7 is 5.7142857142857
The result of dividing 40 by 8 is 5
The result of dividing 40 by 9 is 4.4444444444444
The result of dividing 40 by 10 is 4
The result of dividing 40 by 11 is 3.6363636363636
The result of dividing 40 by 12 is 3.3333333333333
The result of dividing 40 by 13 is 3.0769230769231
The result of dividing 40 by 14 is 2.8571428571429
The result of dividing 40 by 15 is 2.6666666666667
The result of dividing 40 by 16 is 2.5
The result of dividing 40 by 17 is 2.3529411764706
The result of dividing 40 by 18 is 2.2222222222222
The result of dividing 40 by 19 is 2.1052631578947
The result of dividing 40 by 20 is 2
```

Although $a has been assigned the value -3, the output displays the result starting with division by 1. Because you used the continue statement, the values of $a that were less than or equal to 0 were skipped.

Nesting Loops

Nesting loops are a way to use a loop statement within another loop statement. For example, if you have a loop x and have another loop y in the loop x, the loop y will be executed x * y times. Consider the following example:

```
loop x
{
  loop y
  {
//this will be executed ((no. of times x is executed) * (no. of times y
is executed))
```

```
    }
// this statement will be executed (no. of times x is executed)
}
```

This method of using loops within loops is useful when you plan to use dynamically created HTML tables. These loops can also be used with multidimensional arrays. The following code shows the use of nesting loops:

```php
<?php
for ($y = 12; $y <= 14; $y++)
    {
    echo "Multiplication Table of $y","\n";
     for ($x = 1; $x <= 10; $x++)
        {
        echo "$y X $x = ".($y * $x), "\n";
        }
    }
?>
```

Here, one for statement is nested in another one. In the first for statement, the value of 12 is assigned to $y. Then, a condition specifies that until the value of $y is less than or equal to 14, the value of $y should be incremented. Within this for statement, another for statement is included. This for statement declares a variable, $x, and assigns the value 1 to it. Then, a check is made to determine whether the value of $x is less than or equal to 10. Finally, the value of $x is incremented. Within this for statement, a condition also specifies that the value of $x should be multiplied by the value of $y. As a result, the output of the code will print the multiplication tables of 12, 13, and 14 on the screen, as follows:

```
X-Powered-By: PHP/4.0.6
Content-type: text/html
Multiplication Table of 12
12 X 1 = 12
12 X 2 = 24
12 X 3 = 36
12 X 4 = 48
12 X 5 = 60
12 X 6 = 72
12 X 7 = 84
12 X 8 = 96
12 X 9 = 108
12 X 10 = 120
Multiplication Table of 13
13 X 1 = 13
13 X 2 = 26
13 X 3 = 39
13 X 4 = 52
```

```
13 X 5 = 65
13 X 6 = 78
13 X 7 = 91
13 X 8 = 104
13 X 9 = 117
13 X 10 = 130
Multiplication Table of 14
14 X 1 = 14
14 X 2 = 28
14 X 3 = 42
14 X 4 = 56
14 X 5 = 70
14 X 6 = 84
14 X 7 = 98
14 X 8 = 112
14 X 9 = 126
14 X 10 = 140
```

Result

The looping statement that the development team will need to use to generate the report is the for loop statement.

Write the Code

The code for generating the report on the Web page is:

```
<HTML>
<HEAD>
<TITLE>Value of Shares</TITLE>
<H3>Table Showing Cost of Shares</H3>
<BODY>
<TABLE BORDER=1>
<?php
for ($shares = 1; $shares <= 20; $shares++)
{
$cost = $shares * 20;
echo "<TR><TD>The cost of $shares share/s is $cost dollars</TD>","\n";
$dividend = $cost * 0.10;
echo "<TD>The dividend is $dividend dollars</TD></TR>", "\n";
}
?>
</TABLE>
</BODY>
</HTML>
```

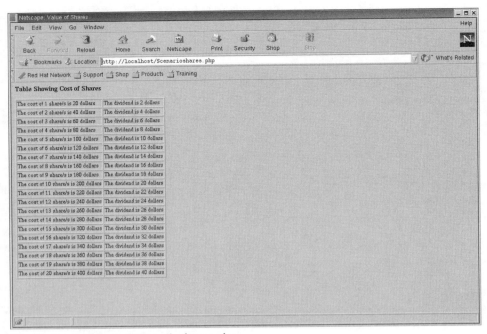

Figure 4.2   Output of Scenarioshares.php.

Execute the Code

To execute the code and view it in the browser, perform the following steps:

1. Save the text file in which you have written the code with a .php extension in /var/www/html as **Scenarioshares.php**.

2. Open Netscape Navigator.

3. In the Address box, type `http://localhost/Scenarioshares.php`.

Figure 4.2 illustrates the output of the code.

Summary

In this chapter, you learned about control structures, and you learned to distinguish between a condition and a statement. You were also introduced to the characteristics of control structures. Next, you learned to use the conditional statements `if`, `else`, `elseif`, and `switch` in your PHP programs. After this, you learned how to use looping statements, such as `while`, `do...while`, and `for`. Then, you learned how to use `break` and `continue` statements. Finally, you learned how to nest loops.

CHAPTER 5

Functions

OBJECTIVES:

In this chapter, you will learn to:

- ✓ Declare a function without arguments
- ✓ Declare a function with arguments
- ✓ Return values by using the return statement
- ✓ Call functions dynamically
- ✓ Define the scope of a variable
- ✓ Use the global statement
- ✓ Use the static statement
- ✓ Assign default values to arguments
- ✓ Pass variables as a reference to the argument of a function

Getting Started

In the previous chapter, you learned about control structures and used them in your scripts to change the flow of a program. The next step in learning about PHP is to know more about functions. They are the heart of any programming language, and PHP is no exception.

This chapter is divided into two parts. The first gives an introduction to functions, and the second discusses how you can use functions effectively in PHP programs.

Introduction to Functions

A function is a piece of independent code that can be used to perform a specific task. To understand what exactly a function does, let us consider the example of a soda-making machine. To get flavored soda from a soda machine, you need to add the necessary ingredients, such as essence and mineral water. The machine then processes these raw materials, and you get your choice of flavor. In the same way, functions can be used to get a desired output. The output entirely depends on the code you specify in it. A function does the following:

Accepts values.   A function accepts values from the arguments passed to it.

Processes them.   A function executes the code specified within it.

Performs an action.   This is the output that is returned after the function is executed. However, returning a value is an optional feature of a function. The output can also act as the input for some other function. It can also be printed on the command line or the browser.

The advantages of using functions in code are that they make code simpler to read and understand and also ensure reusability of code. This is because the same function can be called several times in a particular program, which also avoids repetition to a great extent. To use a particular piece of code specified within a function, the developer just needs to call the respective function.

Features of Functions in PHP

Functions have several features, some of which are specific to PHP:

- Functions are self-contained. That is, they are self-sufficient blocks of code that can operate independently.
- A function needs to be called in a script to be executed.
- Values can be passed with functions. These values can then be used for calculations. The values can also be passed back to the script that called them.
- Functions need not be executed immediately. A function can be declared and then executed whenever required.
- A particular function can be called several times within the same script.
- A function can consist of PHP code, other functions, or a class definition.

You need to remember the following points about the functions available in PHP 4:

- In PHP 4, it is not necessary to define a function before referencing it. This is a new feature.

- PHP doesn't support function overloading. Therefore, you cannot define different functions by using the same function name.
- A function cannot be redefined or undefined after it is declared.
- PHP supports a varying number of arguments.
- PHP supports default arguments.

User-Defined versus Built-in Functions

In PHP, functions can be broadly categorized as *user-defined* or *built-in functions*. User-defined functions, as the name suggests, are functions declared by a user (programmer). The programmer can completely customize these functions and specify exactly what the function does. This attribute of user-defined functions makes them flexible, and developers use them sparingly.

Unlike user-defined functions, built-in functions are prewritten functions that are part of PHP. These functions have a predetermined functionality that doesn't change. There are hundreds of built-in functions available with PHP.

Syntax for Functions

The syntax used to declare functions is as follows:

```
function function_name ($argument1, $argument2)
    {
    //put code here
    }
```

In the preceding syntax:

The `function` statement declares a function and is followed by the name of the function.

`Function_name` is the name that you choose to assign to a function; it distinguishes one function from another in a program. You can also use this function name to reference a function in a program. All functions should have unique function names because PHP doesn't support function overloading. The function name follows the `function` statement.

An argument is a value that you pass to a function. A function can have more than one argument. Whenever you pass an argument, it becomes available in the program as a local variable for that particular function. Arguments should always be enclosed within parentheses. If you choose to not pass arguments, you would still need to use the parentheses. In the preceding syntax, `$argument1` and `$argument2` are the arguments that have been passed.

The function code is the code you specify within a function. As discussed earlier, it is the essence of the function. The output generated after executing the function depends on the code used in it. This code should be enclosed within curly braces.

Using Functions

By now you have a basic understanding of what is meant by a function and why they are used. In this section, you will learn to define user-defined functions in PHP code. You will first learn how to declare a simple function. Then you will learn to declare a function with arguments and also understand how functions are accessed and used within PHP code.

Problem Statement

It's the end of another business month for Mega Music Mart. To keep the employees informed about the profit and loss earned each month, the CEO wants the development team to develop a program that calculates the profit or loss for Mega Music Mart for the month. The CEO also wants this report to be generated on the Web page on the local intranet so that company employees can view the profit or loss status of the company. The report should display:

- The amount of expenses incurred during the month
- The profit earned or loss incurred during the month
- The percentage of profit earned or loss incurred during the month

To perform the calculations, the development team has been provided with the following details:

- The fixed cost incurred during the month is $1,000.
- The variable cost incurred during the month is $500.
- The total revenue earned during the month is $5,000

> **TIP** The sum of fixed cost and variable cost amounts to the total expenses incurred during a financial year.

Task List

To create the Web page, the development team needs to:

✓ **Identify the necessary user-defined functions**

✓ **Write the code**

✓ **Execute the code**

Identify Necessary User-Defined Functions

As discussed earlier, functions are of two types, user-defined and built-in. In this section, we will discuss how user-defined functions can be used in your programs in the best possible way.

Declaring a Simple Function

Now that you know the syntax, let's begin with declaring a simple function. The following code illustrates how a function is declared. To avoid complexity, arguments have not been used in this example.

```php
<?php
function abtmusic ( )
    {
    print "Music is a way of life!";
    }
abtmusic ( );
?>
```

In the this code:

- A function with the name abtmusic is declared.

- No arguments are passed with this function. Therefore, the parentheses are left blank.

- The operation to be performed within the function is specified within curly braces.

- The function is then called by using the function name.

The output of the code is:

```
X-Powered-By: PHP/4.0.6
Content-type: text/html
Music is a way of life!
```

As you can see, when the abtmusic function is called, the print statement is executed, and the message is printed on the command line. Although there is nothing incorrect in the preceding example, functions are usually used to perform operations that are more complex than this. To derive the best advantage from functions, you should be able to pass arguments to them.

Declaring a Function with Arguments

Now that you know how to declare a simple function, let's see how a function with arguments is declared and used. Consider the following code:

```php
<?php
function printcheck ($sometext)
    {
    print ("$sometext \n");
    }
printcheck ("I love music.");
printcheck ("I play the guitar.");
printcheck ("I play for my high school band!");
?>
```

A function named `printcheck` is declared, and an argument, `$sometext`, is passed to the function. As discussed earlier, an argument that is passed once becomes a variable that is local to the function in which it is used. The operation that needs to be performed is specified within curly brackets. As shown in the code, the argument `$sometext` is specified with the `print` statement. Then, different values to the argument are passed in the form of three different text messages. Every time the function `printcheck` is called, a new value is passed to the argument. Therefore, all the three messages are printed to the command line.

The output of the code is:

```
X-Powered-By: PHP/4.0.6
Content-type: text/html
I love music.
I play the guitar.
I play for my high school band!
```

Returning Values

Another important feature of functions is the ability to return a value after performing a specified calculation. You can return a value or an object by using the `return` statement. It can be used to return:

- The value of an expression
- Hard-coded values, that is, values stated in the code
- A value returned by a different function

The following code shows how the `return` statement works:

```php
<?php
function multiply ($a, $b)
    {
    $product = $a * $b;
    return $product;
    }
echo  multiply (3,6),"\n";
?>
```

A function named `multiply` is declared, and two arguments, `$a` and `$b`, are passed to it. Within the curly braces, another variable named `$product` is declared. This variable stores the product of `$a` and `$b`. Then the return statement is used to return the result. The function is called with the values 3 and 6 assigned to `$a` and `$b`, respectively. The output of the code is:

```
X-Powered-By: PHP/4.0.6
Content-type: text/html
18
```

In this case, the `return` statement has been used to return the result of an expression. You can also use it to return hard-coded values:

```
return 9;
```

The `return` statement can be used to return a value returned by another function call. The following code shows how this is done:

```
return ( diff_function ( $anotherarg ) );
```

Here, the return statement will return the value returned by the function `diff_function`.

Calling Functions Dynamically

In PHP, you can call functions dynamically. Using this feature you can:

1. Declare a function
2. Then declare a variable and assign the function name to the variable (as a string)
3. Then use the variable as a function

The following code shows how functions are called dynamically:

```php
<?php
function addition ($a, $b)
    {
    echo ($a + $b), "\n";
    }
$result = "addition";
$result (3,6);
?>
```

A function named `addition` is declared. Next, a variable `$result` is declared and is assigned the name of the function (as a string). Finally, you call the function addition using the variable `$result`. When you call the function, you actually use the variable `$result` as a function. The output of the code is:

```
X-Powered-By: PHP/4.0.6
Content-type: text/html
9
```

As is evident from the output, the values of the arguments `$a` and `$b` that were passed to the function addition are added together. However, you actually called the function by using `$result`.

Scope of a Variable

When using functions in your program, you should be aware of the scope of variables used within it. This refers to the availability of a variable specified within a function. You need to remember the following points with respect to variables in PHP:

- The scope of a variable is limited to the function in which it has been used. As a result, the variable is accessible, or available for use, only within the function and not elsewhere.

- As soon as you specify a variable within a function, this variable becomes local to the function in which it is introduced after the function is declared.

Both these points state that a variable declared within a function is available for use only within that particular function. In addition, a variable declared outside a function cannot be accessed by the function. This feature is especially useful because it prevents the contents of a variable from being overwritten if you use the same variable name more than once and assign different values to it. Consider the following code:

```php
<?php
function music ()
    {
    $a = "Music is great";
    }
print $a;
?>
```

The value of the variable $a is assigned within the function music. Therefore, if you try to print the variable outside the function, the output will be blank because PHP treats the variable outside the function as a different variable to which a value hasn't been assigned.

TIP Using the same variable outside the function doesn't prevent the program from executing. The value of the variable outside the function is just treated as a new variable whose value has not been specified.

The global Statement

As discussed earlier, it is not possible to access a variable that is not defined within the function. This feature is good to some extent, but it makes the program inflexible. You can use the global statement to access variables that are not defined within the function, making the program flexible. Consider the following example:

```php
<?php
$ilike = "Rock";
function music()
    {
    echo "I love listening to $ilike music!", "\n";
    }
music();
?>
```

The variable $ilike is defined before declaring the function music. Therefore, the value specified in the variable $ilike will not be accessible within the function. When you try to access the variable $ilike in the function, the program assumes that $ilike is a new variable that doesn't have any value assigned to it. As a result, the string "Rock," which is assigned to the variable, will not appear in the output:

```
X-Powered-By: PHP/4.0.6
Content-type: text/html
I love listening to  music!
```

The value of the variable $ilike is interpreted as null and an additional blank space appears in the output. You can resolve such problems by using the global statement. Consider this example where the global statement is used:

```
<?php
$ilike = "Rock";
function music ()
    {
    global $ilike;
    echo "I love listening to $ilike music!", "\n";
    }
music ();
?>
```

Again, the value of the variable $ilike is specified outside the function. However, you are using the global statement followed by the name of the variable within the function. As soon as you specify the variable to be a global variable, it becomes accessible inside the function. The output of the code is:

```
X-Powered-By: PHP/4.0.6
Content-type: text/html
I love listening to Rock music!
```

Now, the word *Rock* is also printed. This value was assigned to the variable outside the function but was accessible within the function because you used the global statement.

> **NOTE** Changing the value of the global variable within a function can alter the value of the global variable at different occurrences. Therefore, it is not advisable to do so.

The static Statement

Usually, variables used within functions are short-lived. They are defined when a function is declared, and their purpose is complete as soon as the function is executed. It is advisable to write scripts in such a way that they are a series of independent scripts. However, when you use functions that consist of the global statement, they cannot be referred to as standalone blocks of code. This is because the variable is declared outside the function and is accessed using the global statement. If you use the static statement to define a variable within a function, the variable will remain local to the function. Consider the following example:

```php
<?php
increment();
increment();
increment();
function increment()
    {
    $a=0;
    echo $a;
    $a++;
    }
?>
```

Every time the function increment is called, the variable $a is created and is destroyed as soon as the function is executed. As a result, the value of the variable remains the same. Therefore, the output of the code is as follows:

```
X-Powered-By: PHP/4.0.6
Content-type: text/html
000
```

Consider the following code that uses the static statement to declare the variable within the function:

```php
<?php
increment();
increment();
increment();
function increment()
    {
    static $a=0;
    echo $a;
    $a++;
    }
?>
```

The static statement defines the variable, and the function remembers the value of the variable after it is executed. Therefore, it prints the incremented value of the variable every time the function is called. This is evident from the output:

```
X-Powered-By: PHP/4.0.6
Content-type: text/html
012
```

Arguments

There is more to learn about arguments than what has been covered so far. This section will help you understand the relevance of using arguments and how effectively can they be put to use. While using functions, you can assign default values to arguments and pass variables as a reference to the argument of a function.

Assigning Default Values to Arguments

Assigning default values to arguments means assigning a predefined value to an argument. Generally, when you pass an argument to a function, you specify the value to be used by the argument when you call the function. This is not always the case. Sometimes, you may realize that the value of a particular argument is more or less the same most of the time. In such a situation, you can assign a default value to the argument. Then when you call the function, assigning a value to the argument becomes optional. If you don't assign any value to the argument when calling the function, the function will use the default value that you have assigned. Consider an example where you will specify the font size of the text on your Web page to an argument:

```
<HTML>
<HEAD>
<TITLE>Printing text on a Web Page</TITLE>
</HEAD>
<BODY>
<?php
function textonweb ($content, $fontsize)
{
echo "<FONT SIZE=$fontsize>$content</FONT>";
}
textonweb ("Facts About Me <BR>", 7);
textonweb ("I love music. <BR>", 3);
textonweb ("I love playing the guitar. <BR>", 3);
textonweb ("I play for a rock band! <BR>", 3);
?>
</BODY>
</HTML>
```

Two arguments are passed to the function `textonweb`. The first argument `$content` is passed to hold the text, and the `$fontsize` argument is passed to hold the size of the text. The font size assigned for the heading is 7, and for rest of the text it is 3. In this example, font size 3 is used most often. Therefore, instead of repeatedly specifying the font size for the text, you can specify a default value. After using a default value for the argument `$fontsize`, you would need to specify the font size only if the font size you decide to specify is not 3. The following code assigns a default value to the argument `$fontsize`:

```
<HTML>
<HEAD>
<TITLE>Printing text on a Web Page</TITLE>
</HEAD>
<BODY>
<?php
function textonweb ($content, $fontsize=3)
{
echo "<FONT SIZE=$fontsize>$content</FONT>";
}
textonweb ("Facts About Me <BR>", 7);
textonweb ("I love music. <BR>");
textonweb ("I love playing the guitar. <BR>");
textonweb ("I play for a rock band! <BR>");
?>
</BODY>
</HTML>
```

The default value of the argument $fontsize is 3. Therefore, you would need to specify the value for this argument only if the font size should not be 3, such as when specifying the font size of the heading. Notice that after specifying the default value, the value of the argument $fontsize is left blank, but still the font size used by the program is 3. The output of the program is shown in Figure 5.1.

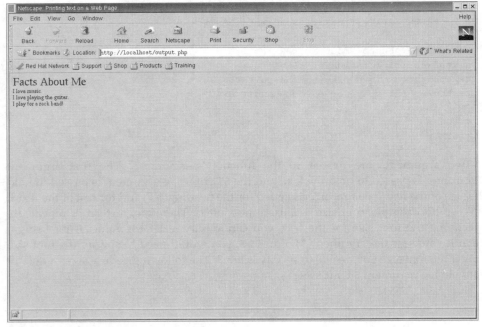

Figure 5.1 Output of the code on the browser.

Passing Variables as a Reference to the Argument of a Function

By now, you know that arguments passed for a function become local variables to that particular function. If you try to make changes to these variables outside of the function, they will not affect the value of the variable within the function. Consider the following example:

```php
<?php
function somefunct ($somearg)
{
    $somearg += 3;
}
$othernum = 12;
somefunct ($othernum);
echo "$othernum","\n";
?>
```

The argument $somearg is passed to the function somefunct. Within the function, the value of $somearg is incremented by 3. Then another variable $othernum is declared outside the function. The value assigned to this function is 12. Then you reference the function somefunct with this variable ($othernum). Now, when you print the value of this variable, the output is 12 because the value of the newly defined variable was declared outside the function somefunct.

You can use the variable defined outside the function as a value to the argument; that is, you can pass an argument to the function by reference. You can do so by using an ampersand. Consider the following code:

```php
<?php
function somefunct ($somearg)
{
    $somearg += 3;
}
$othernum = 12;
somefunct (&$othernum);
echo "$othernum","\n";
?>
```

The ampersand symbol is used with the argument that is being passed as a reference to the function. The output of the code is:

```
X-Powered-By: PHP/4.0.6
Content-type: text/html
15
```

The value of the new variable is now incremented by the number 3.

Write the Code

The code for the scenario is as follows:

```
<HTML>
<HEAD>
<TITLE> Calculating Profit/Loss Percentage</TITLE>
</HEAD>
<BODY BGCOLOR=#EEEEFF>
<H1>Profit/Loss Status for Mega Music Mart</H1>
<TABLE BORDER=1>
<?php
$totalrevenue = 5000;
$fixedcost = 1000;
$variablecost = 500;
$result;
$totalexpense;
totalcost ();
profitorloss();
resultpercent ();
function totalcost ()
    {
    global $fixedcost;
    global $variablecost;
    global $totalexpense;
    $totalexpense = $fixedcost + $variablecost;
    echo "<TR><TD><H2>The expenses for the
month</H2></TD><TD><H2>\$$totalexpense</H2></TD></TR>\n";
    }
function profitorloss()
    {
    global $result;
    global $totalexpense;
    global $totalrevenue;
    $result = $totalrevenue - $totalexpense;
      if ($result == 0)
        {
        echo "<TR><TD><H2>There was no profit no loss</H2></TD></TR>\n";
        }
      elseif ($result < 0)
        {
        echo "<TR><TD><H2>Losses
incurred</H2></TD><TD><H2>\$$result</H2></TD></TR>\n";
        }
      else
        {
        echo "<TR><TD><H2>Profit
gained</H2></TD><TD><H2>\$$result</H2></TD></TR>\n";
```

```
            }
        }
function resultpercent ()
        {
        global $result;
        global $totalrevenue;
        if ($result == 0)
            {
            echo "<TR><TD><H2>There was no profit no loss so percentage
cannot
 be calculated!</H2></TD></TR>\n
            }
        elseif ($result < 0)
            {
            $losspercent = ($result/$totalrevenue * (-100));
            echo "<TR><TD><H2>The loss percentage
is</H2></TD><TD><H2>$losspercent%</H2></TD></TR>\n";
            }
        else
            {
            $profitpercent = ($result/$totalrevenue * 100);
            echo "<TR><TD><H2>The profit percentage
is</H2></TD><TD><H2>$profitpercent%</H2></TD></TR>\n";
            }
        }
?>
</TABLE>
</BODY>
</HTML>
```

Execute the Code

To execute the code and view it on the browser, perform the following steps:

1. Save the text file in which you have written the code with a .php extension in /var/www/html as **Profitloss.php**.

2. Open Netscape Navigator.

3. In the Address box, type http://localhost/Profitloss.php.

Figure 5.2 illustrates the output of the code.

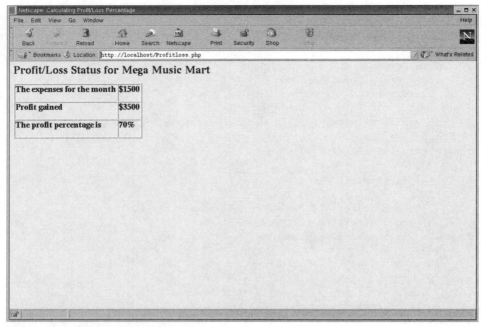

Figure 5.2 Output of Profitloss.php.

Summary

In this chapter, you learned about functions. The chapter began with an introduction to functions. Then, it covered the features of functions and introduced user-defined and built-in functions and explained their differences. Next, you learned about the syntax that is used to declare a function. You also learned how to declare a function with arguments. In addition, you learned when to pass arguments to a function. Then, you learned to use the `return` statement to return values and how to dynamically call a function. Next, the chapter covered the scope of a variable and how to use the `global` and `static` statements. Finally, it discussed other features of arguments, such as assigning default values to arguments and passing references to variables.

Arrays

In this lesson, you will learn to:

- Identify arrays
- Declare arrays
- Distinguish between enumerated arrays and associative arrays
- Declare an enumerated array
- Declare an associative array
- Declare a multidimensional array
- Use the `foreach` statement to loop through an array
- Manipulate arrays using functions
- Sort arrays

Getting Started

In the previous chapter, you learned about functions. You learned to declare a function and distinguish between user-defined and built-in functions. You also learned to use user-defined functions effectively in your programs. Now, it is time to learn about another important concept, arrays.

This chapter is divided into three parts. The first introduces arrays, the second discusses how arrays are used, and the last one discusses how the data in an array can be manipulated.

Introducing Arrays

When creating long, complex programs, it sometimes becomes difficult to access certain elements in a program. For example, there is a limitation on using variables in a program: When you declare a variable, you can assign only one value to it. In certain cases, you may want to declare hundreds of variables, and it may not be possible to remember each and every variable and use it. Arrays help you accomplish this. An array is a special kind of variable that, unlike conventional variables, can store multiple values that are indexed. To understand this definition let us split it into three parts:

- An array is a special kind of variable because it is primarily used for storing values.

TIP Although it is true that multiple values can be stored in a single array, you should ensure that the values you specify in an array are related to each other. The use of unrelated values in the same array can lead to confusion and chaos.

- Unlike conventional variables, arrays can store multiple values. There is no limit on how many values you can store in an array, but you may not want to store so many values that the memory of your computer is unable to handle it.

- Each value that is assigned to an array is accessed using an *index* in the form of a number or a string.

NOTE Indexing is discussed later on in this chapter under the heading *Index*.

Features of Arrays

There are a few underlying features of arrays that help qualify them as one of the most important elements in any complex program:

- Any number of values can be stored in a single array.
- The values stored in an array can be numeric or string.

- After the values are stored in the array, they can be extracted from it at any given time.

- Arrays enhance the scope and flexibility of a program by allowing data to be accessed easily.

- Arrays organize complex data structures that are related in some way.

Although it is correct to state that an array is a kind of variable, it is completely incorrect to assume that the functionality or usage of an array is similar to that of a variable. This is because arrays provide certain benefits that variables do not have:

- An array can store hundreds of values. This saves the time and effort of declaring hundreds of variables to hold each of the values.

- Each of the values specified in an array can be referenced using the index that represents it. The only way you can access a variable is by using its name.

- It is possible to add values to an array after it is created. It is not possible to add values to a variable.

- Arrays are more flexible than variables. There are several built-in functions available with PHP that help manipulate the data in an array.

- Values in an array can be retrieved sequentially and randomly.

Creating a Simple Array

Creating an array is as simple as creating a variable. The only difference is that its main purpose is to hold multiple related values in the same place. Consider the following example of declaring a simple array:

```php
<?php
$music[] = "Heavy Metal";
$music[] = "Hard Rock";
$music[] = "Rap";
$music[] = "Hip Hop";
$music[] = "Jazz";
?>
```

In this code:

- An array by the name $music has been created.

- This array consists of string values.

- Square brackets have been used every time a value is assigned. They hold the index for the value specified.

- Each array declaration ends with a semicolon.

Declaring an Array by Using the array () Function

There is an alternate method of declaring an array. This is by using the `array ()` function. Consider the following example in which the array `$music` is declared using the `array ()` function:

```
$music = array ("Heavy Metal", "Hard Rock", "Rap", "Hip Hop", "Jazz")
```

In this example, the array `$music` holds all the values, and this time all values are contained in one single line.

Index

Throughout our discussion about arrays, there has been reference to an index. An index is the heart of an array. Before discussing what *index* means, it is important to understand what *element* means. Each value that an array contains is called an element. In the preceding array `$music`, the values "Heavy Metal", "Hard Rock", "Rap", "Hip Hop", and "Jazz" are all elements of the array.

In PHP, the elements that are contained in an array are accessed using an index. An index is a way of representing an element in an array. It can also be referred to as a tag that helps distinctly identify an element and access it from an array that contains multiple elements. An index can either be a number or a string. By default all arrays are numerically indexed.

Problem Statement

The development team at Mega Music Mart is used to accepting tough challenges on short notice. This time the development team has decided to do something on its own. The developers want to create a program that accepts user details and uses these details to suggest five different login ID options to the user. The information that should be displayed on the Web page should include:

- The information entered by the user
- Five login ID options that a user can use as a login ID

The following user details should be accepted:

- First name
- Last name
- Location
- Age
- Music choice
- Hobby
- Occupation

The login IDs should be generated in the following way:

- The first login ID option should use the user's first and last names.
- The second login ID option should use the user's location and age.
- The third login ID should use the user's music choice and hobby.
- The fourth login ID should use the user's hobby and occupation.
- The fifth login ID should use the user's the hobby and the occupation and the current year.

Task List

To create the Web page, the development team should be comfortable with creating, looping through, and manipulating arrays. The team will need to:

✔ **Create arrays**

✔ **Write the code**

✔ **Execute the code**

Create Arrays

Before you start using arrays in your program, you will need to learn to create arrays. In this section you will learn how to create enumerated, associative, and multidimensional arrays.

Enumerated Arrays

Arrays that are numerically indexed are called *enumerated arrays*. The first index that represents the first element of a numerically indexed array is always 0. To understand this, consider the following code:

```php
<?php
$testarray[0] = "FirstItem";
$testarray[1] = "SecondItem";
$testarray[2] = "ThirdItem";
$testarray[3] = "FourthItem";
?>
```

Here, 0 represents the first element in the array, which is the first index number of the array. The following elements are sequentially represented by the index numbers 1, 2, and 3, respectively. Even if the index numbers are not specified in an array, the first element in an enumerated array will always be represented by the index number 0, as shown in the following:

```php
$testarray = array ("FirstItem", "SecondItem". ThirdItem",
"FourthItem");
```

This statement also illustrates the declaration of an array. As you can see, the index numbers for each of the elements are not specified. In this case, to access the third element of the array ("ThirdItem"), you would need to use the index number 2 and not 3 because the sequential allocation of index numbers in case of enumerated arrays begins with 0.

Associative Arrays

Arrays that are indexed by using strings are called *associative arrays*. When you use them, you specify a string instead of numbers within the square brackets.

Indexing arrays with strings is very useful at times. Typically, you would index arrays with strings if the data that you want to hold in the array consists of both numeric values and strings. Consider an example of creating an array that holds employee details. It would not be a good idea to use an enumerated array for this purpose because accessing data using numbers could be difficult. Consider the following code:

```
<?php
$emp_det [Name] = "Dave";
$emp_det [Age] = "24";
$emp_det [Code] = "8545";
$emp_det [Designation] = "System Administrator";
?>
```

In this code each element can be referenced using the string index associated with the element. For example, to access the element "Dave", you can specify:

```
echo $emp_det [Name];
// This will print the string "Dave"
```

A few array elements also hold numeric values such as "Age" and "Code". This suggests that you can use names (strings) or numbers as elements when you use associative arrays. Associative arrays can also be created using the array () function. Creating an associative array using the array () function is slightly different. For associative arrays, the string that you use as the index is called the *key*, and you assign a value to this key. Both the key and the value must be specified when creating an associative array. Consider the following example in which an associative array is created using the array () function:

```
$emp_det = array (Name => "Dave", Age => "24", Code => "System
Administrator")
```

In this code:

- The values for each element are defined in a single statement using the array () function.

- The => symbol is used to assign a value to the array.
- The string values are specified within double quotes.
- The key and the value are specified for each element of the array.

TIP It is optional to use double quotes when the string that you specify is a single word. However, if you are using a string that contains more than one word, you need to specify it within double quotes.

Multidimensional Arrays

As discussed earlier, arrays can store numbers as well as names (string values). They can also store other arrays. Such arrays are multidimensional arrays, or an array of arrays.

Consider an example in which you have four arrays, A, B, C, and D. Each consists of four elements and is stored as values of array elements. The array in which these arrays are stored is named $alphabet. Now you want to access the third element of the fourth element of the array $alphabet. You do so as follows:

```
$alphabet [3] [2]
```

By using multidimensional arrays you can:

- Create sophisticated data structures with ease
- Manipulate the values present in the data structure to get the desired output

To understand the concept of multidimensional arrays consider the following code:

```
<?php
$emp_det = array (
                array (Name=> "Dave", Code=> "8545", Hobby=> "Playing
the guitar"),
                array (Name=> "Sally", Code=> "8963", Hobby=> "Reading
books"),
                array (Name=> "Robin", Code=> "1030", Hobby=>
"Trekking"),
                array (Name=> "Brad", Code=> "3319", Hobby=> "Singing"),
                        );
echo $emp_det [0] [Hobby];
?>
```

In this code:

- An array named emp_det is created.
- This array consists of four associative arrays of three elements each.

The output of that code is:

```
X-Powered-By: PHP/4.0.6
Content-type: text/html
Playing the guitar
```

It is evident from the output that the value of the third element of the first array is accessed and printed to the screen. In this example, the array $emp_det is an enumerated array that consists of four associative arrays. Each of these associative arrays consists of three elements. The echo statement is used to access the third element of the first associative array within the array $emp_det.

Looping through Arrays

Another method of accessing the elements in an array and displaying them is by looping. You can use the foreach statement to loop through enumerated, associative, and multidimensional arrays.

Looping through an Enumerated Array

As discussed earlier, the foreach statement comes in handy when looping through an enumerated array. Consider the following example to understand this concept:

```
foreach ($array as $temp)
        {
        //Put code here
        }
```

In the code, $temp is a variable that temporarily stores the value of $array. By doing so you can loop through the array. Examine the following code for a better understanding:

```
<?php
$emp_det []= "Brad";
$emp_det []="Sally";
$emp_det []="Robin";
$emp_det []="Dave";
$emp_det []="Bryan";
$emp_det []="Garry";
        foreach ($emp_det as $temp)
            {
            echo "$temp", "\n";
            }
?>
```

In this code:

- An array named `$emp_det` is created; it stores the names of six employees.
- The `foreach` statement is used to loop through this array by temporarily storing the value of `emp_det` in a temporary variable named `$temp`.
- Each of the values present in `emp_det` is stored in `$temp` one after the other.
- Finally, when we print `$temp`, each element that was present in `$emp_det` is printed one after the other.

The output is:

```
X-Powered-By: PHP/4.0.6
Content-type: text/html
Brad
Sally
Robin
Dave
Bryan
Garry
```

Looping through Associative Arrays

The `foreach` statement is also used for looping through associative arrays, but there is a slight change in the way you use it: You would need to specify the key as well as the value of an element to access a particular element. Consider the following example:

```
foreach ($music as $key => $temp)
        {
        //Put code here
        }
```

In this example:

- `$music` is the name of the array.
- `$key` is the name of the variable that is used to temporarily store the key.
- `$temp` is the name of the variable that is used to store the value assigned to the key.

Consider another example to understand how the `foreach` statement is used to loop through an associative array:

```
<?php
$emp_det = array (
                    Name => "Dave",
                    Age => "24",
                    Code => "8545",
```

```
                              Designation => "System Administrator");
foreach ($emp_det as $key=>$temp)
         {
         echo "$key = $temp","\n";
         }
?>
```

In this code:

- $emp_det is the name of the array that stores the details of Dave.
- The keys used in this array are Name, Age, Code, and Designation.
- The foreach statement is used to loop through this array.
- The variables $key and $temp are temporary variables that store the key and value, respectively.
- The loop is executed until all the details are printed one after the other.

The output is:

```
X-Powered-By: PHP/4.0.6
Content-type: text/html
Name = Dave
Age = 24
Code = 8545
Designation = System Administrator
```

Displaying a Multidimensional Array

After learning how to loop through enumerated arrays and associative arrays, you might want to know how to loop through a multidimensional array. You can combine your knowledge of looping through enumerated and associative arrays to accomplish this. Consider the following code, in which the foreach statement is used to loop through a multidimensional array:

```
<?php
$emp_det = array (
              array (Name=> "Dave", Code=> "8545", Hobby=> "Playing the
guitar
              array (Name=> "Sally", Code=> "8963", Hobby=> "Reading
books"),
              array (Name=> "Robin", Code=> "1030", Hobby=>
"Trekking"),
              array (Name=> "Brad", Code=> "3319", Hobby=> "Singing"),
                 );
foreach ($emp_det as $tempone)
        {
        foreach ($tempone as $key=>$temptwo)
              {
```

```
            echo "$key: $temptwo", "\n";
        }
    echo "\n";
    }
?>
```

In this code:

- Two `foreach` statements have been used.
- The value of `$emp_det` is temporarily stored in `$tempone`. `$emp_det` is an enumerated array that contains associative arrays.
- Then, the value of `$tempone` is temporarily stored in the temporary variables `$key` and `$temptwo` because the arrays specified with the `$emp_det` array are associative arrays.

The output is:

```
X-Powered-By: PHP/4.0.6
Content-type: text/html
Name: Dave
Code: 8545
Hobby: Playing the guitar
Name: Sally
Code: 8963
Hobby: Reading books
Name: Robin
Code: 1030
Hobby: Trekking
Name: Brad
Code: 3319
Hobby: Singing
```

As a result of looping through the multidimensional array, the contents of the array are displayed on the screen.

Manipulating Arrays

You have already learned how to work with enumerated, associative, and multidimensional arrays and to access elements present in these arrays. PHP 4 also has several built-in functions that can be used to manipulate the elements in an array. Using these built-in functions you can:

- Count the number of elements in an array
- Remove the first element from an array
- Add multiple variables to an array
- Join two arrays

- Compare arrays and extract uncommon elements
- Compare arrays and extract common elements
- Eliminate duplicate elements in an array
- Slice arrays
- Sort arrays

The count () Function

The count () function is used to return the number of elements contained in an array. To understand the usage of count () function, consider the following example:

```php
<?php
$employee []= "Dave";
$employee []= "Sally";
$employee []= "Rob";
$employee []= "Brad";
echo count ($employee);
?>
```

The count () function is used to return the number of elements present in the array $employee. The output is:

```
X-Powered-By: PHP/4.0.6
Content-type: text/html
4
```

The count () function can also be used to access certain elements in the array. Consider the following example to understand this concept:

```php
<?php
$employee []= "Dave";
$employee []= "Sally";
$employee []= "Rob";
$employee []= "Brad";
echo $employee [count ($employee)-1];
?>
```

An array $employee that consists of the names of four employees is created. This is an enumerated array. If you want to access the last element of the array, you can use the count () function. Notice that 1 is subtracted from the array so that only the last element of the array is accessed. The output is:

```
X-Powered-By: PHP/4.0.6
Content-type: text/html

Brad
```

Using the array_shift () Function

You can use the `array_shift ()` function to remove the first element of an array that is passed to it as an argument, as shown in the following code.

```php
<?php
$music = array ("Rap", "Hip Hop", "Rock", "Heavy Metal");
    while (count ($music))
            {
            $somevalue = array_shift ($music);
            echo "$somevalue", "\n";
            echo "The elements left are ".count ($music);
            echo "\n";
            }
?>
```

In the code:

- The `array_shift ()` function is used to extract the first element of the array.
- The `while` statement is used to loop through the array.
- The `count ()` function is used to count the number of remaining elements each time the `array_shift ()` function is used.

The output is:

```
X-Powered-By: PHP/4.0.6
Content-type: text/html
Rap
The elements left are 3
Hip Hop
The elements left are 2
Rock
The elements left are 1
Heavy Metal
The elements left are 0
```

Using the array_push () Function

The `array_push ()` function is used to accept an array. All elements that are present in this array are also accepted. Consider the following code in which an array is added and further values are added to it:

```php
<?php
$vocalists = array ("Dave", "Brad", "Cathy");
$musicians = array_push($vocalists, "Robin", "Jack", "Joe");
echo "The total number of musicians are $musicians:", "\n";
```

```
        foreach ($vocalists as $val)
            {
            echo "$val", "\n";
            }
?>
```

In this code:

- An array named $vocalists is created.

- Then another array named $musicians is created in which we use the array_push () function to add the array $vocalists. The $musicians array now consists of three elements of $vocalists as well as the three elements that were specified for $musicians.

- Then the foreach statement is used to loop through the elements and print each element on the screen.

The output is:

```
X-Powered-By: PHP/4.0.6
Content-type: text/html
The total number of musicians are 6:
Dave
Brad
Cathy
Robin
Jack
Joe
```

Using the array_merge () Function

The array_merge () function, as the name suggests, is used to combine two different arrays. For example, there are two arrays, arrayA, which has five elements, and arrayB, which has four. When you use the array_merge () function, you can combine these two arrays. After you use the array_merge () function, the elements of both these arrays will be combined and the resultant array will consist of nine elements. Consider the following example:

```
<?php
$arrayA = array ("Rock", "Pop", "Rap", "Raggae", "Jazz");
$arrayB = array (1, 2, 3, 4);
$arrayAB = array_merge ($arrayA, $arrayB);
echo "The number of elements in \$arrayAB are: ", "\n";
    foreach ($arrayAB as $val)
            {
            echo "$val", "\n";
             }
?>
```

In this code:

- An array $arrayA that contains five elements is created.

- Another array $arrayB that contains four elements is created.

- Finally, an array $arrayAB is created. The array_merge function is used with this array to combine the arrays $arrayA and $arrayB.

- Then the foreach statement is used to loop through the array and display all the elements that it contains one after the other.

The output is:

```
X-Powered-By: PHP/4.0.6
Content-type: text/html
The number of elements in $arrayAB are:
Rock
Pop
Rap
Raggae
Jazz
1
2
3
4
```

Using the array_diff () Function

The array_diff () function is used to extract those elements that are present in the first array but not in the second. When you use the array_diff () function, you must specify the names of the arrays as arguments (the first argument is assumed as the first array) to the function. When you do so, the elements of the two arrays are compared. Then, the elements that are present in the first array but not in the second array are extracted. Consider the following example:

```
<?php
$arrayone = array ("Dave", "Robin", "Bryan", "Cathy");
$arraytwo = array ("Robin", "Mary", "Dave", "Garry");
$diff = array_diff ($arrayone, $arraytwo);
    foreach ($diff as $val)
        {
        echo "$val", "\n";
        }
?>
```

The array_diff () function is used to compare the elements of $arrayone and $arraytwo. The elements that are present in $arrayone and not in $arraytwo are extracted. Then the foreach statement is used to loop through the array and display the output on the screen. The output is:

```
X-Powered-By: PHP/4.0.6
Content-type: text/html
Bryan
Cathy
```

The elements `Bryan` and `Cathy` were not present in `$arraytwo`. Therefore, they were printed on the screen.

Using the array_intersect () Function

The `array_intersect ()` function operates just the opposite of `array_diff ()`. It is used to compare arrays and extract the items that are common. The names of the arrays to be compared are specified as arguments to the `array_intersect ()` function as follows:

```
<?php
$arrayone = array ("Dave", "Robin", "Bryan", "Cathy");
$arraytwo = array ("Robin", "Mary", "Dave", "Garry");
$similarity = array_intersect ($arrayone, $arraytwo);
    foreach ($similarity as $val)
        {
        echo "$val", "\n";
        }
?>
```

The `array_intersect ()` function is used to extract the common elements that are a part of both `$arrayone` and `$arraytwo`. The output is:

```
X-Powered-By: PHP/4.0.6
Content-type: text/html
Dave
Robin
```

The elements Dave and Robin are common to both the arrays. Therefore, they are printed to the screen.

Using the array_unique () Function

The `array_unique ()` function, as the name suggests, is used to eliminate duplicate elements in an array and extract the unique elements to a new array. To detect and eliminate the duplicate elements present in an array you would specify the name of the array as an argument to the `array_unique ()` function, as follows:

```
<?php
$oldarray = array ("Dave", "Robin", "Bryan", "Cathy", "Dave", "Bryan");
$newarray = array_unique ($oldarray);
```

```
       foreach ($newarray as $val)
         {
         echo "$val", "\n";
         }
   ?>
```

The `array_unique` () function is used to eliminate the duplicate elements. There-fore, only a single instance of the duplicate elements will be retained. As a result, when you use the `foreach` statement to loop through the array the output will be:

```
X-Powered-By: PHP/4.0.6
Content-type: text/html
Dave
Robin
Bryan
Cathy
```

Using the array_slice () Function

The `array_slice` () function is used to extract elements from an array. When extracting elements using this function, you must specify:

- The starting position, also known as the *offset*. This is the first element to be extracted from the array. The offset is just the index of the element to be extracted. For example, if you want to extract the fourth element in the array, you would specify the offset as 3.

- The length is the number of elements that need to be extracted, starting from the offset specified.

TIP It is optional to specify the length. If you don't specify the length, all elements starting from the offset are extracted.

When you use the `array_slice` () function, the original array is not altered; rather, the elements are extracted and a new array containing these elements is created. Consider the following syntax: `$newarray = array_slice ($originalarray, 4, 3);`

This statement creates a new array named $newarray and:

- The `array_slice` () function is used to extract the elements from the array `$originalarray`.

- The 4 signifies the offset, or the first element that needs to be extracted. Specifying 4 will extract the fifth element from `$originalarray`.

- The 3 signifies the length. This means that three elements will be extracted starting from the offset specified.

This concept is shown in the following code:

```
<?php
$musicgenre = array (
                      "Rock",
                      "Jazz",
                      "Alternative",
                      "Rap",
                      "Hip Hop",
                      "Heavy Metal",
                      "Classical");
echo "Dave likes listening to:", "\n";
$Dave = array_slice ($musicgenre, 4, 2);
    foreach ($Dave as $valone)
        {
        echo "$valone", "\n";
        }
echo "\n";
echo "Brad loves listening to:", "\n";
$Brad = array_slice ($musicgenre, 1, 3);
    foreach ($Brad as $valtwo)
        {
        echo "$valtwo", "\n";
        }
echo "\n";
echo "Joe likes listening to:", "\n";
$Joe = array_slice ($musicgenre, 3, 3);
    foreach ($Joe as $valthree)
        {
        echo "$valthree", "\n";
        }
echo "\n";
echo "Rick loves listening to:", "\n";
$Rick = array_slice ($musicgenre, -4, 2);
    foreach ($Rick as $valfour)
        {
        echo "$valfour", "\n";
        }
echo "\n";
echo "John likes listening to:", "\n";
$John = array_slice ($musicgenre, 1);
    foreach ($John as $valfive)
        {
        echo "$valfive", "\n";
        }
?>
```

In the code:

■ An array named $musicgenre is created. This array consists of different music genre.

- Then arrays named $Dave, $Brad, $Joe, $John, and $Rick are created.
- These arrays contain the choice of music of each person, respectively.
- The array_slice () function is used to extract the choice of music for each individual.
- The foreach statement is used to loop through each array and display the music choice of each person on the screen.
- Notice that for $Rick the offset specified is -4. This indicates that the elements are counted inversely and the last element of the array $musicgenre is assumed to be the first element.
- Notice that for $John, the offset is specified but not the length. As a result, all elements starting from the second element will be printed.

The output is:

```
X-Powered-By: PHP/4.0.6
Content-type: text/html
Dave likes listening to:
Hip Hop
Heavy Metal
Brad loves listening to:
Jazz
Alternative
Rap
Joe likes listening to:
Rap
Hip Hop
Heavy Metal
Rick loves listening to:
Rap
Hip Hop
John likes listening to:
Jazz
Alternative
Rap
Hip Hop
Heavy Metal
Classical
```

Sorting Arrays

Another useful feature of using arrays is that they can be sorted. This is of great help because sorting an array results in systematic representation of the elements of that array and avoids chaos. Both enumerated and associative arrays can be sorted by using built-in functions of PHP.

Using the sort () Function

The sort () function is used to sort enumerated arrays. To sort an array with the sort () function, you specify the name of the array that you want to sort as an argument to the sort () function. This function can sort string elements as well as numeric elements. Consider the following example in which the sort () function is used to sort string elements:

```php
<?php
$emp_names []= "Dave";
$emp_names []= "Bret";
$emp_names []= "Andy";
$emp_names []= "Cindy";
$emp_names []= "Elizabeth";
sort ($emp_names);
        foreach ($emp_names as $val)
            {
            echo "$val", "\n";
            }
?>
```

In this code:

- An enumerated array named $emp_names is created. This array consists of the names of employees.
- The sort () function is used to alphabetically sort the names of the employees.
- The foreach statement is used to loop through the array and display the names in alphabetical order.

The output is:

```
X-Powered-By: PHP/4.0.6
Content-type: text/html
Andy
Bret
Cindy
Dave
Elizabeth
```

Consider an example in which the elements of the enumerated array are numbers:

```php
<?php
$sortnumbers []= 10000;
$sortnumbers []= 10;
$sortnumbers []= 100;
$sortnumbers []= 1000;
$sortnumbers []= 1;
sort ($sortnumbers);
        foreach ($sortnumbers as $val)
```

```
        {
        echo "$val", "\n";
        }
    ?>
```

The elements specified for the array $sortnumbers are numbers. The output is:

```
X-Powered-By: PHP/4.0.6
Content-type: text/html
1
10
100
1000
10000
```

To reverse sort an enumerated array, use the rsort () function:

```
<?php
$emp_names []= "Dave";
$emp_names []= "Bret";
$emp_names []= "Andy";
$emp_names []= "Cindy";
$emp_names []= "Elizabeth";
rsort ($emp_names);
        foreach ($emp_names as $val)
            {
            echo "$val", "\n";
            }
    ?>
```

The sort () function has been replaced by the rsort () function. Therefore, the elements are sorted in reverse of their original order. The output is:

```
X-Powered-By: PHP/4.0.6
Content-type: text/html
Elizabeth
Dave
Cindy
Bret
Andy
```

Using the asort () Function

The built-in asort () function is used to sort the elements of an associative array. It operates for associative arrays in the same way that the sort () function operates for enumerated arrays. However, the asort () function retains the array's keys in the original state. The array elements are sorted on the basis of the value they possess and not the keys.

Consider the following example to understand this concept:

```php
<?php
$associatedarray = array (
                    FirstName => "Dave",
                    LastName => "Carter",
                    Designation => "Editor",
                    Hobby => "Biking",
                    Sign => "Aries");
asort ($associatedarray);
    foreach ($associatedarray as $key => $val)
        {
        echo "$key = $val", "\n";
        }
?>
```

In this code:

- An array named $associatedarray that contains the details of Dave is created.
- The asort () function is used to sort the particulars of Dave.
- The foreach statement is used to loop through the array and print the output to the screen.

The output is:

```
X-Powered-By: PHP/4.0.6
Content-type: text/html
Sign = Aries
Hobby = Biking
LastName = Carter
FirstName = Dave
Designation = Editor
```

Notice in the output that the keys of the array are not sorted. If the keys were also sorted, it could have led to a lot of chaos. In such a case the Designation of Dave would have become Aries.

TIP An associative array can be sorted in the reverse order to reach the original state. The asort () function can be used to do so.

Using the ksort () Function

In certain situations you might want to sort an associative array on the basis of keys. In such a situation you can use the ksort () function to sort the array. Consider the following example:

```php
<?php
$nameandage = array (
                Dave => 24,
```

```
                          Ashley => 44,
                          Cathy => 34,
                          Eric => 55,
                          Brad => 21,
                          Fred => 48);
ksort ($nameandage);
        foreach ($nameandage as $keys => $val)
            {
            echo "$keys = $val", "\n";
            }
?>
```

In this code:

- An array named $nameandage is created.
- The keys are the names of employees and the value held is the employee's age.
- The ksort () function is used to sort the array on the basis of the keys.
- The foreach statement is used to loop through the array and display the output on the screen.

The output is:

```
X-Powered-By: PHP/4.0.6
Content-type: text/html
Ashley = 44
Brad = 21
Cathy = 34
Dave = 24
Eric = 55
Fred = 48
```

As you can see, the keys have been arranged in alphabetical order and the layout is much more systematic.

Result

To generate the report, the development team will need to:

- Create an associative array that contains the details entered by the user
- Use array_slice () function to extract information from the associative array
- Use the array_merge () function
- Use the foreach statement to display the contents of the arrays

Write the Code

The code for the scenario is:

```
<HTML>
<HEAD>
<TITLE>Displaying Login ID Options</TITLE>
</HEAD>
<BODY BGCOLOR=#EEEEFF>
<H1><CENTER>Generating Login IDs for Dave</CENTER></H1>
<?php
$loginfo = array (
            FirstName => "Dave",
            LastName => "Labrada",
            Sex => "Male",
            Location => "Arizona",
            Age => "24",
            MusicChoice =>  "Rock",
            Hobby => "Shopping",
            Occupation => "Author");
echo "<H3>The information entered by Dave:<BR></H3>";
foreach ($loginfo as $key => $val)
    {
    echo "<B>$key</B> => $val<BR>";
    }
echo "<BR>";
echo "<H3>The login options are:<BR></H3>";
$loginone = array_slice ($loginfo, 0, 2);
$logintwo = array_slice ($loginfo, 3, 2);
$loginthree = array_slice ($loginfo, 5, 2);
$loginfour = array_slice ($loginfo, 6, 2);
$loginfive = array_merge ($loginfour,"2001");
echo "The first login option:<BR>";
foreach ($loginone as $optionone)
    {
    echo "<B>$optionone</B>";
    }
echo "<BR>";
echo "The second login option:<BR>";
foreach ($logintwo as $optiontwo)
    {
    echo "<B>$optiontwo</B>";
    }
echo "<BR>";
echo "The third login option:<BR>";
foreach ($loginthree as $optionthree)
    {
    echo "<B>$optionthree</B>";
    }
echo "<BR>";
echo "The fourth login option:<BR>";
foreach ($loginfour as $optionfour)
    {
    echo "<B>$optionfour</B>";
    }
```

```
echo "<BR>";
echo "The fifth login option:<BR>";
foreach ($loginfive as $optionfive)
    {
    echo "<B>$optionfive</B>";
    }
echo "<BR>";
?>
</BODY>
</HTML>
```

Execute the Code

To execute the code and view it on the browser, perform the following steps:

1. Save the text file in which you have written the code with a .php extension in /var/www/html as **login.php.**

2. Open Netscape Navigator.

3. In the Address box, type `http://localhost/login.php`.

Figure 6.1 illustrates the output of the code.

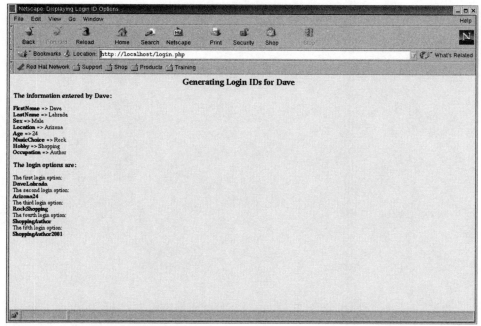

Figure 6.1 Output of login.php.

Summary

In this chapter, you were introduced to the features and benefits of arrays. You learned how to create enumerated, associative, and multidimensional arrays. Then you learned how to loop through these arrays using the foreach statement. Finally, you learned how to manipulate the data present in arrays using the built-in functions that are available with PHP.

Classes

OBJECTIVES:

In this lesson, you will learn to:

- ✔ Identify classes
- ✔ Create a class
- ✔ Identify attributes, objects, and functions
- ✔ Create objects
- ✔ Access attributes and functions
- ✔ Discuss the features of class inheritance
- ✔ Create child classes
- ✔ Access and modify the attributes in a child class
- ✔ Override the functions of a base class
- ✔ Call an overridden function

Getting Started

Programming is the procedure for generating an automated way to perform a task. In the days when high-level programming was introduced, programming languages such as COBOL and BASIC fast gained popularity. However, a drawback was that these languages were not simple to use. The programmer had to write long pieces of code that spanned thousands of lines to achieve a basic functionality. In addition, the features required to perform complex tasks were missing. As a result, developers wanted programming languages that were easy to use and faster. This requirement led to the introduction of object-oriented programming (OOP). Most programming languages today support the concept of object-oriented programming. Over the years, significant modifications have been made in PHP by incorporating object-orientation; PHP 4 is a perfect example.

In the previous chapter, you learned about the concept of arrays and how they are used in PHP. This chapter will focus on the concepts of object-oriented programming and how it is used in relation to PHP. The first portion of this chapter contains a detailed explanation of classes. In the next portion, the concepts related to objects are discussed. Finally, the concept of inheritance is discussed.

Problem Statement

Mega Music Mart wants to introduce a section exclusively for products designed for use by children and needs new software for it. Each product in this section should have a special discount attribute in addition to routine details. The album details should include album code, year of release, name of the artist, and price. The software should also be able to sort the regular collection of album records on the basis of album ID.

This task, which has the following specifications, has been assigned to the development team at Mega Music Mart. The result will be displayed in table format.

- The first table will display the unsorted records of the albums. This table contains seven columns: serial number, album name, year of release, artist, category, price, and album ID.

- The second table will contain the sorted records with album IDs sorted in ascending order.

- The third table will contain the name of each of the albums in the children's section and its discounted price.

Task List

To create the Web page, the development team needs to:

- ✔ **Identify the classes to be defined**
- ✔ **Identify the objects to be created**
- ✔ **Implement class inheritance**
- ✔ **Write the code**
- ✔ **Execute the code**

Identify the Classes to Be Defined

The basis of any object-oriented language is an object. However, to understand objects, you will need to understand the concept of classes. A *class* is a blueprint for an object. Just as a blueprint is used to construct a house, a class is used to create an object. Consider the example where you categorize all the vehicles in a class called *vehicle*. All the vehicles have certain distinguishing features, such as brand name, number of wheels, and seating capacity. In addition, certain tasks, such as repairing and washing, can be performed on these vehicles. You can further group specific vehicles, such as cars and motorbikes, as separate classes. These separate classes can have more specific features. For example, a car can be distinguished on the basis of the number of doors, type of roof, power steering, and power windows. Similarly, motorbikes can be distinguished on the basis of engine type. Now let's see how a class is defined and used in PHP.

Defining a Class

In PHP, a class is defined with the following syntax:

```php
<?php
class class_name
{
    var $property_1;
    var $property_2;
    .
    .
    .
    var $property_n;
function some_function_name()
    {
    //some code
    }
}
?>
```

Creating a Simple Class

A class is a template for creating objects. The following code shows how a class is created in PHP:

```php
<?php
class vehicle
    {
    //this is a simple class
    }
?>
```

A class named `vehicle` is created, and the class keyword is specified before the name of the class.

Identifying Attributes

Attributes are characteristics that are specified in a class. Although attributes can be specified anywhere in the body of a class, it is preferable to specify them at the beginning of the class for clarity. An attribute can be of any scalar data type. In the example of the vehicle class, the brand name, number of wheels, and seating capacity features are attributes.

Let's create this class in PHP with the following code:

```php
<?php
class vehicle
{
var $brand_name;
var $number_of_wheels;
var $seating_capacity;
}
?>
```

In the code:

- A class named vehicle is created.
- The vehicle class has three attributes, $brand_name, $number_of_wheels, and $seating_capacity.
- The attributes are preceded with the var keyword. Each attribute in PHP should be defined using the var keyword.

TIP The attributes in a class are defined by preceding them with the $ sign, which indicates that the attributes are variables. However, attributes are different from conventional PHP variables. When attributes are defined in a class, predefined values cannot be assigned directly; they are assigned to attributes by using constructors, which will be discussed later in this chapter.

Identifying Functions

A *function* is a block of code within a class. Functions are used to perform certain tasks on the attributes of the class. For the example of the vehicle class the tasks performed on vehicles, such as repairing and washing, are functions of the vehicle class. The following code shows how functions are specified within a class:

```php
<?php
class vehicle
{
var $brand_name;
var $number_of_wheels;
var $seating_capacity;
    function repair()
```

```
    {
      echo "The vehicle has been sent for repair";
    }
    function wash()
    {
      echo "The vehicle has been sent for a wash";
    }
}
?>
```

In the code:

- A class named `vehicle` is created.

- The vehicle class has three attributes, $brand_name, $number_of_wheels, and $seating_capacity.

- Two functions named `repair()` and `wash()` are created. These perform the task of displaying a message. However, they must be called to display the message.

Identify the Objects to Be Created

Recall the example of the `vehicle` class that was created earlier. Certain classes, such as `car` and `motorbike`, can be created using the `vehicle` class. Using the `car` class you can create different instances of the `car` class such as `Mercedes`, `Ferrari`, and `Toyota`, which can be objects of the `car` class.

Now let's consider an example of the employees of Mega Music Mart and create a class named `employee`. All the employees of Mega Music Mart can be categorized under this `employee` class. The following attributes of the `employee` class will help you identify and distinguish between the employees:

- Employee code
- Name
- Address
- Department
- Sex
- Salary (per month)
- Date of birth

NOTE Notice that of all the attributes listed, the employee code is the only attribute that will always be distinct for each employee.

These characteristics can be used to identify a particular employee because they will differ from one employee to another. Certain activities can be performed with respect to these employees, such as pay hike or transfer.

Table 7.1   Attributes of the Employee Class

ATTRIBUTES OF EMPLOYEE CLASS	DAVE	ALICE
Employee Code	8545	9964
Name	Dave Osbourne	Alice Tyler
Address	14, Mega Square Apartments	23, Bermuda Square
Department	Software Development	Marketing
Sex	Male	Female
Salary (per month)	$7,500	$5,000
Date of birth	15th September 1977	1st April 1960

Consider two employees, Dave and Alice; they are objects or instances of the employee class. Table 7.1 illustrates the characteristics of Dave and Alice and lists the possible values of their attributes.

Creating an Object

After you create a class, you can begin creating objects of that class. Any number of objects can be created on the basis of an existing class. Objects are created and instantiated with the new statement using the following syntax:

```
$object_name = new class_name;
```

The following code shows how objects are created:

```php
<?php
class employee
    {
    var $emp_code;
    var $name;
    var $address;
    var $department;
    var $sex;
    var $date_of_birth;
    var $salary;
    }
$dave = new employee;
$alice = new employee;
echo gettype ($dave),"\n";
echo gettype ($alice), "\n";
?>
```

In this code:

- A class named employee is created.

- Two objects, $dave, and $alice, are created as instances of the employee class.

- The gettype () function is used to accept an argument and return the data type of the argument. In this case, the gettype () function is used to verify that you created the objects successfully.

The output of the code shows that you have created two objects:

```
X-Powered-By: PHP/4.0.6
Content-type: text/html
object
object
```

Accessing Attributes of Objects

Attributes are the properties of an object. After you specify an attribute in a class and create objects, these objects automatically possess the attributes of the class. Consider the following code:

```php
<?php
class employee
    {
    var $emp_code;
    var $name;
    var $address;
    var $department;
    var $sex;
    var $date_of_birth;
    var $salary;
    }
// Let's assign some values to the attributes of the object $dave.
$dave = new employee;
$dave->emp_code="8545";
$dave->name="Dave Osbourne";
$dave->address="14, Mega Square Apartments";
$dave->department="Software Development";
$dave->sex="Male";
$dave->salary="7500";
$dave->date_of_birth="15-09-1977";
// Let's assign some values to the attributes of the object $alice.
$alice = new employee;
$alice->emp_code="9964";
$alice->name="Alice Tyler";
$alice->address="23, Bermuda Square";
$alice->department="Marketing";
$alice->sex="Female";
```

```
$alice->salary="5000";
$alice->date_of_birth="01-04-1960";
// Let's print the attributes of the object $dave.
echo " Employee Code:",$dave->emp_code," \n ";
echo "Name:",$dave->name," \n ";
echo "Address:",$dave->address," \n ";
echo "Department:",$dave->department," \n ";
echo "Sex:",$dave->sex ,"\n ";
echo "Salary:",$dave->salary," \n ";
echo "Date of Birth:",$dave->date_of_birth ,"\n ";
?>
```

In this code:

- A class named `employee` is created.
- All the attributes are specified in the body of the `employee` class. The keyword `var` is used to specify the attribute.
- Two objects, `$dave` and `$alice`, are created.
- The objects are used to modify and access the values of the attributes by using the `->` operator.

The output is:

```
X-Powered-By: PHP/4.0.6
Content-type: text/html
 Employee Code:8545
 Name:Dave Osbourne
 Address:14, Mega Square Apartments
 Department:Software Development
 Sex:Male
 Salary:7500
 Date of Birth:15-09-1977
```

Accessing the Attributes of a Class by Using Functions

In a class, attributes and functions can coexist, and the attribute specified within the class can be accessed by a function specified within the same class. In a class, you can also refer to the currently instantiated object. This mechanism is simple and is of immense use with PHP. A class designates a special variable to the currently instantiated object. This special variable is $this, which can be used with the -> operator to access class attributes. Consider the following code to understand this concept:

```
<?php
class employee
    {
    var $emp_code;
    var $name;
    var $address;
```

```
    var $department;
    var $sex;
    var $date_of_birth;
    var $salary;
      function showsalary()
            {
            echo "Your salary is accessible from within this
function.\n";
            echo "Your salary is :",$this->salary,"\n";
            }
        }
$dave = new employee;
$dave->emp_code="8545";
$dave->name="Dave Osbourne";
$dave->address="14, Mega Square Apartments";
$dave->department="Software Development";
$dave->sex="Male";
$dave->salary="7500";
$dave->date_of_birth="15-09-1977";
$dave->showsalary();
?>
```

In the preceding code:

- A class named employee is declared.

- The attribute $salary is defined in the employee class.

- The function showsalary() is added to the class and is used to display the salary of the current object.

- The $this->salary in the function signifies that this function will access the value assigned to the attribute $salary.

- The object $dave is instantiated for the employee class and used to call the function defined within the employee class.

The output is:

```
X-Powered-By: PHP/4.0.6
Content-type: text/html
Your salary is accessible from within this function.
Your salary is :7500
```

The output shows that the value assigned to the attribute was accessed by the function in the employee class. As a result, when the object $dave is used to access this function, the value of the attribute $salary is printed.

Changing the Value of an Attribute within a Function

In the previous example, you learned how to access the value of an attribute by using a function that is present in the same class. You can also change the value of the attribute present in a class by using a function that is specified in the same class Consider the following code:

```php
<?php
class employee
     {
    var $emp_code;
    var $name;
    var $address;
    var $department;
    var $sex;
    var $date_of_birth;
    var $salary;
       function payhike($percentagehike)
             {
             echo "Your salary is being incremented.\n";
             echo " Old salary:",$this->salary,"\n";
             $this->salary+=$this->salary * $percentagehike/100;
             echo " New Salary :",$this->salary,"\n";
             }
        }
$dave = new employee;
$dave->emp_code="8545";
$dave->name="Dave Osbourne";
$dave->address="14, Mega Square Apartments";
$dave->department="Software Development";
$dave->sex="Male";
$dave->salary="7500";
$dave->date_of_birth="15-09-1977";
$dave->payhike(10);
echo "Employee Code:",$dave->emp_code," \n";
echo "Name:",$dave->name," \n";
echo "Address:",$dave->address," \n";
echo "Department:",$dave->department," \n";
echo "Sex:",$dave->sex ,"\n";
echo "Salary:",$dave->salary," \n";
echo "Date of Birth:",$dave->date_of_birth ,"\n";
?>
```

In this code:

- The class employee is created.

- The attribute $salary is defined.

- The function payhike() is defined, and variable $percentagehike is defined as an argument to this function.

- The $this->salary += $this->salary * $percentagehike/100 statement is used within this function to increment the value of $this->salary by 10 percent. After specifying this statement, the value of the attribute $salary becomes 8250.

- The function payhike() displays the salary attribute before and after the increment.

- An object named $dave is created with the employee class.

- The function payhike is called. Now, the old value 7500 and the new value 8250 of the attribute $salary appear in the output.

The output of the code is:

```
X-Powered-By: PHP/4.0.6
Content-type: text/html
Your salary is being incremented.
 Old salary:7500
 New Salary :8250
Employee Code:8545
Name:Dave Osbourne
Address:14, Mega Square Apartments
Department:Software Development
Sex:Male
Salary:8250
Date of Birth:15-09-1977
```

Constructors

A constructor is a function. The singular difference between a constructor and a conventional function is that a constructor is a function that is assigned the name of the class within which it is created. For example, if you have a class named employee and you create a function named employee within this class, the function will be called a constructor. A constructor is called automatically each time an object of that class is created. Consider the following code:

```php
<?php
class employee
   {
     var $emp_code;
     var $name;
     var $address;
     var $department;
     var $sex;
     var $date_of_birth;
     var $salary;
     function employee($empname)
      {
        $this->emp_code="default value";
        $this->name=$empname;
        $this->address="default value";
        $this->department="default value";
        $this->sex="default value";
```

```
            $this->date_of_birth="default value";
            $this->salary="default value";
        }
    }
$dave = new employee("Dave Osbourne");
echo "Let's print the values assigned by the constructor.\n";
echo "Employee Code:",$dave->emp_code," \n";
echo "Name:",$dave->name," \n";
echo "Address:",$dave->address," \n";
echo "Department:",$dave->department," \n";
echo "Sex:",$dave->sex ,"\n";
echo "Salary:",$dave->salary," \n";
echo "Date of Birth:",$dave->date_of_birth ,"\n";
?>
```

In this code:

- The class `employee` is created.

- All the attributes for the `employee` class are created.

- The constructor `employee()` is defined, and variable $empname is passed as an argument to this function.

- The `$this->emp_code = "default value"` statements are used within this function to assign default values to various attributes.

- The object $dave of the `employee` class is created. This time, the value for the argument in the `employee` constructor is also specified at the time of instantiation because the name of the class and the name of the function are the same, making the function a constructor.

- The constructor `employee()` accepts the argument $empname and changes the value of the name attribute for the newly created object $dave to Dave Osbourne. The remaining attributes for the $dave object now store the default value.

The output shows that the object was instantiated successfully and that the object function or constructor is also called during instantiation:

```
X-Powered-By: PHP/4.0.6
Content-type: text/html
Let's print the values assigned by the constructor.
Employee Code:default value
Name:Dave Osbourne
Address:default value
Department:default value
Sex:default value
Salary:default value
Date of Birth:default value
```

Implement Class Inheritance

You have learned about the basic structure and working of classes. You will now learn more about classes. Recall the example of the vehicle class. In addition to their inherent features, the two classes car and motorbike carried the attributes in the vehicle class. This is known as *class inheritance*. The car and motorbike classes are child classes of the base class vehicle. Child classes are also known as derived classes. Let's see how class inheritance is implemented in PHP. Child classes are defined using the key word extends.

The syntax for defining a derived or child class is as follows:

```
class some_child_classname extends some_base_classname
{
  var property1_of_childclass;
  var property2_of_childclass;
  .
  .
  .
}
```

Let's create two child classes, car and motorbike, for the base class vehicle:

```php
<?php
class vehicle
{
var $brand_name;
var $number_of_wheels;
var $seating_capacity;
}
class car extends vehicle
{
var $doors;
var $rooftype;
var $powersteering;
var $powerwindows;
}
class motorbike extends vehicle
{
var $engine;
}
//Let's create an object for the car class.
$merk= new car;
$dukat=new motorbike;
?>
```

In this code:

- A class named `vehicle` is created.

- Two other classes, `car` and `motorbike`, are created.

- The keyword `extends` is specified to create two classes, `car` and `motorbike`, as child classes to the `vehicle` class.

- The object `$merk` is created for the `car` class.

- The object `$dukat` is created for the `motorbike` class.

Accessing and Modifying the Attributes in a Child Class

Now, take a look at how to modify and access all the attributes in the child class. Let's create two child classes, `car` and `motorbike`, for the base class `vehicle`:

```php
<?php
class vehicle
{
var $brand_name;
var $number_of_wheels;
var $seating_capacity;
}
class car extends vehicle
{
var $doors;
var $rooftype;
var $powersteering;
var $powerwindows;
}
class motorbike extends vehicle
{
var $engine;
}
//Let's create an object for the car class.
$merk= new car;
$merk->brand_name="Merk Sports";
$merk->number_of_wheels=4;
$merk->seating_capacity=5;
$merk->doors=4;
$merk->rooftype="Convertible";
$merk->powersteering="Yes";
$merk->powerwindows="Yes";
echo " Details for ",$merk->brand_name,"\n";
echo "Name :", $merk->brand_name ,"\n";
echo "Wheels :", $merk->number_of_wheels,"\n";
echo "Seating Capacity :",$merk->seating_capacity,"\n";
echo "Doors: ", $merk->doors,"\n";
echo "Roof Type: ",$merk->rooftype,"\n";
```

```
echo "Power Steering : " , $merk->powersteering,"\n";
echo "Power Windows : " , $merk->powerwindows,"\n";
?>
```

In this code:

- The classes vehicle and car are created.
- The keyword extends is specified to define the class car as a child class to the vehicle class.
- The object $merk is created for the car class.

The values are assigned to the various attributes of $merk, which include the attributes that are inherited by the car class from the vehicle class, and the values of various attributes are printed. The output of this code is:

```
X-Powered-By: PHP/4.0.6
Content-type: text/html
 Details for Merk Sports
Name :Merk Sports
Wheels :4
Seating Capacity :5
Doors: 4
Roof Type: Convertible
Power Steering : Yes
Power Windows : Yes
```

Overriding the Function of a Base Class

You have learned how child or derived classes are created. You may want to know whether or not the functions specified within the base class are always acceptable to the derived classes. A derived class automatically inherits the functions of a base class. However, in programming terminology, it is possible to override the functions of a base class. When you successfully override the functions of the parent class, you can call the functions of the child class while instantiating an object with the child class. The following code shows how this works:

```php
<?php
class vehicle
{
var $brand_name;
var $number_of_wheels;
var $seating_capacity;
function message()
{
 echo "I am in the vehicle class";
}
}
```

```
class car extends vehicle
{
var $doors;
var $rooftype;
var $powersteering;
var $powerwindows;
function message()
{
 echo "I am in the car class";
}
}
//Let's create an object for the car class.
$merk= new car;
$merk->message();
?>
```

In this code:

- The class vehicle is created. This is the base class.

- Another class car is created. This class is the derived or child class and has its own function. The code specified in this function is different from that of the base class.

- The object $merk is instantiated with the derived class car. The output of the code is now based on the function of the derived class.

The output is:

```
X-Powered-By: PHP/4.0.6
Content-type: text/html
I am in the car class
```

Calling an Overridden Function

In certain cases, you may want to use the functions of both the parent and child classes. In such situations, you will need to call the overridden function of the parent class. This is the best part of object-oriented programming: You can have the best of both worlds. The following code shows how overridden functions of a base class are called:

```
<?php
class vehicle
{
    var $brand_name;
    var $number_of_wheels;
    var $seating_capacity;
    function message()
    {
      echo "But now I am in the vehicle class!";
    }
}
```

```
class car extends vehicle
{
     var $doors;
     var $rooftype;
     var $powersteering;
     var $powerwindows;
    function message()
     {
      echo "I am in the car class.", "\n";
      vehicle::message();
     }
}
//Let's create an object for the car class.
$merk= new car;
$merk->message();
?>
```

In this code, the function of the parent class, which was initially overridden by the base class, is called again. The output shows that the function of the base class that was overridden was called again. Therefore, the output of the function of the base class and the derived class was displayed on the screen:

```
X-Powered-By: PHP/4.0.6
Content-type: text/html
I am in the car class.
But now I am in the vehicle class!
```

Write the Code

The development team at Mega Music Mart will need to write the following code to accomplish the task assigned to them. They have decided to use classes to accomplish this task.

```
<HTML>
<HEAD>
<TITLE>Album Details</TITLE>
</HEAD>
<BODY BGCOLOR="#DDDDEE">
<H2><CENTER>Displaying Album Details<CENTER></H2>
<?php
class albumdata
{
 var $data;
        function sortdata()
        {
        global $data;
        for ($i=0;$i<4;$i++)
          {
```

```
                for ($j=0;$j<$i;$j++)
                  {
                    if (($this->data[$j]["ID"]) > ($this->data[$j+1]["ID"]))
                      {
                        $tempname     = $this->data[$j+1]["name"];
                        $tempreleased= $this->data[$j+1]["released"];
                        $tempartist   = $this->data[$j+1]["artist"];
                        $tempcategory= $this->data[$j+1]["category"];
                        $tempprice    = $this->data[$j+1]["price"];
                        $tempID       = $this->data[$j+1]["ID"];

                        $this->data[$j+1]["name"]     = $this->data[$j]["name"];
                        $this->data[$j+1]["released"] =
$this->data[$j]["released"];
                        $this->data[$j+1]["artist"]   =
$this->data[$j]["artist"];
                        $this->data[$j+1]["category"] =
$this->data[$j]["category"];
                        $this->data[$j+1]["price"]    =
$this->data[$j]["price"];
                        $this->data[$j+1]["ID"]       = $this->data[$j]["ID"];

                        $this->data[$j]["name"]     = $tempname;
                        $this->data[$j]["released"] = $tempreleased;
                        $this->data[$j]["artist"]   = $tempartist;
                        $this->data[$j]["category"] = $tempcategory;
                        $this->data[$j]["price"]    = $tempprice;
                        $this->data[$j]["ID"]       = $tempID;
                      }
                  }
              }
          }
  }
class albumdiscounts extends albumdata
{
 var $discount;
 function cal_discount($idx)
 {
     $newprice= $this->data[$idx]["price"] - $this->data[$idx]["price"] *
$this->discount[$idx] / 100;
     return $newprice;
 }

}

$album= new albumdata;

$album->data[0]["name"]    ="Salvation";
$album->data[0]["released"]="1992";
$album->data[0]["artist"]  ="War and Peace";
```

```php
$album->data[0]["category"]="Metal";
$album->data[0]["price"]    ="80";
$album->data[0]["ID"]       =0001;

$album->data[1]["name"]     = "Break Up";
$album->data[1]["released"]= "1986";
$album->data[1]["artist"]   = "Sounds like Metal";
$album->data[1]["category"]= "Metal";
$album->data[1]["price"]    = "107";
$album->data[1]["ID"]       = 0011;

$album->data[2]["name"]     = "Dramatic";
$album->data[2]["released"]= "1998";
$album->data[2]["artist"]   = "RockHeads";
$album->data[2]["category"]= "Hard Rock";
$album->data[2]["price"]    = "200";
$album->data[2]["ID"]       = 0005;

$album->data[3]["name"]     = "Scream";
$album->data[3]["released"]= "1997";
$album->data[3]["artist"]   = "Big Mouths";
$album->data[3]["category"]= "Rock'n Roll";
$album->data[3]["price"]    = "300";
$album->data[3]["ID"]       = 0025;

echo "<H4>Before Sorting</H4>\n";

echo "<table border=1>";
echo "<tr><td><b>S.No.</b></td><td><b>Name</b></td><td><b>Released
</b></td><td><b>
Artist</b></td><td><b>Category</b></td><td><b>Price</b></td><td><b>ID</b>
</td>\n";
for ($i=0;$i<4;$i++)
{
 echo "<tr>\n<td>",$i+1,".",
      "</td>\n<td>", $album->data[$i]["name"] ,
      "</td>\n<td>",$album->data[$i]["released"] ,
      "</td>\n<td>",$album->data[$i]["artist"] ,
      "</td>\n<td>",$album->data[$i]["category"] ,
      "</td>\n<td>",$album->data[$i]["price"] ,
      "</td>\n<td>",$album->data[$i]["ID"],
      "</td>\n</tr>\n";
}
echo "</table>\n";

// $album->sortdata($album->data);
$album->sortdata();
echo "<H4>After Sorting</H4>\n";

echo "<table border=1>";
```

```php
echo "<tr><td><b>S.No.</b></td><td><b>Name</b></td><td><b>Released
</b></td><td> <b>
Artist</b></td><td><b>Category</b></td><td><b>Price</b></td><td><b>ID</b>
</td>\n";
for ($i=0;$i<4;$i++)
{
 echo "<tr>\n<td>",$i+1,".",
      "</td>\n<td>", $album->data[$i]["name"] ,
      "</td>\n<td>",$album->data[$i]["released"] ,
      "</td>\n<td>",$album->data[$i]["artist"] ,
      "</td>\n<td>",$album->data[$i]["category"] ,
      "</td>\n<td>",$album->data[$i]["price"] ,
      "</td>\n<td>",$album->data[$i]["ID"],
      "</td>\n</tr>\n";
}
echo "</table>\n";

$discountedalbums = new albumdiscounts;
$discountedalbums->data[0]["name"]    = "12 Nursery Rhymes";
$discountedalbums->data[0]["released"]= "1988";
$discountedalbums->data[0]["artist"]  = "Candy and Cola";
$discountedalbums->data[0]["category"]= "Leisure";
$discountedalbums->data[0]["price"]   = "300";
$discountedalbums->data[0]["ID"]      = 0032;
$discountedalbums->discount[0]        = 10;

$discountedalbums->data[1]["name"]    = "Learn Counting";
$discountedalbums->data[1]["released"]= "1992";
$discountedalbums->data[1]["artist"]  = "Educate";
$discountedalbums->data[1]["category"]= "Educational";
$discountedalbums->data[1]["price"]   = "300";
$discountedalbums->data[1]["ID"]      = 0037;
$discountedalbums->discount[1]        = 25;

$discountedalbums->data[2]["name"]    = "Snow White";
$discountedalbums->data[2]["released"]= "1994";
$discountedalbums->data[2]["artist"]  = "Story Narrator";
$discountedalbums->data[2]["category"]= "Short Stories";
$discountedalbums->data[2]["price"]   = "300";
$discountedalbums->data[2]["ID"]      = 0094;
$discountedalbums->discount[2]        = 40;

$discountedalbums->data[3]["name"]    = "Fairy Tales";
$discountedalbums->data[3]["released"]= "1991";
$discountedalbums->data[3]["artist"]  = "Tale Tellers";
```

```
$discountedalbums->data[3]["category"]= "Lullaby";
$discountedalbums->data[3]["price"]    = "300";
$discountedalbums->data[3]["ID"]       = 0128;
$discountedalbums->discount[3]         = 25;

echo "<H4>Children's CDs After Discount</H4>\n";
echo "<table border=1>";
echo "<tr><td><b>ID</b></td>",
 "<td><b>Name     </b></td>",
 "<td><b>Released </b></td>",
 "<td><b>Artist   </b></td>",
 "<td><b>Category </b></td>",
 "<td><b>Price    </b></td>",
 "<td><b>Discount </b></td>",
 "<td><b>Discounted Price </b></td></tr>";

for ($i=0;$i<4;$i++)
{
echo "<tr><td>", $discountedalbums->data[$i]["ID"]       ,"</td>";
echo "<td>", $discountedalbums->data[$i]["name"]     ,"</td>";
echo "<td>", $discountedalbums->data[$i]["released"],"</td>";
echo "<td>", $discountedalbums->data[$i]["artist"]   ,"</td>";
echo "<td>", $discountedalbums->data[$i]["category"],"</td>";
echo "<td>", $discountedalbums->data[$i]["price"]    ,"</td>";
echo "<td>", $discountedalbums->discount[$i]         ,"</td>";
echo "<td>", $discountedalbums->cal_discount($i),"</td></tr>";
}

echo "</table>";
?>
</BODY>
</HTML>
```

Execute the Code

To execute the code and view it on the browser, perform the following steps:

1. Save the text file in which you have written the code with a .php extension in /var/www/html as **albumrec.php**.

2. Open Netscape Navigator.

3. In the Address box, type http://localhost/albumrec.php.

Figure 7.1 shows the output of the code.

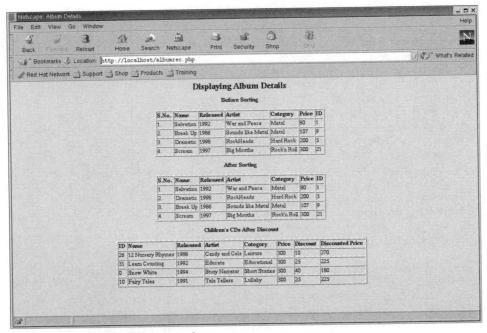

Figure 7.1   Output of albumrec.php.

Summary

In this chapter, you learned about the basic concept of object-oriented programming and its application in PHP. In addition, you learned to create a class, specify attributes, create functions, and instantiate objects. The chapter also covered the concept of inheritance and the procedure for applying it in PHP code. It then outlined the procedures for creating child classes and inheriting the functions of the parent class. Finally, you learned to override the functions of the parent class and access the overridden functions of the parent class when required.

Working with HTML Forms

OBJECTIVES:

In this lesson, you will learn to:

✔ Create HTML forms

✔ Create various form elements using HTML

✔ Parse HTML form data using PHP

Getting Started

In the previous chapters, you learned about all the important programming concepts in PHP. You have learned about variables, functions, arrays, and objects. In this chapter, you will learn how to work with forms, which is an important aspect of PHP and any other scripting language.

Forms are an integral part of any Web site. Regardless of the nature of a Web site, it is difficult to avoid using forms, which are the linking point between the Web site and the user. Forms can be as simple as a login page that consists of login and password text boxes or as complicated as a page that performs complex calculations based on user input. In this chapter, you will learn about forms and how they are used along with PHP to create interactive Web pages.

Form Basics

As discussed previously, almost all Web sites use forms to accept user input. This user input is then processed at the server end and the output is sent to the browser. In addition to this, the user input accepted in a form can also be stored in the database. This section will discuss all the relevant concepts related to Web forms.

Problem Statement

Mega Music Mart has decided to construct a Web site that will contain a user registration form that will be used to extract user details. The task of creating a registration form has been assigned to the development team at Mega Music Mart. The form should contain the following fields for information about a user:

✔ **Name**

✔ **Address**

✔ **Date of birth**

✔ **Gender**

✔ **Music preferences**

The team will also need to display this information in another Web page that will display in a table the following details entered by the user:

✔ **Name**

✔ **Address**

✔ **Date of birth**

✔ **An appropriate title based on the user's gender displayed before the name**

✔ **Music preferences**

Task List

Identify form elements:

✔ **Parse HTML form data in PHP**

✔ **Create the registration form**

✔ **Write the PHP code**

✔ **Execute the code**

Identify Form Elements

Three following basic elements are used with HTML forms whether you are creating a simple login page or a complex shopping cart:

FORM. Contains all the code related to a form, that is, all the tags that are specific to a form

INPUT. Specifies the code used to create the form controls that accept user input; can contain text boxes, buttons, check boxes, and radio buttons

SELECT. Displays lists in a form

The FORM Element

The main purpose of a form is to accept user input in a systematic and structured manner. The FORM element contains all code specific to a form, which is a collection of text boxes, radio buttons, check boxes and buttons; therefore, the INPUT and SELECT elements are also included in the FORM element. The METHOD and ACTION attributes are also used with the form element.

The METHOD Attribute

The METHOD attribute is used to transmit form data, which is the data that is supplied by a user. There are two methods that can be used to transmit form data: GET and POST.

NOTE The GET and POST methods are discussed in detail later in this chapter.

The ACTION Attribute

The ACTION attribute is used to specify the target, which is where the form data is to be transmitted. Typically, the target is a file that contains code for processing the form data. After processing the form data, the file generates the desired output and displays it.

Syntax for METHOD and ACTION Attributes

Almost every HTML form that accepts user input begins with a FORM tag that contains METHOD and ACTION attributes. The syntax for using these attributes is:

```
<form METHOD= "GET/POST" ACTION= "name_of_the_target_file">
```

The GET and POST Methods

By now, you know that by specifying the name of the target file in the ACTION attribute of the FORM element, the form data can be transmitted to the target file to be processed. Now let's look at the features of these methods and how they differ from each other. The following are the features of the GET method:

- It is simple to use.
- It appends the information entered by a user to the URL in the form of a query string.

- The query string is appended to the ? symbol that is present in the URL.

- The data entered by a user in the query string is separated by the & symbol.

- This method is not suitable for sending huge volumes of data because certain browsers limit the size of a URL that can be used.

- This method is not used to transmit sensitive or confidential information because the information entered by a user is visible on the Address or the Status bar.

The features of the POST method are:

- It can be used to transmit voluminous data.

- The string that contains the values entered by a user is not appended to the URL. Instead, it is stored within the body of the request.

- The information entered by a user is not displayed in the Address or the Status bar.

- It is ideal to use this method to transmit a user's confidential information because the information is not visible while it is being transmitted.

The INPUT Element

As discussed earlier, the INPUT element is specified within the FORM element. The main purpose of the INPUT element is to accept user-specific input, to make the Web page interactive and user friendly. All a user has to do is to fill in the required fields and click a button to submit the information.

The INPUT element consists of controls, such as text boxes, buttons, radio buttons, and check boxes. These controls contain the following attributes:

TYPE.   Specifies the type of control that will be used to accept input from the user.

NAME.   Specifies a name for the control. This name is used to identify a particular control in the form.

VALUE.   Holds the value entered by a user or the default value for a particular control.

When using the INPUT element with HTML forms, you can create four types of controls that accentuate the user interface: submit button, text boxes, radio buttons, and check boxes.

Submit Button

The submit button is used in an HTML form to submit information that is entered by a user to the target file. A form in HTML would be meaningless without this button. The syntax for specifying a submit button is:

```
<INPUT TYPE="submit" NAME="submit" VALUE="TESTBUTTON">
```

In the preceding syntax:

- The TYPE attribute signifies that this is a submit button.

- The NAME attribute signifies the name of the submit button.

- The VALUE attribute contains the text that is displayed on the button in the HTML page.

Text Boxes

Text boxes are the most commonly used controls and are used by almost all types of forms. They allow users to enter text in an HTML form. There are three types of text boxes in HTML: the Text field, the Text area, and the Password field. The attributes of all text fields are similar.

Text fields are used to accept single-line text input from a user, and they have two main attributes, name and value. The name attribute becomes the variable name in PHP, and the value attribute becomes the value for this variable. Consider the following code that displays two text fields on an HTML form:

```
<HTML>
<HEAD>
<TITLE>A Form with Two Text Fields</TITLE>
</HEAD>
<BODY>
<H2> A Form with Two Text Fields</H2
<FORM METHOD="POST" ACTION="hellouser.php">
First Name
<INPUT TYPE="TEXT" NAME="fname" VALUE="" >
<BR>
Last Name
<INPUT TYPE="TEXT" NAME="lname" VALUE="" >
<INPUT TYPE="submit" NAME="submit" VALUE="ACCEPT">
</FORM>
</BODY>
</HTML>
```

Figure 8.1 shows what the form looks like when you use the preceding code.

A Text area allows multiline text input in HTML forms. For example, the text area control is used to enable a user enter an address. Consider the following code that displays a text area control for the user:

```
<HTML>
<HEAD>
<TITLE>A Form with Text Area Control</TITLE>
</HEAD>
<BODY>
```

```
<H2> A Form with Text Area Control</H2>
<FORM METHOD="POST" ACTION="hellouser.php">
First Name
<INPUT TYPE="TEXT" NAME="fname" VALUE="">
<BR>
Last Name
<INPUT TYPE="TEXT" NAME="lname" VALUE="">
<br>
Address
<TEXTAREA NAME="address" VALUE="">
</TEXTAREA>
<br>
<INPUT TYPE="submit" NAME="submit" VALUE="ACCEPT">
</FORM>
</BODY>
</HTML>
```

Figure 8.2 displays an HTML form that contains a text area control. This control is basically the Address field.

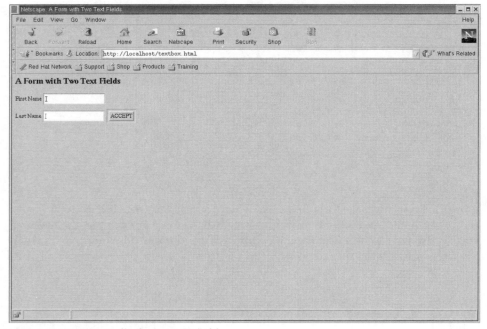

Figure 8.1   A form displaying text fields.

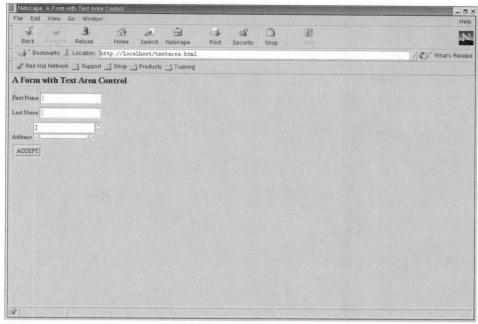

Figure 8.2 A form displaying a text area control.

A Password field allows a user to enter confidential information such as a password. An asterisk appears in the text box for each character of text entered. Consider the following HTML code that displays a login page:

```
<HTML>
<HEAD>
<TITLE>A Form with a Password Field</TITLE>
</HEAD>
<BODY>
<H2> A Form with a Password Field</H2>
<FORM METHOD="POST" ACTION="hellouser.php">
Login ID
<INPUT TYPE="TEXT" NAME="fname" VALUE="guest">
<BR>
Password
<INPUT TYPE="PASSWORD" NAME="lname" VALUE="default">
<INPUT TYPE="submit" NAME="submit" VALUE="ACCEPT">
</FORM>
</BODY>
</HTML>
```

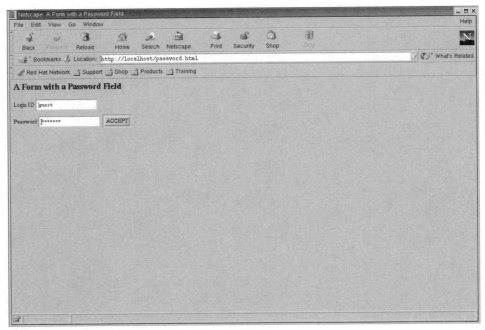

Figure 8.3   A form displaying the Password field.

Figure 8.3 shows a form displaying the Password field.

Radio Buttons

Radio buttons are controls that allow the user to choose a single option from the available predefined options. For example, a user can specify gender by selecting the Male or Female radio button.

Consider the following code that displays two radio buttons. The user has the option of selecting Yes or No depending on music listening preferences.

```
<HTML>
<HEAD>
<TITLE>Radio Buttons</TITLE>
</HEAD>
<BODY>
<H2>Radio Buttons</H2>
Do you like Rock music?
<FORM METHOD="POST" ACTION="hellouser.php">
Yes
<INPUT TYPE="RADIO" NAME="likemusic" VALUE="yes">
<BR>
No
<INPUT TYPE="RADIO" NAME="likemusic" VALUE="no">
<INPUT TYPE="submit" NAME="submit" VALUE="ACCEPT">
</FORM>
</BODY>
</HTML>
```

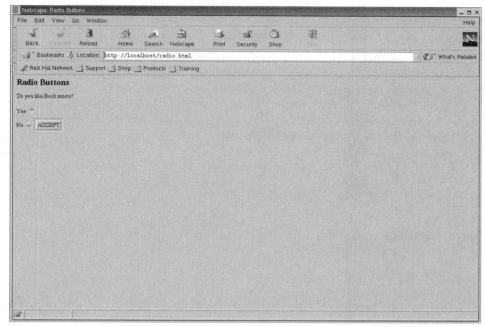

Figure 8.4   A form displaying radio buttons.

Figure 8.4 displays a set of radio buttons.

Check Boxes

Check boxes are controls that offer a user a choice of one or more options from a set of available predefined options. For example, you can have a list of music genres for a user with a check box in front of each option. In such a situation, a user may choose all the desired options.

```
<HTML>
<HEAD>
<TITLE>Check Boxes</TITLE>
</HEAD>
<BODY>
<H2>Check Boxes</H2>
<FORM METHOD="POST" ACTION="hellouser.php">
<INPUT TYPE="checkbox" NAME="pop" VALUE="1">POP
<BR>
<INPUT TYPE="checkbox" NAME="rock" VALUE="1">ROCK
<BR>
<INPUT TYPE="checkbox" NAME="metal" VALUE="1">METAL
<BR>
<INPUT TYPE="checkbox" NAME="jazz" VALUE="1">JAZZ
<INPUT TYPE="submit" NAME="submit" VALUE="ACCEPT">
</FORM>
</BODY>
</HTML>
```

Figure 8.5 displays check boxes.

Combo Boxes

Combo boxes are menu type controls that allow a user to select one of the listed options. Combo boxes are defined in HTML by using the <SELECT> and </SELECT> container tags. For each option that is to be displayed in the combo box menu, a separate option tag is placed between these container tags. A combo box allows one or more options to be selected from a predefined set. An example of using a combo box is to choose Male or Female from a combo box follows:

```
<HTML>
<HEAD>
<TITLE>Combo Boxes</TITLE>
</HEAD>
<BODY>
<H2>Combo Boxes</H2>
<FORM METHOD="POST" ACTION="hellouser.php">
Gender
<SELECT NAME="gender">
<OPTION VALUE="Male"> Male
<OPTION VALUE="Female"> Female
</SELECT>
<INPUT TYPE="submit" NAME="submit" VALUE="ACCEPT">
</FORM>
</BODY>
</HTML>
```

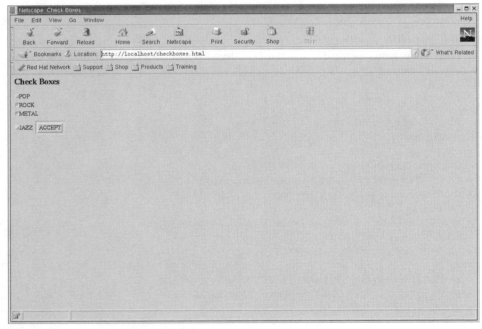

Figure 8.5 An example of check boxes.

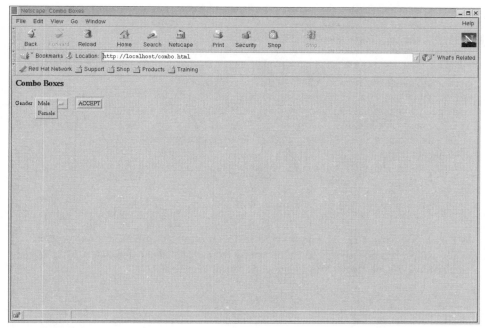

Figure 8.6 Combo boxes.

Figure 8.6 displays combo boxes.

Parsing HTML Form Data in PHP

By now you have an idea about creating controls for your HTML form. It is now time to understand how PHP handles the data entered in the form. Parsing form data using PHP is fairly easy because unlike most other languages PHP parses data transmitted using both GET and POST methods. The only thing that should be kept in mind is that the variable name in PHP should be the same as the NAME attribute of any HTML form tag. For example, if the NAME attribute of a text box is texbox, the value in this text box will be accessible in PHP as variable $texbox.

Creating an HTML Form

A profit calculator should contain two text boxes that accept the revenue and expenses as input from a user. It should also contain a submit button that a user can use to submit the values entered. To begin with, let's create a simple HTML form that accepts user input in the predetermined fields. Consider the following code:

```
<HTML>
<HEAD>
<TITLE>PROFIT CALCULATOR</TITLE>
</HEAD>
<BODY>
<H4><CENTER>PROFIT CALCULATOR</CENTER></H4>
<FORM METHOD="get" ACTION="verify.php">
<P><CENTER>REVENUE: <INPUT TYPE="text" NAME="revenue"
SIZE=10></CENTER></P>
<P><CENTER>EXPENSES: <INPUT TYPE="text" NAME="expenses"
SIZE=10></CENTER></P>
<P><CENTER><INPUT TYPE="submit" NAME="submit"
VALUE="ACCEPT"></CENTER></P>
</BODY>
</HTML>
```

In this code, form data is transmitted to the file **verify.php**. The next section will examine the PHP code that will be required to perform the calculation by using the values entered in the form. The form is shown in Figure 8.7.

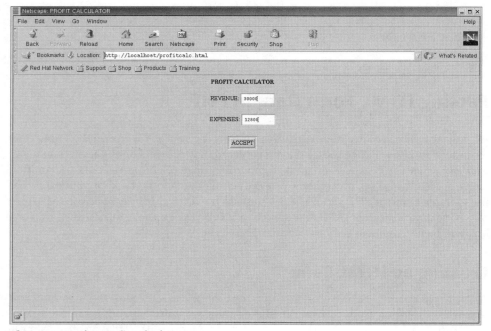

Figure 8.7 The profit calculator.

Creating the PHP File

The next step is to write the code for the PHP file that receives the data submitted by the HTML form. This file will contain the PHP code that will process the data received and produce an output HTML page. The PHP code should accept the values entered in the Revenue and Expenses fields, calculate the profit or loss, and display a message.

```
<HTML>
<BODY>
<?php
if ($revenue > $expenses)
    {
    $profit = $revenue - $expenses;
    echo "You have earned a profit of $profit dollars!";
    }
elseif ($revenue == $expenses)
    {
    echo "Neither profit nor loss";
    }
elseif ($revenue < $expenses)

    {
    $loss = $expenses - $revenue;
    echo "You have incurred a loss of $loss dollars.";
    }
?>
</BODY>
</HTML>
```

Create the Registration Form

The development team of Mega Music Mart will now create a registration form that accepts the desired user input. The code for the HTML registration form is:

```
<html>
<head>
<title>Index</title>
</head>
<body>
<h2 align="center">User Registration Form</h2>
<form name="form1" method="post" action="output.php"
enctype="multipart/form-data">
  <table width="53%" border="0" align="center" cellpadding="5"
cellspacing="0" bgcolor="#CCCCCC">
    <tr>
      <td width="49%">Name </td>
      <td colspan="2">
```

```
      <div align="left">
        <input type="text" name="name" size="25" maxlength="25">
      </div>
    </td>
  </tr>
  <tr>
    <td width="49%" bgcolor="#FFFFFF"> </td>
    <td height="2" colspan="2" bgcolor="#FFFFFF"> </td>
  </tr>
  <tr>
    <td width="49%" height="57">Address</td>
    <td height="57" colspan="2">
      <textarea name="address" cols="25" rows="4"></textarea>
    </td>
  </tr>
  <tr>
    <td width="49%" bgcolor="#FFFFFF"> </td>
    <td height="2" colspan="2" bgcolor="#FFFFFF"> </td>
  </tr>
  <tr>
    <td width="49%">Date of Birth</td>
    <td height="2" colspan="2">
      <select name=birth_month>
        <option selected
            value=1>January
        <option value=2>February
        <option
            value=3>March
        <option value=4>April
        <option value=5>May
        <option
            value=6>June
        <option value=7>July
        <option value=8>August
        <option
            value=9>September
        <option value=10>October
        <option
            value=11>November
        <option value=12>December</option>
      </select>
      <select
          name=birth_day>
        <option selected value=1>01
        <option
            value=2>02
        <option value=3>03
        <option value=4>04
        <option
            value=5>05
        <option value=6>06
```

```
               <option value=7>07
               <option
                   value=8>08
               <option value=9>09
               <option value=10>10
               <option
                   value=11>11
               <option value=12>12
               <option value=13>13
               <option
                   value=14>14
               <option value=15>15
               <option value=16>16
               <option
                   value=17>17
               <option value=18>18
               <option value=19>19
               <option
                   value=20>20
               <option value=21>21
               <option value=22>22
               <option
                   value=23>23
               <option value=24>24
               <option value=25>25
               <option
                   value=26>26
               <option value=27>27
               <option value=28>28
               <option
                   value=29>29
               <option value=30>30
               <option value=31>31</option>
           </select>
           <input maxlength=4 name=birth_year size=4>
           (Year) </td>
     </tr>
     <tr bgcolor="#FFFFFF">
       <td width="49%" height="2"> </td>
       <td height="2" width="17%"> </td>
       <td height="2" width="34%"> </td>
     </tr>
     <tr>
       <td width="49%">Gender</td>
       <td height="2" width="17%">
         <input type="radio" name="gender" value="M">
         Male </td>
       <td height="2" width="34%">
         <input type="radio" name="gender" value="F">
         Female</td>
     </tr>
```

```html
        <tr>
          <td width="49%" bgcolor="#FFFFFF" height="5"> </td>
          <td height="5" colspan="2" bgcolor="#FFFFFF"> </td>
        </tr>
        <tr>
          <td width="49%">Music Preference</td>
          <td height="2" colspan="2">
            <table width="100%" border="0">
              <tr>
                <td>
                  <input type="checkbox" name="pop" value="1">
                  Pop </td>
                <td>
                  <input type="checkbox" name="rock" value="1">
                  Rock </td>
              </tr>
              <tr>
                <td>
                  <input type="checkbox" name="jazz" value="1">
                  Jazz </td>
                <td>
                  <input type="checkbox" name="metal" value="1">
                  Metal </td>
              </tr>
              <tr>
                <td>
                  <input type="checkbox" name="instrumental" value="1">
                  Instrumental</td>
                <td> </td>
              </tr>
            </table>
          </td>
        </tr>
        <tr>
          <td width="49%" height="2" bgcolor="#FFFFFF"> </td>
          <td colspan="2" height="2" bgcolor="#FFFFFF"> </td>
        </tr>

        <tr>
          <td colspan="3">
            <div align="center">
              <input type="submit" name="Submit" value="Submit">
            </div>
          </td>
        </tr>
      </table>
    </form>
  </body>
</html>
```

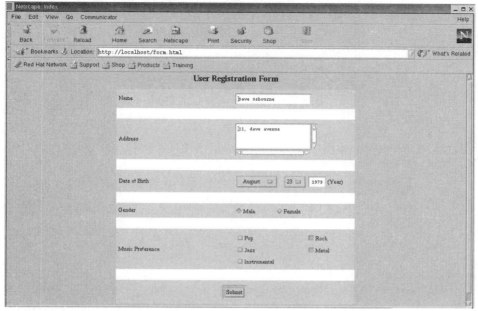

Figure 8.8   The user registration form.

Figure 8.8 shows how the user registration form appears in the browser.

Write the PHP Code

Now the team will write the PHP script that will be accessed by the HTML form. The form will send user input to the PHP file. The PHP code will then process the user input and display the required information. This can be made possible by writing the following code in the PHP file:

```
<html>
<head>
<title>Display Output </title>
</head>
<body>
<h2> Dear
<?php
if ($gender=='M')
{
 echo "Mr.";
}
```

```php
elseif ($gender=='F')
{
echo "Ms.";
}
echo "  ",$name;
?>  ! You have entered the following information:</h2>
<table width="75%" border="1">
  <tr>
    <td>Address </td>
    <td>
      <?php echo $address; ?>
    </td>
  </tr>
  <tr>
    <td>Date of Birth</td>
    <td>
      <?php echo $birth_month," ",$birth_day,"  ",$birth_year; ?>
    </td>
  </tr>
  <tr>
    <td colspan=2>You prefer listening to:
<?php
if (!(empty($pop)))
      {
       if($pop==1)         { echo " Pop ";       }
      }
if (!(empty($jazz)))
      {
       if($jazz==1)        { echo " Jazz ";      }
      }
if (!(empty($rock)))
      {
       if($rock==1)        { echo " Rock ";      }
      }
if (!(empty($instrumental)))
      {
       if($instrumental==1){ echo " Instrumental ";}
      }
if (!(empty($metal)))
      {
       if($metal==1)       { echo " Metal ";    }
      }
?>
</td>
  </tr>

</table>
</body>
</html>
```

Execute the Code

To check whether the code specified in the PHP file is functional, perform the following steps:

1. Open Netscape Navigator.
2. In the Address box, specify the URL as `http://localhost/filename.htm` to open the form in Netscape Navigator.
3. Fill in all the form's fields.
4. Press the submit button to view output.

Figure 8.9 shows how the output will look after you fill in the required details and press the submit button.

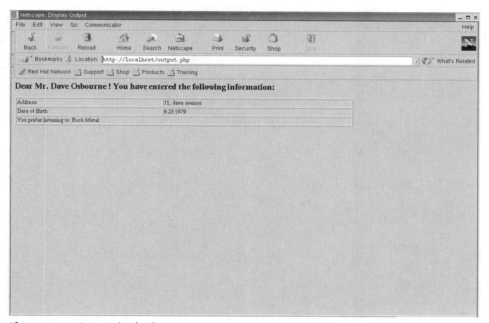

Figure 8.9   Output in the browser.

Summary

In this chapter, you learned the basics of working with forms. You learned to create form controls and use them in HTML forms. You also learned how to accept user input and use PHP code to process the information entered by the user.

Using the File System

OBJECTIVES:

In this chapter, you will learn to:

- ✔ Open, close, and check an external file
- ✔ Read from and write to an external file
- ✔ Write and append an external file
- ✔ Delete an external file
- ✔ Define access permissions for files
- ✔ Access and store data into an external file
- ✔ Create a directory
- ✔ Open a directory
- ✔ Access the files in a directory
- ✔ Read the files in a directory
- ✔ Remove a directory

Getting Started

Web sites that offer relevant, up-to-date information, such as news sites, attract many users. Visitors to a news Web site expect to be updated promptly on the latest happenings around the world. If a news Web site fails to do this, users will stop using that site. However, from a developer's point of view, changing the information that is embedded in the HTML code is a tedious task. A simpler alternative is to store dynamic data in an external file and then retrieve this data when required. After you update the data in this file, it can be retrieved and displayed on the Web page. The need for dynamic information makes access to files an essential part of Web applications programming.

In addition to storing site-related information in an external file, you can use a file to store the data entered by a user in an HTML form. This enables you to store data entered by users for future reference. However, files cannot handle voluminous data efficiently. For that, you must use databases, which are discussed in the next chapter.

This chapter is divided into two portions. The first provides an introduction to the functions that you can use to access and manipulate the data stored in external files, and the second covers how to effectively use functions in PHP programs to handle directories.

File Accessing

There are several built-in functions in PHP that allow developers to perform a number of operations on files. This section will help you understand how these built-in functions are used. Now let's see what is the new problem that Mega Music Mart is facing.

Problem Statement

Mega Music Mart wants to introduce a news page on its Web site that would display the latest information about global events related to music. This page would need to be updated regularly. An essential part of the project is creating two sections for the Web site:

Administrator-Only Section. This section will be accessible only to the administrator. It should allow the administrator to perform the following tasks:

- Update the news from time to time
- Delete the old news
- Review the posted news articles

In addition, it would allow the administrator to enter information in two parts. The first part would contain the headline, and the second part would contain the main content of the news.

Customer Section. This section would allow the users to view the news on a Web page but not to change or update the news.

Specifications. To complete the task assigned to them, the development team is given the following specifications:

- Maintain the news items for each day in a separate file
- Name the file in the format newsdd-mm-yyyy.txt
- Keep all news files in the news directory

To implement the project, the development team decides to create four scripts: An index page would display two HTML forms to the administrator.

- The first HTML form would allow the administrator to create a file to store the news headlines for the particular day and the main news content. If the file for the particular day exists, the old data should be overwritten.

- The second form on the same page should allow the administrator to view a list of all previously stored news files in a drop-down menu and view or delete any news file. While using this form, if the administrator chooses to view a previously stored news file, the result page should display the file name and the file size in addition to the headline and news content.

- The main Mega Music Mart news page would locate the news file for the day and display the content.

Task List

On a broad level, the tasks that need to be performed to obtain the best results are the following:

✔ **Identify the file-related functions**

✔ **Write the PHP code**

✔ **Execute the code**

Creating a Test File

Code samples specified in this chapter assume that a test file named **testfile.txt** is created. The purpose of creating this test file is to check how file-related functions work. You will need to create this file if you want the output of your code to match the output specified in the book. This file should be located in /home/username directory. In this chapter, dave is the username in the examples that explain all file-related concepts. To create the file named **testfile.txt**, follow these steps:

1. Create a file named **testfile.txt** by using the vi editor in the directory /home/dave.

NOTE The directory /home/dave will exist only when you add a user named dave. The user can be added by using the useradd command in Linux.

2. Type the following text in **testfile.txt:**

```
Hi all.
This is a test file that has been created to test the file-related
functions in PHP. This file will be used as an example throughout this
chapter.
Thank You.
```

NOTE Save the file and exit the **vi** editor.

Identify the File-Related Functions

PHP has several built-in functions that allow you to create and manipulate the data stored in an external file. They can also be used to perform a wide range of tasks with external files, including:

- Opening, closing, and checking a file
- Reading from a file
- Writing and appending content to file
- Deleting a file
- Working with directories

Opening a File

Before you learn to manipulate the data stored in an external file, you need to open it. To do so, you use the fopen() function, which requires two parameters, the *path* of the external file and the *mode* in which you want to open the file. The mode is basically the permission with which you open the file. For example, a file can be opened in read-only, write, or append mode. The syntax of the fopen() function is as follows:

```
fopen (filename, mode);
```

In the preceding syntax:

- The fopen() function is used with two parameters, *filename* and *mode*.
- The filename represents the path of the file if the file is not present in the current directory. For example if the current directory is /home/dave and the file is located in this directory, you can specify just the filename. However, you can also specify a different location for the file by specifying the complete path for the file.

NOTE The files that you execute in the browser will be stored in the /var/www/html directory. Therefore, if you specify a filename without the path, the PHP script will search for the specified file in the /var/www/html directory.

■ The mode of a file can be read, write, or append.

Table 9.1 lists the modes that you can specify while opening an external file.

TIP Another mode that can be used to open a file is b. This mode works on those platforms that can differentiate between text and binary formats. Therefore, this mode works with Windows platforms and not with Unix and Linux platforms.

The following code opens an external file named **testfile.txt,** which is present on the local hard drive:

```php
<?php
$openfile ="/home/dave/testfile.txt";
$result = fopen ($openfile,"r") or die ("Couldn't open the file");
echo "File opened successfully";
?>
```

Table 9.1   The File-related Modes

CODE	MODE
'r'	Opens the file with the read-only permission. The file pointer is placed at the beginning of the file.
'r+'	Opens the file with read and the write permissions. The file pointer is placed at the beginning of the file.
'w'	Opens the file with write permission. The file pointer is placed at the beginning of the file. If the file exists, the data present in the file is lost. If the file does not exist, a new file is created.
'w+'	Opens the file with the read and write permissions. The file pointer is placed at the beginning of the file. If the file exists, the data present in the file is lost. If the file does not exist, a new file is created.
'a'	Opens the file with the write permission. The file pointer is positioned at the end of the file. If the file exists and contains data, the new content is appended to the existing file. If the file does not exist, a new file is created.
'a+'	Opens the file with the read and write permissions. The file pointer is positioned at the end of the file. If the file exists, new content is appended to the file. If the specified file does not exist, a new file is created.

In this code:

- The variable $myfile stores the path of the external file that you want to open. In this case, the path specified is the home directory of the user dave. If you want to open a file that is present in the current directory, you do not need to specify the absolute path of the file. This means that if the user dave executes the preceding PHP code from his home directory, he does not need to specify the absolute path of the file. The file will be opened even if only the filename is specified.

- The function fopen() is used to open the specified file.

- Two parameters, $myfile and r, are used with the fopen() function.

- The $myfile variable specifies the path of the file that needs to be opened.

- The value r specifies that the file will be opened in read-only mode.

- The function die () is used to close the program if the external file cannot be opened.

- A message is specified within the die() function. This message appears if the specified file is not found at the specified location.

- The message File opened successfully is displayed if the external file is opened.

The output of this is:

```
X-Powered-By: PHP/4.0.6
Content-type: text/html
File opened successfully
```

If the external file is not present at the specified location, an error message will appear. To test what happens when a file with the specified names is not present, you can rename the file **testfile.txt** to **Testfile.txt**. When you do this, the file **Testfile.txt** is not found at the specified location and an error message appears. In this case, the output will be:

```
X-Powered-By: PHP/4.0.6
Content-type: text/html
<br>
<b>Warning</b>: fopen("Testfile.txt","r") - No such file or directory
in <b>check.php</b> on line <b>3</b></b><br>
Couldn't open the file
```

Notice that a warning message precedes the message Couldn't open the file. This message indicates that PHP was unable to open the file because it was not present in the specified location. You can avoid the warning message from being displayed by adding the symbol @ with the fopen() function as follows:

```
<?php
$myfile = "/home/dave/MyFile.txt";
$openfile = @fopen ($myfile,"r") or die ("Couldn't open the file");
echo "File was opened";
?>
```

When you execute this code, only the message `Couldn't open the file` will be displayed. The output will be:

```
X-Powered-By: PHP/4.0.6
Content-type: text/html
Couldn't open the file
```

Closing a File

After you finish working with a file, you close it with the `fclose()` function. This function returns a boolean value; if the file is closed successfully, it returns true and if not, it returns false. The `fclose()` function takes only one argument, which is the file pointer. The syntax of `fclose()` function is:

```
fclose(filepointer);
```

Checking a File

Before you start working extensively with external files, it is a good idea to check files. This may help avoid possible errors. The operations that you can perform are:

- Checking that a file exists
- Checking the mode of the file
- Checking the size of the file

Checking That a File Exists

You can avoid possible file system errors by checking whether a file exists before trying to access it. To do this, use the `file_exists()` function, which accepts the path of the external file as a parameter. The function returns true if the external file exists. Otherwise, it returns false. Consider the following code:

```php
<?php
$myfile = "/home/dave/testfile.txt";
if (file_exists ($myfile))
  {
   $msg="File already exists. ";
  }
else
  {
   $myfile = @fopen ($myfile, "w+") or die ("Couldn't create the file");
   $msg= "File created! ";
   fclose ($myfile);
  }
?>
<?echo "$msg"; ?>
```

In the preceding code:

- The `file_exists()` function is used to check whether the file **testfile.txt** exists.
- The `fopen()` function is used with the w+ mode to create the file if it doesn't exist.
- The `fclose()` function is used to close the file.

The output is:

```
X-Powered-By: PHP/4.0.6
Content-type: text/html
File already exists.
```

The output indicates that the file **testfile.txt** exists in the directory /home/dave. Therefore, the file couldn't be opened.

Now let's examine what happens when the file is not present in the specified directory. The output then is:

```
X-Powered-By: PHP/4.0.6
Content-type: text/html
File created!
```

Here the file did not exist but was created because you used the fopen() function and opened the file in w+ mode.

Checking the Mode of a File

You can determine if you can read, write, or execute the code in a file by checking the file's mode using the following functions:

- `is_readable()` checks whether you can read a file.
- `is_writable()` checks whether you can write to a file.
- `is_executable()` checks whether you can execute a file.

These functions all accept the path of the file as a parameter and return a boolean value of true if the test is successful and false if the test fails. Consider the following code:

```php
<?php
$myfile = "/home/dave/testfile.txt";
if (is_readable ($myfile))
  {
   echo "The file can be read!", "\n";
  }
else
  {
echo "The file cannot be read.", "\n";
  }
if (is_writable ($myfile))
  {
    echo "The file can be used for writing!", "\n";
```

```
    }
  else
  {
  echo "The file cannot be used for writing.", "\n";
  }
  if (is_executable ($myfile))
  {
    echo "The file is executable!", "\n";
  }
  else
  {
    echo "The file is not executable.", "\n";
  }
?>
```

In this code:

- The variable $myfile is used to store the location of the file **testfile.txt**.
- The is_readable() function is used to check whether the file is readable.
- The is_writable() function is used to check whether the file can be written.
- The is_executable() function is used to check whether the file can be executed.

The output is:

```
X-Powered-By: PHP/4.0.6
Content-type: text/html
The file can be read!
The file can be used for writing!
The file is not executable.
```

The output indicates that the file **testfile.txt** is located in the home directory of the user dave and has read and write but not executable permissions. The permissions of the file can be checked using the following command:

```
[dave@localhost dave]$ ls -l testfile.txt
```

The output of this command is:

```
-rw-rw-r—    1 dave      dave        167 Dec 29 21:26 testfile.txt
```

The output indicates that dave has the read and the write permissions for the file named **testfile.txt**.

Determining the Size of a File

If you are planning to store a large amount of data in a file, it is good practice to check the size of the file before you begin using it. To do so, you can use the filesize() function, which returns the size of the file in bytes. It accepts the name of the file as the parameter and returns the size of the file. Consider the following code:

```php
<?php
$myfile = "/home/dave/testfile.txt";
if (file_exists ($myfile))
 {
  $checksize=filesize ($myfile);
  echo "$checksize";
 }
else
 {
   echo "The file doesn't exist!";
 }
?>
```

In this code:

- The variable $myfile is used to store the location of the file named **testfile.txt.**

- The file_exists () function is used to check whether a file by the name **testfile.txt** exists.

- The filesize () function is used to determine the size of the file named **testfile.txt.**

The output of this code is:

```
X-Powered-By: PHP/4.0.6
Content-type: text/html
167
```

Copying the Contents of an External File into a Variable

The data stored in an external file takes longer to load on a Web page. Therefore, if you need to repeatedly use data from an external file, a possible approach to avoid this time delay is to use a variable to store the content of the external file. Then, after you complete your work, you can release the memory space.

To store the content of a file into a variable, use the fread () and filesize () functions. The following code copies the content of the external file and stores it in the variable $file_content. If the copying is successful, the code will display the message Copying the file contents was successful. Consider the following code:

```php
<?php
$myfile = "/home/dave/testfile.txt";
$openfile = @fopen ($myfile,"r") or die ("Couldn't open the file");
$file_content = fread ($openfile, filesize ($openfile));
echo "The file content copied successfully!";
echo $file_content;
?>
```

In this code:

- The fopen () function is used with the filesize () function.

- The filesize () function is used to retrieve the size of the file in bytes.

- The fopen() function is used to open the file and read the number of bytes retrieved by using the filesize() function.

The output of the code is:

```
X-Powered-By: PHP/4.0.6
Content-type: text/html
The file content copied successfully!
```

Clearing Cache

Many functions such as filesize(), is_readable(), and file_exists() are small functions and take minimal memory space. However, the disk access is sometimes very slow. Therefore, the results of these functions are cached for faster access. It is advisable to clear the cache from time to time so that there is enough space where the results of these functions can be stored. The clearstatcache() function is used to clear the cache. However, there is no need to use the clearstatcache() function if you are not using a function repeatedly.

Reading from a File

After you have opened a file, you might want to read data from it. PHP provides several functions for this. They enable you to read the bytes, lines, or characters in a file. The following code reads the data from an external file and then displays it onscreen:

```php
<?php
$myfile = "/home/dave/testfile.txt";
$openfile = fopen ($myfile,"r") or die ("Couldn't open the file");
$file_size=filesize($myfile);
$file_content = fread ($openfile,$file_size);
fclose ($openfile);
echo $file_content;
?>
```

In this code:

- The variable $myfile is used to store the location of the file named **testfile.txt.**
- The $openfile variable will open the file **testfile.txt** as a read-only file. If the file is not found at the specified location, the program will close.
- The $file_size variable is used to store the size of the file retrieved by the filesize() function.
- The variable name $file_content is used to store the data retrieved by the fread() function from the external file.

The output of the code is:

```
X-Powered-By: PHP/4.0.6
Content-type: text/html
Hi all.
```

```
This is a test file that has been created to test the file-related
functions in PHP. This file will be used as an example throughout this
chapter.
Thank You.
```

It is evident from the output that **testfile.txt** was successfully opened and the content was accessed, read, and displayed on the screen.

Using fgets() and feof() Functions

An alternative method of reading content from an external file is by using `fgets()` and `feof()` functions. The `fgets()` function is used to access the contents of a file line by line, and it requires two parameters. The first is the pointer returned by the `fopen()` function, and the second is an integer. This integer represents the number of characters the `fgets()` function should read before it encounters the end of the first line.

You can use the `fgets()` function in conjunction with the `feof()` function. The `feof()` function is used to track when the program reaches the end of the file after reading all the lines. The `feof()` function returns true if the program reaches the end of the file and false if it doesn't. The following code illustrates the method for retrieving data line by line by using the `fgets()` and the `feof()` functions:

```php
<?php
$myfile = "/home/dave/testfile.txt";
$openfile = fopen ($myfile, "r") or die ("Couldn't open the file");
while (!feof ($openfile))
{
$lines= fgets($openfile, 1024);
echo "$lines", "\n";
}
?>
```

In this code:

- The variable `$myfile` is used to store the path of the file named **testfile.txt.**

- The `fopen()` function is used to open the file named **testfile.txt** as a read-only file.

- The `feof()` function is used with the while loop to read the contents of the file until the end of the file.

- The `while` loop continues until it reaches the end of the file.

- The `fgets()` function within the `while` loop extracts 1024 bytes of the file, which are stored in the variable `$lines`.

- Finally, the contents of the variable `$lines` are displayed on the screen.

The output is:

```
X-Powered-By: PHP/4.0.6
Content-type: text/html
Hi all.
This is a test file that has been created to test the file-related
```

functions in PHP. This file will be used as an example throughout this
chapter.
Thank You

Reading Specific Data from a File

In the preceding section, you retrieved the entire content of the file using various built-
in functions in PHP. However, at times you may need to retrieve specific data from a
file. For example, you may have stored the comments entered by a user on the feedback form in a certain section of a file. You can retrieve this information stored with the
fread() and fseek() functions. This is because although the fread() function
allows you to read specific data in the external file, you need to place the pointer at a
specific location in the external file. To do so in relation to the current position of the
pointer, use the fseek() function, which requires two parameters, a file pointer and
an integer that defines the starting point. Consider the following code that places the
pointer directly on the second line and then extracts the text from the second line:

```php
<?php
$myfile = "/home/dave/testfile.txt";
$openfile = fopen ($myfile, "r") or die ("Couldn't open the file");
$filesize =filesize($myfile);
fseek ($openfile,8);
$sp_data = fread ($openfile, ($filesize - 8)
);
print $sp_data;
?>
```

The output is:

```
X-Powered-By: PHP/4.0.6
Content-type: text/html
This is a test file that has been created to test the file-related
functions in PHP. This file will be used as an example throughout this
chapter.
Thank You.
```

As is evident, the code extracts only the second line. Therefore, the text Hi all!
doesn't appear when the contents of the file named testfile.txt are displayed.

Reading a Specific Character

A feedback form on your Web site might have questions that are answered as Y or N
for Yes or No. To make any calculation on such variables, you just need to retrieve the
specific character using the fgetc() function, which requires one parameter, the
pointer for the file. The length of the file is only 1 byte because one character is always
1 byte. Therefore, you do not need to specify the size of the file. Consider the following
code:

```php
<?php
$myfile = "/home/dave/testfile.txt";
$openfile = fopen ($myfile, "r") or die ("Couldn't open the file");
```

```
fseek ($openfile,88);
$chunk = fgetc ($openfile);
echo $chunk;
?>
```

In this code:

- The variable $myfile is used to store the location of the file named **testfile.txt.**
- The fopen() function is used to open the file in read-only mode.
- The fseek() function is used to place the pointer at the twelfth byte of the external file.
- The variable $chunk stores the character retrieved using the fgetc() function.

The output of the code is:

```
X-Powered-By: PHP/4.0.6
Content-type: text/html
P
```

Writing and Appending Content in a File

There may be times when you want to update the information in a file either by replacing the content in the file or adding to it. The functions that write to a file are fwrite() and fputs(), which are similar and both accept two parameters, a file pointer and a string. The string holds the text that you want to write or append to the file.

The code for writing and adding to the file is the same. The difference lies in the way you call the fopen() function. When opening a file for writing, the file needs to be opened in the write (w) mode. Appending to the file uses the write mode. The following code opens the file in append mode, adds the line This is great music, reads from the same file, and displays the text that you have added to the file:

```
<?php
$myfile = "/home/dave/newfile.txt";
$openfile = fopen ($myfile,"w") or die ("Couldn't open the file");
fwrite ($openfile,"This is great music \n");
fclose ($openfile );
$openfile = fopen ($myfile,"r") or die ("Couldn't open the file");
$file_size=filesize($myfile);
$file_contents = fread ($openfile,$file_size);
$msg ="$file_contents";
fclose ($openfile);
echo $msg;
?>
```

In this code:

- The variable $myfile contains the location of the file **newfile.txt.**
- The fopen() function is used to open the file in write mode.

- The fwrite() function is used to write text in the file.
- The fclose() function is used to close the file.
- The fopen() function is used to open the file in read-only mode to view the text was written to the file.
- The filesize() function is used to determine the size of the newly created file.
- The fread() function is used to read the contents of the new file.
- The fclose() function is used to close the file.

The output is:

```
X-Powered-By: PHP/4.0.6
Content-type: text/html
This is great music
```

The following code shows you how to add text to the file. The only difference in the code is the way the file is opened. When adding text without changing the existing contents of the file, you need to open the file in the append mode, as follows:

```php
<?php
$myfile = "/home/dave/testfile.txt";
$openfile = fopen ($myfile,"a") or die ("Couldn't open the file");
fwrite ($openfile,"Have a nice day! \n");
fclose ($openfile );
$openfile = fopen ($myfile,"r") or die ("Couldn't open the file");
$file_size=filesize($myfile);
$file_contents = fread ($openfile,$file_size);
$msg ="$file_contents";
fclose ($openfile);
echo $msg;
?>
```

In this code:

- The variable $myfile is used to store the location of the file named **testfile.txt.**
- The fopen() function is used to open the file in append mode so that the existing content of the file is not changed.
- The fwrite() function is used, and the file pointer and string are specified as arguments to the fwrite() function.
- The fclose() function is used to close the file.
- The fopen() function is used again to open the file in read-only mode so that the text added to the file can be viewed.
- The filesize() function is used to determine the size of the file.
- The fread() function is used to read the entire contents of the file.
- The fclose() function is used again to close the file.

The output of this code is:

```
X-Powered-By: PHP/4.0.6
Content-type: text/html
Hi all.
This is a test file that has been created to test the file-related
functions in PHP. This file will be used as an example throughout this
chapter.
Thank You.
Have a nice day!
```

Deleting a File

When you no longer require a file, you can delete it using the unlink() function, which permanently deletes a file from the disk. However, you need to have the necessary permissions to use this function. The syntax for using the unlink() function is:

```
$result = unlink($filename);
```

In the preceding syntax:

- $filename is the name of the file to be deleted. If the file to be deleted is not in the directory in which the PHP script resides, $filename will represent the complete path of the file, including the filename.

- $result is a variable that stores true or false depending on the result of using the unlink() function. The $result will be false for the following reasons:

  - $filename doesn't exist.

  - Lack of adequate permissions to delete the file. In this case, you can change the file permissions by using either the chmod() function or the chmod command at the command prompt.

Consider the following code:

```php
<?php
$myfile = "/home/dave/testfile.txt";
if (file_exists($myfile))
  {
   $result=unlink ($myfile);
   echo $result;
  }
?>
```

In this code:

- The variable $myfile is used to store the location of the file named **testfile.txt**.

- The file_exists() function is used to check whether the file with the specified name exists.

- The unlink() function is used to delete the file.

The output is:

```
X-Powered-By: PHP/4.0.6
Content-type: text/html
1
```

The output shows that specified file was deleted because 1 indicates true.

Working with Directories

Directories are an inseparable part of any file system. Until now, we have discussed the functions that are used to work with the individual external files. However, there are several situations that require operations where directories need to be created or deleted.

In this section of the chapter, you will learn to:

- Set permissions
- Create and delete a directory
- Create and destroy a directory handle
- Read contents from a directory

NOTE The source code provided in the section will not work in the absence of adequate permissions to access the /home directory.

Setting Permissions

To test the source code in this section you will need to alter the permissions for the /home directory as follows:

1. Make sure that you are logged in as the root user, the only user who can alter the permissions for the /home directory.

2. Type the following command:

   ```
   # chmod 777 /home
   ```

NOTE It is not advisable to grant the permission 777 to the /home directory because this will give read, write, and execute permissions for the /home directory to all users on the computer. This permission has been granted here to demonstrate how the directory functions operate.

If you want to execute PHP code in the browser, you will need to set adequate permissions for the /var/www/html directory because all PHP files are saved in the /var/www/html directory so that the output can be viewed in the browser.

Creating a Directory Using mkdir()

PHP provides a function named mkdir() to create directories. This function in PHP is similar to its Linux counterpart, the mkdir command. However, the user must have adequate permissions to be able to create a directory by using this function.

The syntax for the mkdir() function is:

```
$result = mkdir($dirname, $permissions);
```

In this syntax:

- $dirname is the name of the directory that will be created. All the directory-naming rules of Linux apply to this argument.
- $permissions is an octal number used to define the permissions that will be set for this directory, such as 0777.
- $result is a variable that stores the success or failure of the mkdir() function. The $result can be false because:
  - The argument $dirname is empty.
  - The value specified as $dirname is an invalid value for a directory name.
  - A directory of the specified name already exists.
  - PHP doesn't have access to the file system to create a new directory in the working directory.

The following code creates a directory called dummydir in the /home directory:

```php
<?php
if (!(file_exists("/home/dummydir")))
{
if(!(is_dir("/home/dummydir")))
 {
  $result = mkdir("/home/dummydir",0700);
  echo " Result = ".$result;
 }
}
?>
```

In this code:

- The file_exists() function is used to search for a file called dummydir in the /home directory.
- If no directory or file named dummydir is present, a new directory named dummydir is created in the /home directory using the mkdir() function. The directory permissions are set as an octal number, 0700.
- A result, true or false is displayed on the success or failure of the mkdir() function.

The output of the code is:

```
X-Powered-By: PHP/4.0.6
Content-type: text/html
 Result = 1
```

The output indicates that the directory was created successfully. You can check whether dummdir was created by using the ls command, which displays a list of the files and directories present in the current directory.

Deleting a Directory by Using rmdir()

The rmdir() function can be used to delete directories; it is similar to its Linux counterpart, the rmdir command. However, before using this function, the required permissions to delete a directory should be attained. The syntax for the rmdir() function is:

```
$result = rmdir($dirname);
```

In this syntax:

- $dirname is the name of the directory to be deleted. If this directory is located in another directory, $dirname is the complete path of the directory.

- $result is a variable that stores the success or failure of the rmdir() function. The value of $result can be false or true; it could be false because:

  - $dirname doesn't exist.

  - The permissions required to delete a directory are not assigned.

The following code deletes the dummydir directory from the /home directory:

```php
<?php
if (file_exists("/home/dummydir"))
{
if(is_dir("/home/dummydir"))
 {
  $result = rmdir("/home/dummydir");
  echo " Result = ".$result;
 }
}
?>
```

In this code:

- The script searches for a file called dummydir in the /home directory using the file_exists() function.

- If a file by the specified name exists, the program checks whether it is a file or a directory.

- If it is a directory, the program attempts to remove the directory by using the rmdir() function.

- A result, true or false, is displayed depending on success or failure of using the rmdir() function.

The output is:

```
X-Powered-By: PHP/4.0.6
Content-type: text/html
 Result = 1
```

This shows that the directory named dummydir was successfully deleted. You can check that dummdir was deleted by using the ls command.

Creating and Destroying a Directory Handle

In PHP, it is possible to extract filenames from a directory using the opendir() function as follows:

```
$dirhandle = opendir($dirname);
```

In this syntax:

- $dirname is the name of the directory that needs to be accessed. If this is not the current working directory, $dirname should represent the complete path of the directory.

- $dirhandle is the variable that represents the $dirname directory; that is, it is a variable that allows you to handle the $dirname directory. The $dirhandle will be false if the directory doesn't exist or you don't have the appropriate permissions for this directory.

A directory handle can be closed using the closedir() function, which accepts only one parameter, the previously created $dirhandle. The syntax for the closedir() function is:

```
closedir($dirhandle);
```

In this syntax, $dirhandle is a directory handle that was created earlier by using the opendir() function. The following creates a handle for the /home directory:

```
<?php
if(file_exists("/home"))
{
if(is_dir("/home"))
 {
  $dh = opendir("/home") or die(" Directory Open failed !");
  echo "Directory was opened successfully";
```

```
    closedir($dh);
  }
}
?>
```

In this code:

■ If a directory /home exists, the function opendir() attempts to create a handle for the /home directory and store it in the variable $dh.

■ If the directory handle is created successfully, the program prints a success message with the next statement.

■ If the opendir() function fails, the program closes.

> **NOTE** The opendir() function will not be successful if the user does not have the appropriate permissions for the /home directory.

■ The closedir() function is used to close the directory handle.

The output of the code is:

```
X-Powered-By: PHP/4.0.6
Content-type: text/html
Directory was opened successfully
```

Reading Contents from a Directory

The readdir() function is used to read the file entries in a directory. It accepts the directory handle as an argument and returns one filename at a time. The function also returns the . and the .. entries for each directory.

```
<?php
if(file_exists("/home"))
{
if(is_dir("/home"))
  {
   $dh = opendir("/home") or die(" Directory Open failed !");
   while ($file = readdir($dh))
   {
     echo "$file\n";
 }
echo "Directory was opened successfully";
   closedir($dh);
 }
}
?>
```

In this code:

- Checks are performed to see if the directory exists.
- The opendir() function is used to create a handle for the /home directory.
- The readdir() function returns the first file entry that is stored in the $file variable.
- The $file is displayed on the screen.
- The while loop continues to execute the two previous steps until there are no more file entries left in the $dh handle.
- The directory handle is closed using the closedir() function.

The output is:

```
X-Powered-By: PHP/4.0.6
Content-type: text/html

.
..
user1
user2
user3
user4
user5
dave
Directory was opened successfully
```

NOTE The output of the preceding code may differ depending on the contents of the /home directory on your computer.

Write the PHP Code

To implement the task assigned to it, the development team at Mega Music Mart has decided to create four PHP scripts. The first script should display a combination of two forms. One form should allow the administrator to specify the news headline and the news content and submit the headline and content to the file. The second form should allow the administrator to choose one of two options, View or Delete. The View option should allow the administrator to view the contents of the file, and the Delete option should allow the administrator to delete the file.

NOTE Ensure that the necessary permissions are set for the /var/www/html directory before you execute any of the following code. To do so, logon as root and type the command chmod 777 /var/www/html.

The first PHP script that the team has created is **index.php.** It contains the following code:

```
<html>
<head>
<title>News Admin Area</title>
</head>
<body bgcolor="#FFFFFF" text="#000000">
<p> </p>
<table width="600" border="1" align="center" bordercolor="#000000"
cellspacing="0">
  <tr>
    <td width="300" height="146" bgcolor="#CCCCCC">
      <form name="form1" method="post" action="writenews.php">
        <table width="48%" border="0" align="center">
          <tr>
            <td>
              <center>
                <b>Add Today's News Headline</b>
              </center>
            </td>
          </tr>
          <tr>
            <td>
              <center>
                <input type="text" name="headline" size="35">
              </center>
            </td>
          </tr>
          <tr>
            <td>
              <center>
                <b>Main Article</b>
              </center>
            </td>
          </tr>
          <tr>
            <td>
              <center>
                <textarea name="news" cols="30" rows="7"></textarea>
              </center>
            </td>
          </tr>
          <tr>
            <td>
              <div align="center">
                <input type="submit" name="Submit" value="Submit">
              </div>
            </td>
```

```
      </tr>
    </table>
  </form>
</td>
<td width="300" height="146" bgcolor="#CCCCCC">
  <form name="form2" method="post" action="oldnews.php">
    <p align="center"> <b>Select Old News </b></p>
    <p align="center">
      <select name="select" size="1">
        <option value="0">Select Old News</option>
<?php
if (!((file_exists("news")) || (is_dir("news"))))
 {
   mkdir("news",0700);
 }
 else
 {
   $filelist = opendir('news/');
   while ($file=readdir($filelist))
    {
//      if (is_file($file))
//        {
      echo "<option value=\"".$file."\">".$file."( ".filetype($file)." )
</option>";
//        }
    }
 }
?>
      </select>
    </p>
    <p align="center">
      <input type="radio" name="radio" value="view">
      View Contents
    <p align="center">
      <input type="radio" name="radio" value="delete">
      <b>Delete !!</b><br>(no confirmation)</p>
    <p align="center">
      <input type="submit" name="Submit2" value="Submit">
    </p>
    </form>
</td>
</tr>
</table>
<p> </p>
</body>
</html>
```

After writing the PHP code for the interface that allows the administrator to enter or modify the daily news, the development team needs to write the code for a file that will accept the information entered by the administrator and then process it. The team has created a file named **writenews.php** that contains the following code:

```php
<html>
<head>
<title>New News Item</title>
</head>
<body bgcolor="#FFFFFF" text="#000000">
<?php
   if((empty($headline)) || (empty($news)))
     {
       die("Incomplete form submitted");
     }
 if (!((file_exists("news")) || (is_dir("news"))))
 {
  mkdir("news",0700);
 }
 $gd
=getdate();
 $filename= "news/news" . $gd["mday"] ."-" . $gd["mon"] ."-" .
$gd["year"]
.".txt";
 if ((file_exists("news")) || (is_dir("news")))
 {
 $file= fopen($filename,"w+");
 }
 else
 {
 echo "Only 1 news per day allowed.";
 }
$headline.="\n";
$news.="\n";
fputs($file,$headline);
fputs($file,$news);
fclose($file);
?>
<p> </p>
<p> </p>
<form name="form1" method="post" action="writenews.php">
  <table width="48%" border="0" align="center" bgcolor="#CCCCCC">
    <tr>
      <td>
        <center><b>News Headline</b></center>
      </td>
    </tr>
    <tr>
      <td>
        <center>
<?php
```

```
    echo $headline;
?>
        </center>
      </td>
    </tr>
    <tr>
      <td>
        <center><b>Main Article</b></center>
      </td>
    </tr>
    <tr>
      <td>
        <center>
          <?php
            if(!(empty($news)))
              {
                echo $news;
              }
          ?>
        </center>
      </td>
    </tr>
    <tr>
      <td>
        <div align="center">
          <A href="index.php"> Back to main page</a>
        </div>
      </td>
    </tr>
  </table>
</form>
</body>
</html>
```

NOTE The `getdate()` function in the preceding code is used to return an associative array that contains the current date information.

Then, the development team will need to write the code to enable the administrator to view or delete the existing files. To accomplish this the team has created a PHP script named **oldnews.php** that contains the following code:

```
<html>
<head>
<title>View or Delete News Item</title>
</head>
```

```
<body bgcolor="#FFFFFF" text="#000000">
<?php
 $select= "news/".$select;
 if (is_dir($select))
 {
  die("Please choose a news file not directory !");
 }
 if (!(file_exists($select)))
 {
  die("News file missing !");
 }
 if ($radio=="view")
 {
  $data=file($select);
  echo "<table width=\"400\" bgcolor=\"#cccccc\" border=\"1\"
bordercolor=\"#000000\" align=\"center\" cellspacing=\"0\">";
  echo "<tr> <td><b> File :</b>".$select."</td><td align=\"right\"><b>
Size
:</b>".filesize($select)."</td></tr>";
  echo " <tr><td colspan=\"2\"><h1>".$data[0]."</h1></td></tr>";
  echo "<tr><td colspan=\"2\">";
  for ($i=1;$i<count($data);$i++)
  {
   echo $data[$i]."<br>";
  }
  echo "</table>";
 }
 if($radio=="delete")
 {
   unlink($select) or die("File could not be deleted");
   echo "<h3> File ".$select." deleted successfully.</h3>";
 }
?>
</body>
</html>
```

Finally, the development team creates the Web page on which the news will be displayed. They have created a file named **megamart.php** to achieve this. The file contains the following code:

```
<html>
<head>
<title>Customer Section</title>
</head>
<body bgcolor="#FFFFFF" text="#000000">
<center><h1> Mega Mart News Page</h1></center>
<?php
```

```
$gd=getdate();
$filename= "news/news" . $gd["mday"] ."-" . $gd["mon"] ."-" .
$gd["year"]
.".txt";
if (!((file_exists($filename)) || is_file($filename) ||
is_readable($filename)))
 {
  die("News file ERROR !");
 }
 $data=file($filename);
 echo "<table align=\"center\">";
 echo " <tr><td><h1>".$data[0]."</h1></td></tr>";
 echo "<tr><td>";
 for ($i=1;$i<count($data);$i++)
 {
  echo $data[$i]."<br>";
 }
 echo "</table>";


?>
</body>
</html>
```

Execute the Code

To execute the code:

1. Open Netscape Navigator.
2. In the Address box, type http://localhost/index.php. Figure 9.1 displays the output of the file **index.php**. This form accepts information from the administrator, enters it into a file, and allows the contents of the file to be viewed or deleted.
3. Type the news headlines in the Add Today's News Headline text box.
4. Type the news content in the Main Article text box.
5. On the left pane, click the submit button. Figure 9.2 shows the Web page that appears after you submit the news item.
6. Click Back to return to the main page link.
7. In the form on the right pane, from the Select Old News list box, select a file.
8. Select the View Contents option and click the Submit button. A Web page that displays the contents of the newly created file appears (Figure 9.3). It also displays the location and the size of the file.

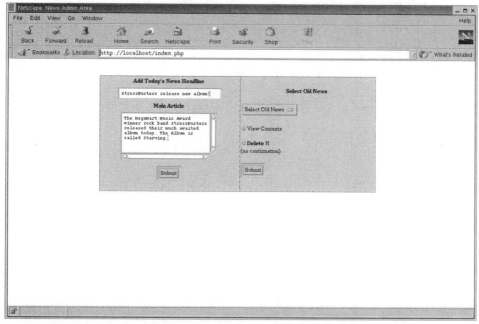

Figure 9.1   The Web page after adding the news headline and news content.

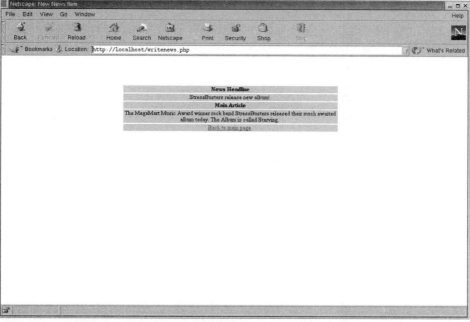

Figure 9.2   The Web page after submitting the news item.

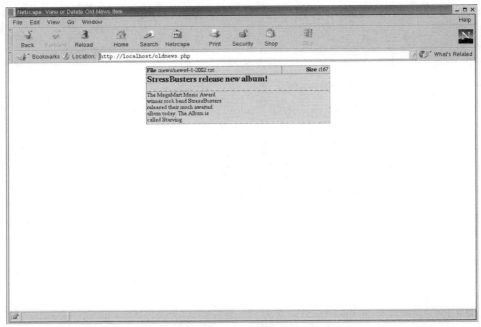

Figure 9.3 The Web page displaying the content of the news file.

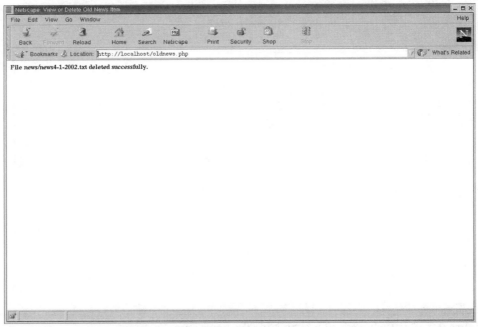

Figure 9.4 The Web page that displays the message indicating that the file has been deleted.

Figure 9.5   The news page that will be viewed by the customers.

9. Click the Back button on the browser.

10. In the form, on the right pane, from the Select Old News list box, select the news file.

11. Select the Delete option and click the Submit button on the right pane. A Web page appears that displays a message indicating that the file has been deleted (Figure 9.4).

NOTE To check the whether the file has been deleted, repeat steps 5 and 6. A Web page appears indicating that the file no longer exists.

12. In the Address box, type `http://localhost/megamart.php`. A Web page appears as shown in Figure 9.5. This is the page that will be viewed by the customers.

Summary

In this chapter, you learned to work with built-in functions that are used in relation to files and directories. First, you learned to use built-in functions to access and work with the files on a local machine. Then, you learned to open, access, and use the directories present on a local computer.

Database Concepts

OBJECTIVES:

In this lesson, you will learn to:

- ✔ Define a database
- ✔ Identify the need for using databases
- ✔ Identify database-related concepts
- ✔ Identify the databases that can be used with PHP
- ✔ Install MySQL
- ✔ Identify the features of MySQL
- ✔ Configure MySQL to work with PHP

Getting Started

In this fast-evolving world of e-commerce, the need to store and manage a large amount of data is prevalent. Consider a site that provides free email services to its users. Have you ever wondered where the information specific to each user is stored? In addition, how is this information retrieved every time the user logs on? The answer to both these questions is databases.

In previous chapters, you learned about basic PHP programming. This chapter will deal with database concepts. They are essential to understand because when you start programming with PHP and creating Web sites, you need to apply these concepts to store, manage, and retrieve information.

This chapter begins with an introduction to databases and explains why they are important. Next, the chapter discusses PHP support for databases. This chapter also deals with the concepts of installing and configuring MySQL to work with PHP.

Problem Statement

The project leader of the development team at Mega Music Mart has asked the development team to incorporate databases into the structure of its Web site. The team is to make a presentation that describes the structure of the database that will be used to store site-related information. The presentation should contain the following information:

- Number of tables that will be used in the database
- Names of the tables that will be used
- Information that will be stored in each table

The database administrator will manage the database by creating and managing user accounts for the database.

Task List

✔ **Install and configure the database server**

✔ **Gather the information that needs to be stored**

✔ **Use database normalization to identify the tables that need to be created**

Identify and Work with Databases

A *database* can be defined as a repository that stores information, and it needs to be monitored and managed on a regular basis. The advantage of using databases is that a piece of desired information can be extracted from voluminous data by using programs.

Tables

Databases are primarily composed of *tables*, which are collections of rows and columns that contain data. They are different from normal files, which store data arbitrarily, because tables store data that is preformatted. A table's columns are called *fields* and its rows are called *records*.

Fields

A field is a space that is allocated for storing values that belong to the same category. Consider a form that requires an applicant to fill in personal details; typically, it requires information such as the name, address, and telephone number of an applicant. A table stores names, addresses, and telephone numbers separately under different heads. This helps to group related data under different columns in the same table. These heads, or *fields*, can contain numeric or textual data. Every field has a name, called the *field name,* that distinguishes it from other fields. Fields can be categorized as:

Required.   It is mandatory to enter data in a required field.

Optional.   These fields can be left blank.

Records

A record is a collection of fields. For example, a record can consist of three required fields: name, age, and sex. A record is created when these three fields are filled with respective values. If a user, Alice, registers with your site, then her name, age, and sex will form one record.

TIP The task of maintaining databases is known as *database management.* Database management helps to store and retrieve useful information quickly.

Benefits of Using Databases

There are innumerable benefits of implementing databases in your site. Some of the major ones are:

- Accessing information easily
- Extracting specific information from a large amount of information
- Organizing data systematically
- Storing voluminous data in a programmer-friendly format
- Handling repetitive tasks that involve processing data
- Update information promptly

Database Management System

As you already know, a database is used to store voluminous information. This information can be the details of a shopping cart or a picture gallery or even sensitive information related to a corporate network. To handle huge databases effectively, you need to have a centralized mechanism with which to manage them. Here arises the need for using a *database management system (DBMS)*.

Relational Database Management System

In a database it is preferable to use multiple tables instead of placing all types of information in a single table. This helps a user extract or retrieve information quickly. The tables in a database can be related to each other so that the various types of information in different tables can be retrieved when required. A *relational database management system* allows you to define relationships between the tables in a database. This increases the speed and flexibility of data retrieval, and data from different tables can be combined when requested by a client.

Support Provided by PHP for Databases

PHP supports a wide range of database servers, such as:

mSQL. A fast, reliable, and lightweight database. You can obtain more information about mSQL from www.hughes.com.au.

MySQL. An extremely powerful, open source, relational database. Its main feature is its fast, robust, and stable design, which makes it a popular choice for Linux developers. You can find more information about MySQL at www.mysql.com.

PostgreSQL. Another powerful, open source, relational database that is also popular. It is comparable with almost any of the popular database servers used today. You can find more information about PostgreSQL from www. postgresql.com.

Microsoft SQL Server 2000. A powerful database developed by Microsoft. It is fast and preferred by millions of developers who work on the Windows platform. You can obtain more information about Microsoft SQL Server at www.microsoft.com/sql.

Oracle. A popular database that is being used worldwide. Popular Web sites, such as Yahoo and Amazon, use the Oracle database server. For more information about Oracle, visit www.oracle.com.

NOTE Although PHP supports a wide range of database servers, we will use MySQL for all database-related tasks in this book.

Installing and Configuring MySQL

MySQL is a powerful database server developed by MySQL AB. It is open source and can be downloaded from www.mysql.com. MySQL can be installed and configured for use with both Windows and Linux platforms. The features of MySQL are:

- MySQL is a database management system that allows you to handle databases with ease.

- MySQL is a relational database management system. As a result it allows you store data in separate tables rather than putting all data in a single table.

- It can be downloaded free of cost from its official site. By modifying the source code of MySQL, you can customize it to meet the needs of a user.

- It has built-in support for a number of applications and languages such as Python, Perl, and PHP.

- It can be installed on many operating systems, including Linux and Windows.

- It consists of a thread-based memory allocation system, which is fast.

- It supports fixed- and variable-length records.

- It has an efficient security system that allows host-based verification. Passwords are encrypted during transit to ensure maximum security.

- It supports a wide variety of character sets, such as big5, ujis, and ISO-8859-1.

- It is capable of handling very large databases.

- Support is available for almost all MySQL programs. In Linux systems, the `--help` argument can be used with the program name to display a page that contains online help.

- It supports many column types, such as `FLOAT`, `CHAR`, `TEXT`, `DATE`, `TIME`, `DATETIME`, `VARCHAR`, `YEAR`, `TIMESTAMP`, `SET`, and many more.

- It is backed by a strong and prompt open source community that rectifies any reported bugs in short notice.

- It contains B-TREE disk tables with index compression. A B-TREE is a mechanism that stores and locates files. These files are essentially records or keys in a database. A B-TREE algorithm is used to reduce the number of times a database needs to locate a desired record, thereby increasing the speed of the database.

- It consists of an optimized class library. All MySQL functions are implemented by using this class library and as a result are very fast.

- It supports TCP/IP and Unix sockets and Named Pipes for connectivity.

Installing MySQL

If you have chosen Linux as the platform for MySQL and installed Linux with the Custom-Everything option, you need not install MySQL separately because MySQL is included with Red Hat Linux. However, there are a few steps that you need to perform before you can start using MySQL:

1. Ensure that you have logged on as a root user.

2. At the command prompt, type the command `ntsysv` to see the Services screen.

3. Select the option `mysqld` as shown in Figure 10.1 and click OK.

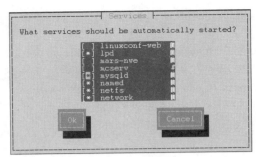

Figure 10.1   The Services screen.

4. Type the following command at the command prompt to start the MySQL daemon:

```
# /etc/rc.d/init.d/mysqld start
```

Figure 10.2 shows the result of this command.

Installing MySQL Separately

If you didn't install MySQL while installing Linux, you can install it separately. The recommended way to install MySQL for beginners is by using its Red Hat Package Manager (RPM) file. The latest RPM files can be downloaded from www.rpmfind.com, and they are also available on the Red Hat Linux 7.2 CD. The following RPM files are available for MySQL:

MySQL-versionname.i386.rpm.   Installs MySQL Server. You will require this file unless you want to use the MySQL Server that is installed on a remote computer.

MySQL-client-versionname.i386.rpm.   Installs the client-only version of MySQL. It is advisable that you always install this package along with MySQL Server.

MySQL-devel-versionname.i386.rpm.   Installs all the necessary libraries and includes files that are required to compile other client programs.

MySQL-versionname.src.rpm.   Contains the entire source code for all the preceding application packages.

```
[root@server1 /root]# /etc/rc.d/init.d/mysqld start
Starting MySQL:                                          [  OK  ]
```

Figure 10.2   Starting mysqld.

To install MySQL using the RPM file:

1. Download the latest RPM files or copy the required files from the Red Hat 7.2 CD to the /root directory.

2. Issue the following command to install MySQL Server and MySQL client:

```
# rpm -ivh MySQL-versionname.i386.rpm MySQL-client-
versionname.i386.rpm
```

After you install MySQL using the RPM files, all necessary data is transferred to the /var/lib/mysql directory. Appropriate entries are also made in the /etc/rc.d directory. This configures the system to start MySQL at boot time.

Testing MySQL

Before you begin using MySQL, it's a good idea to make sure that it was installed properly. To do this, let's start working with MySQL by using some basic commands. To begin issuing commands for MySQL, you first need to invoke the MySQL monitor at the command prompt by issuing the following command:

```
# mysql
```

After you invoke the MySQL monitor, the following message appears on the screen:

```
[root@localhost root]# mysql
Welcome to the MySQL monitor.  Commands end with ; or \g.
Your MySQL connection id is 3 to server version: 3.23.41
Type 'help;' or '\h' for help. Type '\c' to clear the buffer.
mysql>
```

This interface enables you to type commands to create and explain tables and also insert and select data. You should end all MySQL commands with a semicolon or \g. Otherwise, you will encounter an error message.

Working with MySQL

There are several commands that you can use to handle database-related tasks in MySQL. With them you can perform a series of tasks such as create a database, create tables, add records, and update and delete data. Let's begin with understanding how to use the mysqladmin command.

The mysqladmin Command

The mysqladmin command is used in MySQL for basic administration. Its syntax is:

```
#mysqladmin [options] command1 command2......commandn
```

Table 10.1 Options Used with the mysqladmin Command

COMMAND	TASK PERFORMED
create <database_name>	Creates a new database with the name specified
drop <database_name>	Deletes the specified database
Extended-status	Displays the status in a table with two columns, Variable name and Value
flush-hosts	Clears all hosts that are cached
flush-logs	Clears all server logs
flush-tables	Clears all tables
flush-threads	Clears all threads from the thread cache
ping	Checks whether the mysql daemon is functional and displays mysqld is alive if it is
Refresh	Clears all tables and then opens and closes log files
Status	Displays a short status message at the command prompt
Variables	Displays all available variables at the command prompt
Version	Displays the version information about MySQL Server
Shutdown	Shuts down MySQL Server

A database administrator can perform many tasks with the mysqladmin command at the command prompt; they are listed in Table 10.1.

Creating a Database

You can create a database by typing the create <databasename> command at the command prompt. This command is used with the mysqladmin command. You do not need the mysql prompt to create a database. Type the following command at the command prompt:

```
#mysqladmin create newdatabase
```

This creates a database named newdatabase.

An alternate way of creating a database is by using the create command, but you can use it only when the MySQL monitor is invoked. To create a database using the create command, type the following command:

```
mysql>create database if not exists latestdatabase;
```

This will create a database named latestdatabase. The output of the command is:

```
Query OK, 1 row affected (0.01 sec)
```

When you no longer need a database, you can delete or drop it, but you should only do so when you are absolutely sure about what you are doing. This is because after you drop a database, all the tables and the records within these tables are also deleted. To drop the database named latestdatabase, type the following command:

```
mysql>drop database if exists latestdatabase;
```

You can also delete a database by using the mysqladmin command. To delete an existing database using the mysqladmin command, type:

```
[root@localhost root]# mysqladmin drop newdatabase
```

NOTE It has been assumed that the database named newdatabase exists.

A confirmation message is displayed as shown:

```
[root@localhost root]# mysqladmin drop newdatabase
Dropping the database is potentially a very bad thing to do.
Any data stored in the database will be destroyed.
Do you really want to drop the 'newdatabase' database [y/N]
```

To continue deleting the database, type y. The following message appears when you permanently delete the database named newdatabase:

```
Do you really want to drop the 'newdatabase' database [y/N] y
Database "newdatabase" dropped
```

Working with Tables

To create a table in an existing database, you will first need to invoke the MySQL monitor. To do this, type mysql at the command prompt. After you invoke the MySQL monitor, you can type commands to perform various tasks on an existing database.

Accessing an Existing Database

To create a table, you first need to access the database in which you want to add a table. To access an existing database, type the following command at the MySQL monitor:

```
mysql>use userdetails
```

NOTE This command will work only if you create the database named userdetails before executing the preceding command.

This command will provide access to the database named `userdetails`. If you successfully access the database, you will see the following message stating that the database has changed; it indicates that you have accessed the database named `userdetails`:

```
Database changed
```

Understanding Field Types

Before beginning to create tables in a database, it is essential to know more about the field types that are supported by MySQL. The following is a list of the most commonly used ones:

INT.   Signifies that the type of the field is integer. This type of field can store a maximum of 4,294,967,295 unsigned numeric values.

TINYINT.   Signifies a very small integer. This type of field can store up to 255 unsigned numeric values.

SMALLINT.   Signifies a small integer value. This type of field can store up to 65,535 unsigned numeric values.

BIGINT.   Signifies a very large integer value. This type of field can store a maximum of 18,446,744,073,709,551,615 unsigned numeric values.

FLOAT.   Used to store decimal values.

DATE.   Used to store the date in yyyy-mm-dd format. The range of this field is from 1000-01-01 to 9999-12-31.

DATETIME.   Used to store the date as well as the year.

YEAR.   Used to store the year.

CHAR.   Used to store string type data.

VARCHAR.   Similar to CHAR field type and is used to store string type data.

BLOB or **TEXT.**   Is also used to store characters. The maximum number of characters that can be stored in this field is 65,535.

Creating Tables

Now you can begin creating tables in a database named `userinfo`. The syntax for creating a table is:

```
mysql> create table_name (first_field_name fieldtype,
second_field_name fieldtype, ..........n_field_name fieldtype
```

The command to create a table, `userinfo`, with four fields, `name`, `age`, `sex`, and `location` is:

```
mysql> CREATE TABLE userinfo
  (name VARCHAR(30) NOT NULL,
```

```
age INT UNSIGNED NOT NULL,
sex CHAR(1) NOT NULL,
location VARCHAR(200) NOT NULL,
email VARCHAR(40) PRIMARY KEY);
```

With this command:

- A table named `userinfo` is created.
- The table has four fields, `Name`, `Age`, `Sex`, and `Location`.
- The `name` field is of `VARCHAR` type because names are of variable length. It has been assumed that all full names should not be more than 30 characters.
- The `age` field has been declared integer because age is numerical. The `UNSIGNED` attribute specifies that the value cannot be negative.
- The `sex` field would either contain the value M or F. Therefore, it is a fixed-length character type variable, which can hold only one character.
- The `location` field will be used to store the address of an individual. Therefore, it is of variable length. A maximum of 200 characters can be used to store the address.
- The `email` field is used to store the email ID, which is unique for each customer. Therefore it has been marked as the primary key.
- The `NOT NULL` attribute signifies that value cannot be null for any record in that field.

After you execute the preceding command, the following message will be displayed:

```
Query OK, 0 rows affected (0.00 sec)
```

This indicates that the table was created successfully.

Testing That the Table Was Created Successfully

To test whether the table was successfully created, type the following command:

```
mysql> show tables;
```

This command will display the tables present in the database named `newdatabase`. The output of the command shows that a table named `userinfo` was created in `userdetails`:

```
mysql> show tables;
+----------------------+
| Tables_in_userdetails |
+----------------------+
| userinfo             |
+----------------------+
1 row in set (0.00 sec)
```

Viewing the Fields of a Table

You can also view the fields that you have added to the table `userinfo` by typing the following command:

```
mysql> explain userinfo;
```

This command helps an administrator keep track of the number of fields and their types. The output of the command is:

```
mysql> explain userinfo;
+----------+------------------+------+-----+---------+-------+
| Field    | Type             | Null | Key | Default | Extra |
+----------+------------------+------+-----+---------+-------+
| name     | varchar(30)      |      |     |         |       |
| age      | int(10) unsigned |      |     | 0       |       |
| sex      | char(1)          |      |     |         |       |
| location | varchar(200)     |      |     |         |       |
| email    | varchar(40)      |      | PRI |         |       |
+----------+------------------+------+-----+---------+-------+
5 rows in set (0.00 sec)
```

The details of the table that you have created are:

Field. The name of the field that you have specified.

Type. The type of field that you have created. The text fields are denoted by the word `text` and the integer fields are denoted by the word `int`. The storage limit of a field can be defined at the time of creation by following the field type with the maximum number of characters or numbers that it can hold. This number should be specified within parentheses when issuing the `create table` command.

Null. Signifies whether the value of a particular field can be null or not.

Key. Specifies whether the particular field is a *primary key* or not. A field is marked as a primary key when each value of this field is unique and this particular field is also a part of other tables. In MySQL, only one primary key can exist in a table, and the field marked as the primary key must be unique and have a nonnull value.

Default. Contains the default value of the field.

Extra. Contains extra information about how MySQL will resolve a query.

Inserting Data into a Table

After you create a table, the `insert` statement can be used to insert data into it. The syntax for using the `insert` statement is:

```
mysql> insert into table_name values ('value_for_first_field',
'value_for second_field', ......'value_for_nth_field'
```

To insert data in the table userinfo, type the following command:

```
mysql> insert into userinfo values ('Dave', '24', 'M', 'Arizona',
'davem@music.com');
```

This command will add a record with the values Dave, 24, Male, Arizona, and davem@music.com in the respective fields. The output of the command is:

```
Query OK, 1 row affected (0.03 sec)
```

Similarly, you can enter all these details for other users. To add the details for another user named Alice, use the insert statement:

```
mysql> insert into userinfo values ('Alice', '43', 'F', 'Dallas',
'alicec@music.com');
```

Reading Data from a Table

After entering the data into the table, you may want to view it from time to time. The select statement is used to view the contents of a table. As you begin using MySQL, you will realize that this is the most commonly used statement. The select statement can be used to selectively display records present in a table based on the criteria that you can define in the command. The syntax of the select statement is:

```
mysql>select [field_name] from [table_name]
where [some_expression] order by [field_name];
```

However, to select all the records, you can simply issue the following command:

```
mysql>select * from table_name;
```

This command will read and display all the records in the table. To display all the records of the table userinfo, type the following command:

```
mysql>select * from userinfo;
```

The output is:

```
mysql> select * from userinfo;
mysql> select * from userinfo;
+-------+-----+-----+----------+------------------+
| name  | age | sex | location | email            |
+-------+-----+-----+----------+------------------+
| Dave  |  24 | M   | Arizona  | davem@music.com  |
| Alice |  43 | F   | Dallas   | alicec@music.com |
+-------+-----+-----+----------+------------------+
2 rows in set (0.03 sec)
```

All the records present in the table are displayed on the screen. You can display specific fields from a table by typing the following command:

```
mysql>select field_name from table_name;
```

This will display only the contents of the specified field. For example, if you want to display the contents of the Name field from the table userinfo, type:

```
mysql>select name from userinfo;
```

The output is:

```
mysql> select name from userinfo;
+-------+
| name  |
+-------+
| Dave  |
| Alice |
+-------+
2 rows in set (0.00 sec)
```

Updating Data

The update command is used when you want to modify one or more columns of an existing record. Its syntax is:

```
mysql> update table_name set field_name = '[newvalue]';
```

You can update the field name in the userinfo table by using this command. Let's update the field named location by changing the location specified in each record. The command to achieve this is:

```
mysql> update userinfo set location = 'New York';
```

The output is:

```
Query OK, 2 rows affected (0.00 sec)
Rows matched: 2   Changed: 2   Warnings: 0
```

After updating the location, you can view the updated record as follows:

```
mysql> select location from userinfo;
+----------+
| location |
+----------+
| New York |
| New York |
+----------+
2 rows in set (0.00 sec)
```

You can also update specific rows by using the where clause as follows:

```
mysql> update table_name set field_name = '[newvalue]' where [some
expression];
```

> **TIP** If used properly, the update command is very useful and powerful
> because you can use mathematical functions that perform complex calculations
> and string functions on the existing records and then use the update command
> to modify the values of the records.

Deleting Contents from a Table

To delete one or more records from an existing table, use the delete command. The where clause is used with the delete command to specify a condition. You need to be careful when using the delete command because after data is deleted, it cannot be recovered.

To delete selective rows from a table, use the following syntax:

```
delete [field_name] from table_name [where where_definition]
```

To delete the entire contents of an existing table, use the following command.

```
mysql> delete from table_name;
```

Modifying the Elements of a Table

The alter command is used to modify the elements of a table. The following tasks can be performed with the alter command:

Adding a column to a table:

```
mysql> alter table table_name add newcolumn fielddefinition;
```

Changing the type of column:

```
mysql> alter table table_name change column_name newfielddefinition;
```

Indexing a column in a table:

```
mysql> alter table table_name add index column_name (column_name);
```

Adding a unique column in a table:

```
mysql> alter table table_name add unique column_name (column_name);
```

Deleting a column from a table:

```
alter table table_name drop column_name;
```

Gather the Information That Needs to be Stored

The development team and database administrator have decided what information needs to be stored in the database:

- Personal details of a customer, such as the name and the address
- The account history of the customer, including the number of purchases made to date
- The login ID and password of the customer
- Details of the bills generated by the accounts department
- Details of the items sold in each bill

To store all these details, they decided that the following fields should be present in a table in the database:

- Name of the customer
- Address of the customer
- Customer ID
- Password
- Date of birth
- Gender
- Music preference
- Billing number
- Billing address
- Billing amount
- Billing date
- Item 1
- Item 2
- Item 3
- Item 4
- Item 5

NOTE It has been assumed that a customer visiting this site will not shop for more than five items at once.

Use Database Normalization to Identify the Tables That Need to be Created

Although it is possible to store all the fields in a single table of a database, it is not advisable to do so. The contents of a database should be carefully organized, or the data will occupy more than the available space in the database and overburden the system memory. Therefore, a decision regarding what needs to be stored in which table should be made at the outset. The process of carefully organizing and distributing the information to be stored in different tables is called *database normalization*. Let's consider the fields listed in the previous section to understand why database normalization is essential.

Assume all the fields mentioned are to be included in a single table. In this case, whenever the details of a new customer are added, only the first six fields will be filled in because the customer has not yet made any purchases. As a result, all the fields for the billing information of products purchased will be wasting space.

Similarly, if that same customer visits the site again and buys three products, only the customer ID field and the billing information are filled in the respective fields, again leaving some fields blank. The fields that contain the customer's personal information are left blank because the customer did not have to provide personal information again. For all future purchases made by the customer, only the fields that contain the billing information will be filled in.

Whenever you specify a field in a table, the database server allocates some space to that field. If the fields that contain user information are left blank when an existing user buys something from the site, a lot of space is wasted. This situation can be avoided by intelligently distributing the information to be stored in a database in multiple tables.

As a solution to this problem, the development team and the database administrator of Mega Music Mart have decided that there will be three different tables to store different types of information. The first table will only contain fields that store a customer's personal details as follows:

- Customer ID
- Name
- Address
- Date of birth
- Gender
- Music preference

The second table will primarily contain the customer's account details. This table will help track the history of purchases made by a customer over a period of time and will include the following fields:

■ Bill ID

■ Customer ID

■ Amount for purchases

■ Date of purchase

The third table will contain the billing details in the following fields:

■ Bill ID

■ Item ID

■ Price

■ Quantity of the products bought

The fourth table will contain the following fields:

■ Customer ID

■ Password

It is important to store the customer ID and the password in a separate table for security reasons; all other tables are frequently accessed and are more prone to security threats. Also notice that the field Customer ID is common to all tables. The Customer ID is the primary key for the database and is used to establish a relationship with all other tables of the database.

Now the design is ready for presentation.

Summary

In this chapter, you learned about databases and why they are essential. Then, you learned about their general features. Next, you learned about the support provided by PHP for different databases. Finally, you learned to install, configure, and perform basic tasks such as creating a database and creating a table in MySQL.

Database Interactivity Using PHP

OBJECTIVES:

In this lesson, you will learn to:

- ✓ Establish a connection with MySQL Server
- ✓ Send SQL commands to MySQL
- ✓ Receive information from MySQL
- ✓ Create a database in MySQL using PHP
- ✓ Create a table in MySQL using PHP
- ✓ Insert data in a MySQL table using PHP
- ✓ Read data from a database using PHP

Getting Started

In the previous chapter, you learned about the basic concepts of MySQL. All Web-based applications or scripts operate by accepting and processing or storing the data and producing the output. Files and databases are the most widely used methods for storing data permanently. You have learned how to store and retrieve data from files; now, you will use databases to do so. Databases are back-end storage media that are used to store scripts and Web applications that are used when an amount of data needs to be stored in a systematic and organized way.

You have learned how to accept information from users by using HTML forms and how to process the information in PHP scripts. Now, you will learn how this data is stored and about the features provided by PHP to interact with a MySQL database. You will also learn how SQL statements are sent to a server and how responses are received.

Using PHP to Work with MySQL

Now let's understand how PHP interacts with a database server. We will do this with the help of a case study of Mega Music Mart.

Problem Statement

Mega Music Mart wants to create a user registration form for its customers and store their personal information. The software development team decides to make a set of HTML forms and PHP scripts to accept personal information from customers and store them in a MySQL database. The team must also create a script that allows customers to update their personal information. According to the specifications provided to the development team, the following information should be accepted from the user:

- Name
- Address
- Date of birth
- Gender
- Music preferences

After accepting this information:

- A customer ID should be assigned to the registrant using a PHP script.
- The information entered by the user should be stored in a database with the unique customer ID.
- Registrants should be able to update their personal information on the site by using the customer ID assigned to them.
- After updating, the information should be displayed on another Web page.

To accomplish this task, the development team will need to:

- Create an HTML form to allow the user to enter information.
- Write a PHP script to accept this information. This PHP script should establish a connection with MySQL Server and extract the last customer ID assigned from the `customerid` field in the `customerinfo` table.
- The value of the customer ID should be incremented by 1 so that a new user can be assigned a unique customer ID.

- A new record should be entered in the database with the incremented customer ID.

- Another HTML form should be created to accept the customer ID from the user. The customer will use the assigned customer ID to gain access to personal information.

- A PHP script should accept the customer ID and establish a connection with the database.

- This PHP script should extract all the customer's relevant information from the respective record.

- This script should also display the user's personal information on an HTML form so that the customer can update the information.

Task List

To accomplish the assigned task, the development team will need to perform the following steps:

✔ **Create the table for storing user details**

✔ **Create the HTML form that accepts user information**

✔ **Write the information accepted in the user registration form to a database**

✔ **Create the HTML form that accepts the customer ID**

✔ **Write the PHP code that processes the customer ID**

✔ **Write the PHP code that updates the record in the database**

Using PHP Built-In Functions

PHP uses a set of built-in functions to interact with a database. There are separate functions that can be used to establish a connection with a database server, create a database, and use it. More so, you can also send SQL queries, create tables, and insert, read, and update data in tables using PHP built-in functions. This section will follow a step-wise approach to discuss how database interactivity can be achieved using PHP.

Connecting to MySQL Server

To perform database-related tasks, you must first log on to the server. After logging on, you can start using MySQL Server. However, you will be able to perform only those tasks that you are authorized to perform. The permissions to perform particular tasks are assigned to users at the time their login ID is created by the database administrator. This process of logging on is known as connecting to MySQL Server.

PHP provides a built-in function that can be used to connect to a MySQL Server, the `mysql_connect ( )` function, which is used to establish a new connection with a MySQL Server. It accepts a set of optional arguments to enable a user to log on to it and returns a *connection identifier*. A connection identifier is used internally by PHP to refer to a connection. If a PHP script contains more than one mysql_connect() function and the first function successfully establishes a connection with MySQL Server, the second time the PHP compiler encounters the function it does not establish another new connection. Instead, it uses the connection identifier of the previous connection.

The syntax for using the mysql_connect() function is:

```
$linkid = mysql_connect($hostname, $username, $password);
```

In this syntax:

- $hostname specifies the host name on which the MySQL server is running. This argument also accepts valid Internet Protocol (IP) addresses. If no value is specified, the value localhost is assumed, which means that the MySQL server resides in the local machine.

- $username specifies the user name of a valid account. This name should exist in the MySQL server.

- $password specifies the password for the account. A blank password will be assumed if this argument is left blank.

- $linkid contains the connection identifier of a connection; it can be used to refer to a MySQL connection. If the attempt to connect to MySQL Server is successful, $linked contains the value true; otherwise, it contains the value false.

Now let's write the PHP code to establish a connection with MySQL:

```php
<?php
$host="";
$uname="root";
$pass="";
$connection= mysql_connect($host,$uname,$pass);
if (!$connection)
{
 die("A connection to the Server could not be established!");
}
else
{
echo "User root logged into to MySQL server ",$host," successfully.";
}
?>
```

In this code:

- The value assigned to $host is null. Therefore, the value localhost will be assumed.

- The variables $uname and $pass are declared. The value of $uname is root, and the value of $pass is blank.

- The variable $connection is declared. This variable contains the result of the mysql_connect() function.

- The `mysql_connect()` function first tries to locate a MySQL server and then tries to establish a connection by using `$uname` and `$pass`.

The output is:

```
X-Powered-By: PHP/4.0.6
Content-type: text/html
User root logged into to MySQL server   successfully
```

Creating a Database in MySQL

Before you start working with MySQL, you need to create a database. PHP provides a built-in function, `mysql_create_db()`, to create databases in MySQL. Its syntax is:

```
$result = mysql_create_db($databasename);
```

In the syntax:

- The argument `$databasename` is used to specify the name of the database to be created.
- The variable `$result` is used to store the result of the attempt to create the database. This variable contains the value true if the database is created successfully; otherwise, it contains the value false.

Let's create a database using PHP:

```php
<?php
$host="";
$uname="root";
$pass="";
$connection= mysql_connect($host,$uname,$pass);
if (!$connection)
{
 die("A connection to the server could not be established!");
}
$result=mysql_create_db("megabase");
If (!$result)
{
 die("database could not be created!");
}
echo "Database megabase was created successfully.";
?>
```

In this code:

- A connection is established with MySQL using the `mysql_connect()` function.
- A new database named megabase is created using the `mysql_create_db()` function.

- The variable $result is used to store the result of the mysql_connect() function. The value of this variable is true if the database is created successfully and false otherwise.

The output is:

```
X-Powered-By: PHP/4.0.6
Content-type: text/html
Database megabase was created successfully.
```

Selecting a Database

Now that you have learned how to create a database using PHP, you may want to start working with it to create tables and records. However, before you begin working with an existing database, you will need to select it. PHP provides the mysql_select_db() built-in function to select a database in MySQL; it provides the functionality of the use <databasename>; statement in MySQL.

The syntax of the mysql_select_db() function is:

```
$result = mysql_select_db($databasename)
```

In this syntax:

- The $database argument is used to specify the name of the existing database that you want to select. The variable $result stores the result returned by the mysql_select_db() function. The result is true if the database is selected successfully and false otherwise. There could be many reasons for a failure, such as:

  - The specified database does not exist in MySQL Server.

  - Another user who is simultaneously trying to access the database locks the specified database for use.

Let's select the database named megabase using a PHP script:

```
<?php
$host="";
$uname="root";
$pass="";
$connection= mysql_connect($host,$uname,$pass);
if (!$connection)
{
 die("A connection to the server could not be established!"); }
$result=mysql_select_db("megabase");
If (!$result)
{
 die("database could not be selected");
}
echo "Database megabase is ready for use.";
?>
```

In this code:

- A database connection is established using the `mysql_connect()` function.

- A database named `megabase` is selected using the `mysql_select_db()` function.

- A variable named `$result` is declared; it stores the result of the `mysql_select_db()` function. The value of `$result` is true if the database is selected successfully and false otherwise.

- The `die()` function is used to display an appropriate error message if the attempt to select the specified database is unsuccessful.

The output is:

```
X-Powered-By: PHP/4.0.6
Content-type: text/html
Database megabase is ready for use.
```

Sending SQL Queries to a MySQL Database

It is not possible to directly enter or retrieve data from MySQL; SQL queries are used for this. PHP provides the built-in `mysql_query()` function to send SQL queries to MySQL Server. It accepts any SQL query as an argument and sends it to MySQL Server. The result returned is accessed using various other functions that are discussed later in the chapter.

The syntax for using the `mysql_query()` function is:

```
$result = mysql_query($sqlquery);
```

In this syntax:

- The argument `$sqlquery` is any valid SQL query. The SQL query should always end with the semicolon.

- The variable `$result` stores the result of the statement. If the query is successful `$result` will contain the value true; otherwise, it will contain false. The value of `$result` can be false for the following reasons:

  - The query is not a valid SQL query.

  - The resource addressed did not exist.

  - The user name used to establish the connection with MySQL was not authorized to access this resource.

Let's send a simple SQL query to MySQL using the `mysql_query()` function:

```php
<?php
$host="";
$uname="root";
$pass="";
$database="megabase";
```

```
$connection= mysql_connect($host,$uname,$pass)
    or die("Database connection failed!");
$result=mysql_select_db($database)
    or die("Database could not be selected");
$query = "drop table if exists junktable";
$result = mysql_query($query) or die("Query failed.");
?>
```

In this code:

- A database connection is established using the mysql_connect() function.
- A database named megabase is selected using the mysql_select_db() function.
- The argument $query is used to store the SQL query.
- The mysql_query() function executes the SQL query.
- The variable $result contains the value true if the query was sent successfully; otherwise, $result contains false.

Creating a Table in MySQL

Unlike binary files, information cannot be stored directly into databases. A database stores only formatted data. As a result, the information in a database is stored in tables, which have predefined columns called fields.

Consider an example where the development team at Mega Music Mart wants to store information for a newsmaillist for its customers. To do this, the team creates a table with the following fields:

- name
- email
- customerid

NOTE This example is not a part of the main scenario. It is used to help you learn how to use PHP built-in functions to interact with MySQL.

Now let's write a program in PHP to create a table in a MySQL database:

```
<?php
$host="";
$uname="root";
$pass="";
$database="megabase";
$tablename="newsmail";
$connection= mysql_connect($host,$uname,$pass)
    or die("Database connection failed!");
```

```
$result=mysql_select_db($database)
   or die("Database could not be selected");
$query = "create table if not exists " . $tablename ." (name varchar(20)
Not Null, email varchar(40) Not Null, customerid varchar(20) Not Null
Primary Key)";
$result = mysql_query($query);
if (!$result)
{
die(" Query could not be executed.");
}
else
{
echo $tablename ." created in the megabase database.\n";
}
?>
```

In this code:

- The argument $tablename is used to specify the name of the table that will be created in the database.

- A database connection is established using the mysql_connect() function.

- The database megabase is selected using the mysql_select_db() function.

- The $query argument is used to store a SQL query.

- The SQL query is to create a table with three fields: name, email, and customerid. The name field has a variable length, which means that it can have an indefinite number of characters.

- The email field doesn't have a fixed length.

- The customerid field is numerical and is marked as the primary key for the table because it can be used to identify a customer uniquely.

- The variable $result contains the value true if the operation of the query is successful; otherwise, it contains false. The program displays an error message if $result is false.

The output of the code is:

```
X-Powered-By: PHP/4.0.6
Content-type: text/html
newsmail created in the megabase database.
```

Inserting Data in a MySQL Table

Now we have a database and a table ready for use. It's time to add some information to it, but first, we need to collect or retrieve the information. Therefore, let's create a simple HTML form to accept the data and save it as **newsmail.htm** in the /var/www/html directory:

```
<html>
<head>
<title>Newsmail Registration Form</title>
<meta http-equiv="Content-Type" content="text/html; charset=iso-8859-1">
</head>
<body bgcolor="#FFFFFF" text="#000000">
<p> </p><form name="newsmailform" method="post"
action="addnew.php">
  <table width="250" border="0" align="center" cellpadding="3">
    <tr>
      <td colspan="2" bgcolor="#dddddd">
        <div align="center"><b>Enter Newsmail Information</b></div>
      </td>
    </tr>
    <tr bgcolor="#eeeeee">
      <td width="100" bgcolor="#eeeeee">
        <div align="right">Name </div>
      </td>
      <td width="150">
        <input type="text" name="name">
      </td>
    </tr>
    <tr bgcolor="#eeeeee">
      <td width="100" bgcolor="#eeeeee">
        <div align="right">E-mail</div>
      </td>
      <td width="150">
        <input type="text" name="email">
      </td>
    </tr>
    <tr bgcolor="#eeeeee">
      <td width="100" bgcolor="#eeeeee">
        <div align="right">CustomerID</div>
      </td>
      <td width="150">
        <input type="text" name="customerid">
      </td>
    </tr>
    <tr>
      <td colspan="2" bgcolor="#dddddd">
        <div align="center">
          <input type="submit" name="Submit" value="Submit">
        </div>
      </td>
    </tr>
  </table>
</form>
</body>
</html>
```

In this code:

- A HTML form is created.
- The form accepts three types of inputs using text fields.
- The first text field accepts the user's name.
- The second text field accepts the user's email ID.
- The third text field accepts the user's customer ID.
- The input from the user is submitted to a PHP script by using the POST method.

Figure 11.1 shows how the HTML form appears in the browser.

Now that the information to be added to the database is ready, let's look at the steps involved in writing the data into the table. This data will be entered as a new row in the newsmail table. The new row will contain the three fields specified earlier. To write the information in the database, you will need to:

- Establish a connection with MySQL Server by using the mysql_connect() function
- Select a database by using the mysql_select_db() function
- Send the INSERT query to MySQL Server by using the mysql_query() function, which returns a value to signify the success or failure of the insertion

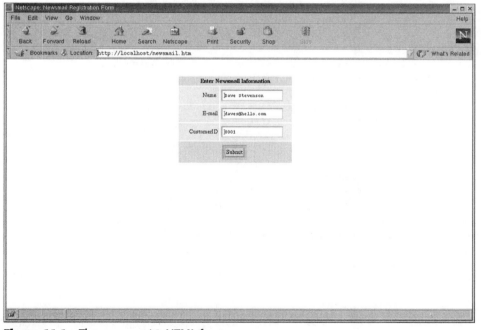

Figure 11.1 The newsmail HTML form.

Now, let's create the PHP script to see how these steps are implemented in PHP and the data is sent to MySQL Server. Let's name the PHP script **addnew.php**.

```
<html>
<head>
<title>New Record in News Mail Table</title>
<meta http-equiv="Content-Type" content="text/html; charset=iso-8859-1">
</head>
<body bgcolor="#FFFFFF" text="#000000">
<p> </p>
<?php
$host="";
$uname="root";
$pass="";
$database="megabase";
$tablename="newsmail";
$connection= mysql_connect($host,$uname,$pass)
    or die("Database connection failed! <br>");
$result=mysql_select_db($database)
    or die("Database could not be selected");
$query = "INSERT INTO newsmail VALUES('". $name ."','". $email . "','".
$customerid . "')";
$result = mysql_query($query);
if (!$result)
{
die(" Query could not be executed.<br>");
}
else
{
echo "<table border=\"0\" align=\"center\" cellspacing=\"1\"
cellpadding=\"5\" width=\"300\">";
echo "   <tr> ";
echo "     <td colspan=\"2\" bgcolor=\"#dddddd\"> ";
echo "        <center><b>".mysql_affected_rows()." record entered into the
table</b></center>";
echo "     </td>";
echo "   </tr>";
echo "   <tr bgcolor=\"#eeeeee\"> ";
echo "     <td width=\"100\" bgcolor=\"#eeeeee\"> ";
echo "        <div align=\"right\">Name</div>";
echo "     </td>";
echo "     <td width=\"200\">".$name. "</td>";
echo "   </tr>";
echo "   <tr bgcolor=\"#eeeeee\"> ";
echo "     <td width=\"100\" bgcolor=\"#eeeeee\"> ";
```

```
echo "        <div align=\"right\">E-mail</div>";
echo "      </td>";
echo "      <td width=\"200\">".$email. "</td>";
echo "   </tr>";
echo "   <tr bgcolor=\"#eeeeee\"> ";
echo "      <td width=\"100\" bgcolor=\"#eeeeee\"> ";
echo "        <div align=\"right\">CustomerID</div>";
echo "      </td>";
echo "      <td width=\"200\">".$customerid. "</td>";
echo "   </tr>";
echo "   <tr> ";
echo "      <td colspan=\"2\" bgcolor=\"#dddddd\"> </td>";
echo "   </tr>";
echo "</table>";
}
?>
</body>
</html>
```

In this code:

- A database connection is established using the mysql_connect() function.
- The database megabase is selected using the mysql_select_db() function.
- A SQL query is stored in $query.
- The SQL query is used to fill a row in the newsmail table. It contains the values for the columns in the newsmail table. The values are sent in the same order in which the columns were created.
- The variable $result contains the value true if the data is written to the table; otherwise, it is false.
- The code displays an error message if the value of $result is false. The value of $result can be false for the following reasons:
  - The table newsmail is locked for use by another user.
  - The table consists of the requested customerid.
  - The user connected to MySQL doesn't have the write permission for this table.
  - MySQL Server was too busy and rejected the request.
- If the value of $result is true, the confirmation and report are created. The report of the newly added record is shown in Figure 11.2.
- The function mysql_affected_rows() is used to return the number of rows affected by the last SQL query.

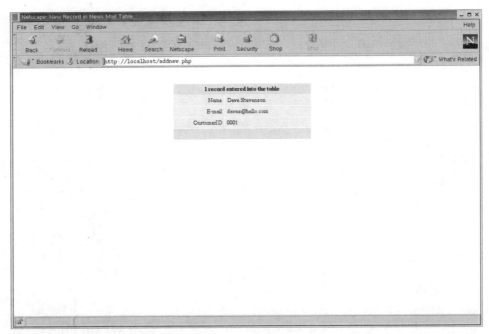

Figure 11.2 The addnew.php report.

Reading Rows from a MySQL Table

Data is extracted from a MySQL table with the following steps:

1. A connection is established with the MySQL Server.
2. A database is selected using the mysql_select_db() function.
3. A SELECT query is sent to the MySQL Server using the mysql_query() function.
4. The data is returned as a result identifier.

PHP provides many functions to extract rows from the result identifier. The following functions are used to return the result as an array:

- mysql_fetch_row() returns the result as an enumerated array.
- mysql_fetch_array() returns the result as an associative array.

The mysql_fetch_row() Function

The mysql_fetch_row() function returns one row at a time from the result. The row is returned in the form of an enumerated array so that each field of the row is an element in the array. The syntax for using the mysql_fetch_row() function is:

```
$row=mysql_fetch_row($result);
```

In this syntax:

- The variable $result is the result identifier returned by the mysql_query() function after the execution of the select query.

- The variable $row is the row in the form of an enumerated array returned by the mysql_fetch_row() function. The first element of $row is the first column or field of the returned row; the second element is the second field and so on. The last element of this enumerated array is the last field of the returned row.

- The mysql_fetch_row() function returns a single row at a time; if the select statement returns 50 rows, the mysql_fetch_row() function will be called 50 times to process all the returned data.

Let's create a PHP script to read the data from the newsmail table in the megabase database by using the mysql_fetch_row() function and let's name this file **frow.php**:

```
<html>
<head>
<title>Newsmail Table Browser</title>
<meta http-equiv="Content-Type" content="text/html; charset=iso-8859-1">
</head>
<body bgcolor="#FFFFFF" text="#000000">
<h2 align="center">The Newsmail Table Browser</h2>
<?php
$host="";
$uname="root";
$pass="";
$database="megabase";
$tablename="newsmail";
$connection= mysql_connect($host,$uname,$pass)
    or die("<br>Database connection failed! <br>");
$result=mysql_select_db($database)
    or die("<br>Database could not be selected<br>");
$query = "SELECT * from newsmail";
$result = mysql_query($query);
echo "<table width=\"500\" border=\"0\" align=\"center\"
cellpadding=\"5\" cellspacing=\"3\">
";
echo " <tr bgcolor=\"#DDDDDD\">
";
echo "   <td width=\"150\"> <center><b>Name       </b></center></td>\n";
echo "   <td width=\"150\"> <center><b>E-mail      </b></center></td>\n";
echo "   <td width=\"100\"> <center><b>CustomerID</b></center></td>\n";
echo "   </tr>\n";
while ($row=mysql_fetch_row($result))
{
echo "   <tr bgcolor=\"#EEEEEE\">\n";
echo "      <td>$row[0]</td>\n";
echo "      <td>$row[1]</td>\n";
echo "      <td>$row[2]</td>\n";
echo "   </tr>\n";
```

```
}
echo "</table>\n";
?>
</body>
</html>
```

In this code:

- A database connection is established using the `mysql_connect()` function.

- The database named `megabase` is selected using the `mysql_select_db()` function.

- A SQL query is stored in `$query`.

- The SQL query is used to extract all records from the newsmail table in the megabase database.

- The variable `$result` contains the true result identifier if the data was successfully extracted from the table; otherwise it contains false. The program displays an error message and exits if `$result` is false. The failure could be for the following reasons:

  - The table did not exist.

  - The table `newsmail` was locked by another user.

  - The user who established a connection to MySQL doesn't have the read permission for this table.

  - MySQL Server was busy and rejected the request.

- The variable `$rows` is declared.

- The `mysql_effect_rows()` function is called. The first record in `$result` is extracted, converted to an array, and stored in `$rows`.

- The `$row` is now a single-dimensional array of three elements, and the first element in `$row` is now the first column of the first record in the `newsmail` table.

- Data in `$row` is displayed on the Web page in a table.

- The `mysql_effect_rows()` function is called repeatedly until all the rows returned by the MySQL query are displayed.

- The function `mysql_affected_rows()` is used to return the number of rows affected by the last SQL query.

The output of the PHP code is shown in Figure 11.3.

The mysql_fetch_array() Function

The `mysql_fetch_array()` function is quite similar to the `mysql_fetch_row()` function, which returns a single row at a time from the result identifier. However, unlike the `mysql_fetch_row()` function, which returns the row in the form of an enumerated array, `mysql_fetch_array()` returns the row in the form of an associative array. As a result each field of the row is an element in the returned array. The label of each element in this associative array is the name of the field in the table.

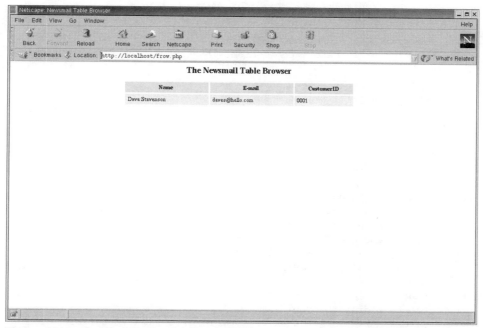

Figure 11.3 The output of code using the `mysql_fetch_row()` function.

The syntax for using the `mysql_fetch array()` function is:

```
$row=mysql_fetch_array($result);
```

In this syntax:

- The argument `$result` is the result identifier returned by the `mysql_query()` function after the SELECT query is executed.

- The variable `$row` is the row in the form of an associative array returned by the `mysql_fetch_array()` function.

- The value of the first element of `$row` is the same as the value of the first field of the returned record, and the label of the first element is the name of the first field. Similarly, the value of all the other elements is the same as the corresponding fields in the row, and the labels of the second and third elements are same as the names of the second and third fields.

The main advantage of using the `mysql_fetch_array()` function is that the programmer doesn't have to remember the order of columns in the table.

Let's create PHP code to read the data from the newsmail table in the database megabase by using the `mysql_fetch_array()` function, and let's name the file that contains the code **farray.php**:

```html
<html>
<head>
<title>Newsmail Table Browser</title>
<meta http-equiv="Content-Type" content="text/html; charset=iso-8859-1">
</head>
<body bgcolor="#FFFFFF" text="#000000">
<h2 align="center">The Newsmail Table Browser</h2>
<?php
$host="";
$uname="root";
$pass="";
$database="megabase";
$tablename="newsmail";
$connection= mysql_connect($host,$uname,$pass)
    or die("Database connection failed! <br>");
$result=mysql_select_db($database)
    or die("Database could not be selected");
$query = "SELECT * from " . $tablename;
$result = mysql_query($query);
echo "<table width=\"500\" border=\"0\" align=\"center\"
cellpadding=\"5\" cellspacing=\"3\">";
echo " <tr bgcolor=\"#DDDDDD\"> ";
echo "   <td width=\"150\"> <center><b>Name       </b></center></td>\n";
echo "   <td width=\"150\"> <center><b>E-mail      </b></center></td>\n";
echo "   <td width=\"100\"> <center><b>CustomerID</b></center></td>\n";
echo "   </tr>\n";
while ($row=mysql_fetch_array($result))
{
echo "   <tr bgcolor=\"#EEEEEE\">\n";
echo "      <td>".$row["name"]."</td>\n";
echo "      <td>".$row["email"]."</td>\n";
echo "      <td>".$row["customerid"]."</td>\n";
echo "   </tr>\n";
}
echo "</table>\n";
?>
</body>
</html>
```

In this code:

- A database connection is established using the `mysql_connect()` function.

- The database named `megabase` is selected using the `mysql_select_db()` function.

- A SQL query is stored in `$query`.

- The SQL query is used to extract all the records from the `newsmail` table in the `megabase` database.

- The variable `$result` contains the result identifier and checks that the data was successfully extracted from the table. The program displays an error message and exits if the value of `$result` is false. The failure could be for the following reasons:

- The table does not exist.
- The table `newsmail` was locked by another user.
- The user who established a connection with MySQL doesn't have the read permission for this table.
- MySQL server was too busy and therefore rejected the request.

- The variable $row is declared.
- The `mysql_fetch_array()` function is called. The first record in $result is extracted and converted to an associative array and stored in $row.
- The $row is now a single-dimensional array of three elements, and the value of the first element in $row is now the value of the first column of the first record in the `newsmail` table. In addition, the label name of the first element of $row is name, which is the name of the first field of the `newsmail` table.
- Data in $row is displayed on the Web page in a table.
- The `mysql_fetch_array()` function is called repeatedly until all the rows returned by the MySQL query are displayed.
- The `mysql_affected_rows()` function is used to return the number of rows affected by the last SQL query.

The output of this PHP code is shown in Figure 11.4.

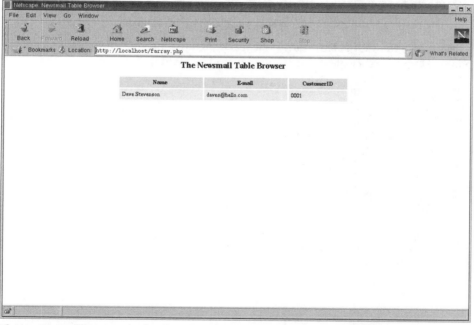

Figure 11.4 The output of code using the `mysql_fetch_array` function.

Updating Data in a Table

Updating data in a MySQL table is quite simple; it is done using the `update` statement, following these steps:

1. An HTML form is displayed to identify the row whose data needs to be updated. This form should accept any field in the database, which is unique in all records, such as the email column.

2. This field is submitted to another PHP script.

3. The second script establishes a connection with MySQL Server.

4. A database is selected using the `mysql_select_db()` function.

5. A `select` query is sent to MySQL Server using the `mysql_query()` function. The `select` query carries a `where` clause so that only a single row is returned in the result identifier.

6. The data is returned as a result identifier.

7. The second script now displays an HTML form.

8. The values of each field in the present row are filled in with the default values in various HTML form controls. This HTML form containing the present values is shown on the Web browser.

9. The user changes the values in this HTML form as required and submits the information to another PHP script.

10. The third PHP script establishes a new connection to the MySQL server and updates the rows by sending the `update` SQL query using the `mysql_query()` function.

11. The result identifier is true on success and false on failure.

Let's create the first HTML form that reads the customer ID and submits it to the update HTML form script, and let's name it **reademail.htm**:

```
<html>
<head>
<title>Update Record</title>
<meta http-equiv="Content-Type" content="text/html; charset=iso-8859-1">
</head>
<body bgcolor="#FFFFFF" text="#000000">
<p> </p>
<form name="newsmailform" method="post" action="displayform.php">
  <table width="250" border="0" align="center" cellpadding="3">
    <tr>
      <td colspan="2" bgcolor="#dddddd" height="23">
        <center><b>Enter the Customer ID</b></center>
      </td>
    </tr>
```

```
<tr bgcolor="#eeeeee">
  <td width="100" bgcolor="#eeeeee">
    <center>Customer ID</center>
  </td>
  <td width="150">
    <input type="text" name="customerid">
  </td>
</tr>
<tr>
  <td colspan="2" bgcolor="#dddddd">
    <center>
      <input type="submit" name="Submit" value="Submit">
    </center>
  </td>
</tr>
</table>
</form>
</body>
</html>
```

The HTML form is shown in Figure 11.5.

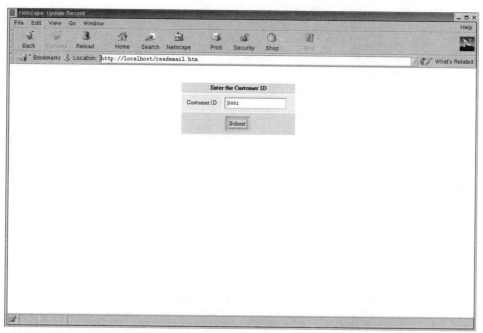

Figure 11.5 An HTML form that reads and submits customer IDs.

Now, let's create a PHP script that reads the data from a MySQL database and feeds the values in HTML form controls, and let's name this file **displayform.php**:

```
<html>
<head>
<title>Newsmail Updation Form</title>
<meta http-equiv="Content-Type" content="text/html; charset=iso-8859-1">
</head>
<body bgcolor="#FFFFFF" text="#000000">
<p> </p><form name="newsmailform" method="post"
action="update.php">
  <table width="250" border="0" align="center" cellpadding="3">
    <tr>
      <td colspan="2" bgcolor="#dddddd">
        <div align="center"><b>Update Personal Infomration</b></div>
      </td>
    </tr>
<?php
$host="";
$uname="root";
$pass="";
$database="megabase";
$tablename="newsmail";
$connection= mysql_connect($host,$uname,$pass)
   or die("Database connection failed! <br>");
$result=mysql_select_db($database)
   or die("Database could not be selected");
$query = "SELECT * from newsmail where customerid='" .$customerid ."'";
$result = mysql_query($query);
if($row=mysql_fetch_array($result))
{
echo "<tr bgcolor=\"#eeeeee\"> ";
echo " <td width=\"100\" bgcolor=\"#eeeeee\"> ";
echo " <div align=\"right\">Name </div>";
echo " </td>";
echo " <td width=\"150\"> ";
echo " <input type=\"text\" name=\"name\" value=\"".$row["name"]."\" >";
echo " </td>";
echo " </tr>";
echo " <tr bgcolor=\"#eeeeee\"> ";
echo " <td width=\"100\" bgcolor=\"#eeeeee\"> ";
echo " <div align=\"right\">E-mail</div>";
echo " </td>";
echo " <td width=\"150\"> ";
echo " <input type=\"text\" name=\"email\" value=\"".$row["email"]."\"
>";
echo " </td>";
echo " </tr>";
echo " <tr bgcolor=\"#eeeeee\"> ";
echo " <td width=\"100\" bgcolor=\"#eeeeee\"> ";
```

```
echo "  <div align=\"right\">CustomerID</div>";
echo "  </td>";
echo "  <td width=\"150\"> ";
echo "<input type=\"text\" name=\"customerid\"
value=\"".$row["customerid"]."\" >";
echo "        </td>";
echo "      </tr>";
echo "      <tr> ";
echo "        <td colspan=\"2\" bgcolor=\"#dddddd\"> ";
echo "          <div align=\"center\"> ";
echo "            <input type=\"submit\" name=\"Submit\"
value=\"Submit\">";
echo "          </div>";
echo "        </td>";
echo "</tr>";
}
?>
  </table>
</form>
</body>
</html>
```

Figure 11.6 shows the form that appears when you submit the customer ID. It allows you to update your personal information.

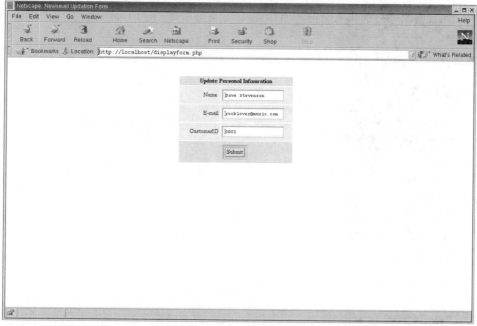

Figure 11.6   The form that appears when you submit your customer ID.

Now, the third PHP script that accepts the new input from the second script and updates the record in the MySQL database needs to be created. Let's name this file **update.php**:

```
<html>
<head>
<title>New Record In News Mail Table</title>
<meta http-equiv="Content-Type" content="text/html; charset=iso-8859-1">
</head>
<body bgcolor="#FFFFFF" text="#000000">
<p> </p>
<?php
$host="";
$uname="root";
$pass="";
$database="megabase";
$tablename="newsmail";
$connection= mysql_connect($host,$uname,$pass)
    or die("Database connection failed! <br>");
$result=mysql_select_db($database)
    or die("Database could not be selected");
$query = "UPDATE newsmail SET name=\"". $name ."\" ,
email=\"".$email."\" where customerid=\"".$customerid."\"";
$result = mysql_query($query);
if (!$result)
{
die(" Query could not be executed.<br>");
}
else
{
echo "<table border=\"0\" align=\"center\" cellspacing=\"1\"
cellpadding=\"5\" width=\"300\">";
echo "   <tr> ";
echo "     <td colspan=\"2\" bgcolor=\"#dddddd\"> ";
echo "        <center><b>".mysql_affected_rows()." record updated
successfully</b></center>";
echo "     </td>";
echo "   </tr>";
echo "   <tr bgcolor=\"#eeeeee\"> ";
echo "     <td width=\"100\" bgcolor=\"#eeeeee\"> ";
echo "        <div align=\"right\">Name</div>";
echo "     </td>";
echo "     <td width=\"200\">".$name. "</td>";
echo "   </tr>";
echo "   <tr bgcolor=\"#eeeeee\"> ";
echo "     <td width=\"100\" bgcolor=\"#eeeeee\"> ";
echo "        <div align=\"right\">E-mail</div>";
```

```
echo "    </td>";
echo "    <td width=\"200\">".$email. "</td>";
echo "  </tr>";
echo "  <tr bgcolor=\"#eeeeee\"> ";
echo "    <td width=\"100\" bgcolor=\"#eeeeee\"> ";
echo "      <div align=\"right\">CustomerID</div>";
echo "    </td>";
echo "    <td width=\"200\">".$customerid. "</td>";
echo "  </tr>";
echo "  <tr> ";
echo "    <td colspan=\"2\" bgcolor=\"#dddddd\"> </td>";
echo "  </tr>";
echo "</table>";
}
?>
</body>
</html>
```

The output of the PHP script is shown in Figure 11.7.

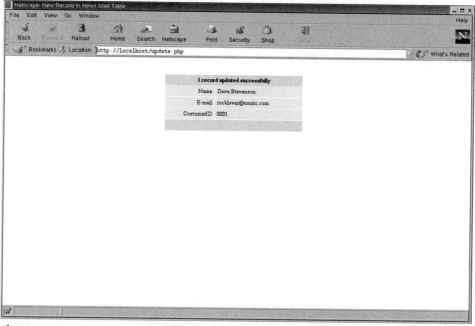

Figure 11.7   Output of the PHP script that shows the updated record.

Create the Table for Storing User Details

The development team decides to create a table named `customerinfo` that will store all user-specific information. The following steps create the table:

1. Select the database by using the following command:

```
mysql> use megabase;
```

2. To create the table, type the following command at the `mysql` prompt:

```
mysql> CREATE TABLE customerinfo (customerid VARCHAR(20) NOT NULL, name
VARCHAR(50) NOT NULL, address VARCHAR(200) NOT NULL, dob DATE NOT NULL,
gender CHAR(1) NOT NULL, pop CHAR(1) NOT NULL, rock CHAR(1) NOT NULL,
jazz CHAR(1) NOT NULL, metal CHAR(1) NOT NULL,
instrumental CHAR(1) NOT NULL,
PRIMARY KEY (customerid));
```

Create the HTML Form That Accepts User Information

The development team decides to use the user registration form created earlier to accept the input from the user. A file named **register.htm** is created that contains the HTML code for the form that accepts user information. The HTML code is:

```
<html>
<head>
<title>User Registration Form</title>
</head>
<body>
<h2 align="center">User Registration Form</h2>
<form name="form1" method="post" action="output.php"
enctype="multipart/form-data">
  <table width="53%" border="0" align="center" cellpadding="5"
cellspacing="0" bgcolor="#CCCCCC">
    <tr>
      <td width="49%">Name </td>
      <td colspan="2">
        <div align="left">
          <input type="text" name="name" size="25" maxlength="25">
        </div>
      </td>
    </tr>
```

```
    <tr>
      <td width="49%" bgcolor="#FFFFFF"> </td>
      <td height="2" colspan="2" bgcolor="#FFFFFF"> </td>
    </tr>
    <tr>
      <td width="49%" height="57">Address</td>
      <td height="57" colspan="2">
        <textarea name="address" cols="25" rows="4"></textarea>
      </td>
    </tr>
    <tr>
      <td width="49%" bgcolor="#FFFFFF"> </td>
      <td height="2" colspan="2" bgcolor="#FFFFFF"> </td>
    </tr>
    <tr>
      <td width="49%">Date of Birth</td>
      <td height="2" colspan="2">
        <select name=birth_month>
          <option selected
  value=1>January
          <option value=2>February
          <option
value=3>March
          <option value=4>April
          <option value=5>May
          <option value=6>June
          <option value=7>July
          <option value=8>August
          <option value=9>September
          <option value=10>October
          <option value=11>November
          <option value=12>December</option>
        </select>
        <select
          name=birth_day>
          <option selected value=1>01
          <option
value=2>02
          <option value=3>03
          <option value=4>04
          <option
 value=5>05
          <option value=6>06
          <option value=7>07
          <option value=8>08
          <option value=9>09
          <option value=10>10
```

```
            <option value=11>11
            <option value=12>12
            <option value=13>13
            <option value=14>14
            <option value=15>15
            <option value=16>16
            <option value=17>17
            <option value=18>18
            <option value=19>19
            <option value=20>20
            <option value=21>21
            <option value=22>22
            <option
value=23>23
            <option value=24>24
            <option value=25>25
            <option value=26>26
            <option value=27>27
            <option value=28>28
            <option
value=29>29
            <option value=30>30
            <option value=31>31</option>
          </select>
          <input maxlength=4 name=birth_year size=4>
          </td>
      </tr>
      <tr bgcolor="#FFFFFF">
        <td width="49%" height="2"> </td>
        <td height="2" width="17%"> </td>
        <td height="2" width="34%"> </td>
      </tr>
      <tr>
        <td width="49%">Gender</td>
        <td height="2" width="17%">
          <input type="radio" name="gender" value="M">
          Male </td>
        <td height="2" width="34%">
          <input type="radio" name="gender" value="F">
          Female</td>
      </tr>
      <tr>
        <td width="49%" bgcolor="#FFFFFF" height="5"> </td>
        <td height="5" colspan="2" bgcolor="#FFFFFF"> </td>
      </tr>
      <tr>
        <td width="49%">Music Preferences</td>
```

```
            <td height="2" colspan="2">
              <table width="100%" border="0">
                <tr>
                  <td>
                    <input type="checkbox" name="pop" value="1">
                    Pop </td>
                  <td>
                    <input type="checkbox" name="rock" value="1">
                    Rock </td>
                </tr>
                <tr>
                  <td>
                    <input type="checkbox" name="jazz" value="1">
                    Jazz </td>
                  <td>
                    <input type="checkbox" name="metal" value="1">
                    Metal </td>
                </tr>
                <tr>
                  <td>
                    <input type="checkbox" name="instrumental" value="1">
                    Instrumental</td>
                  <td> </td>
                </tr>
              </table>
            </td>
          </tr>
          <tr>
            <td width="49%" height="2" bgcolor="#FFFFFF"> </td>
            <td colspan="2" height="2" bgcolor="#FFFFFF"> </td>
          </tr>
          <tr>
            <td colspan="3">
              <div align="center">
                <input type="submit" name="Submit" value="Submit">
              </div>
            </td>
          </tr>
        </table>
    </form>
  </body>
</html>
```

The resulting HTML form after the user Dobin has entered her personal details is shown in Figure 11.8.

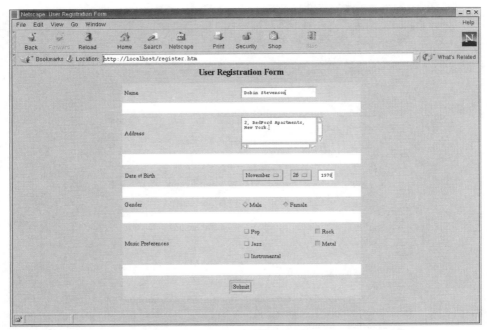

Figure 11.8   The user registration form after filling in the necessary details.

Write the Information Accepted in the User Registration Form to a Database

The development team will now write the PHP code that will be used for writing the information entered in the form by a user into the `customerinfo` table and to display a report that indicates success or failure. A file named **output.php** is used to create the PHP code.

```
<html>
<head>
<title>New Record Added</title>
<meta http-equiv="Content-Type" content="text/html; charset=iso-8859-1">
</head>
<body bgcolor="#FFFFFF" text="#000000">
<p> </p>
<?php
//--begin--convert birthdate---
  if (($birth_year < 2000) && ($birth_year > 1900))
    {$birthdate=$birth_year."-";}
```

```php
         else { echo  "Invalid birthyear"; exit;}
   if (($birth_month <  13) && ($birth_month >  0))
     {$birthdate.= $birth_month."-";}
       else { echo  "Invalid birth month"; exit;}
   if (($birth_day   < 32) && ($birth_month >  0))
     {$birthdate.= $birth_day;}
       else { echo  "Invalid birth day";exit;}
//--end--convert birthdate---
$host="";
$uname="root";
$pass="";
$database="megabase";
$tablename="customerinfo";
$connection= mysql_connect($host,$uname,$pass)
    or die("Database connection failed! <br>");@@@AU: Okay?@@@@@@AU: Yes.
Thank You.@@@
$result=mysql_select_db($database)
    or die("Database could not be selected");
$query = "SELECT max(customerid) as customerid from customerinfo";
$result = mysql_query($query);
if(!($row=mysql_fetch_array($result)))
{
 die("No existing customerid found!");
}
$customerid = $row["customerid"] + 1;
$query = "INSERT INTO customerinfo VALUES('".$customerid."','". $name.
"','". $address . "','" . $birthdate . "','".$gender."','";
if(!empty($pop)
)
{
 $query .= $pop . "','";
}
else
{
 $query .= "0','";
}
if(!empty($rock))
{
 $query .= $rock . "','";
}
else
{
 $query .= "0','";
}
if(!empty($jazz)
)
{
 $query .= $jazz . "','";
}
else
```

```php
{
 $query .= "0','";
}
if(!empty($metal))
{
 $query .= $metal . "','";
}
else
{
 $query .= "0','";
}
if(!empty($instrumental)
)
{
 $query .= $instrumental . "')";
}
else
{
 $query .= "0')";
}
//echo $query;
$result = mysql_query($query);
if (!$result)
{
 die(" Query could not be executed.<br>");
}
?>
<center>
    <h3> New Record Added</h3>
</center>
<table width="75%" border="1" bgcolor="#abcdef" cellspacing="1"
cellpadding="5">
  <tr>
    <td><h3> CustomerID</h3> </td>
    <td>
      <?php echo $customerid; ?>
    </td>
  </tr>
  <tr>
    <td>Full Name </td>
    <td>
      <?php echo $name; ?>
    </td>
  </tr>
 <tr>
    <td>Address </td>
    <td>
      <?php echo $address; ?>
```

```
          </td>
       </tr>
       <tr>
         <td>Date of Birth</td>
         <td>
           <?php echo $birthdate; ?>
         </td>
       </tr>
       <tr>
         <td>You like
</td>
         <td>
<?php
if (!(empty($pop)
))
         {
           if($pop==1)           { echo " Pop ";      }
         }
if (!(empty($jazz)))
           {
             if($jazz==1)        { echo " Jazz ";     }
           }
if (!(empty($rock)
))
           {
             if($rock==1)        { echo " Rock ";     }
           }
if (!(empty($instrumental)
))
           {
           if($instrumental==1){ echo " Instrumental ";}
           }
if (!(empty($metal)
))
           {
             if($metal==1)       { echo " Metal ";    }
           }
?>
</td>
   </tr>
</table>
<center> <A href="login.htm"> Click here</a> to update your
information.</center>
</body>
</html>
```

The output of this code is shown in Figure 11.9.

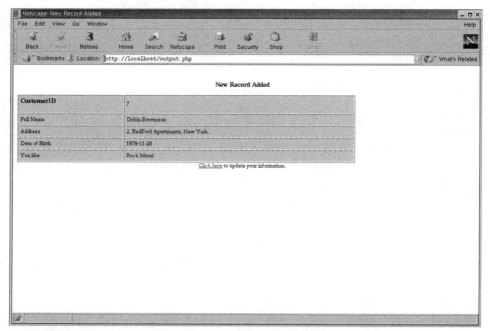

Figure 11.9 The output of the PHP code in the browser.

Create the HTML Form That Accepts the Customer ID

Now, the development team needs to create a login page in HTML that will accept only the user's customer ID. A file named **login.htm** contains the code for the HTML form that accepts the customer ID.

```
<html>
<head>
<title>Enter the CustomerID</title>
<meta http-equiv="Content-Type" content="text/html; charset=iso-8859-1">
</head>
<body bgcolor="#FFFFFF" text="#000000">
<p> </p>
<form name="newsmailform" method="post"
action="display_update_form.php">
  <table width="250" border="0" align="center" cellpadding="3">
    <tr>
      <td colspan="2" bgcolor="#dddddd" height="23">
```

```
        <center><b>Enter the CustomerID</b></center>
      </td>
    </tr>
    <tr bgcolor="#eeeeee">
      <td width="100" bgcolor="#eeeeee">
        <center>CustomerID</center>
      </td>
      <td width="150">
        <input type="text" name="customerid">
      </td>
    </tr>
    <tr>
      <td colspan="2" bgcolor="#dddddd">
        <center>
          <input type="submit" name="Submit" value="Submit">
        </center>
      </td>
    </tr>
  </table>
</form>
</body>
</html>
```

The HTML form that accepts the customer ID from a user is shown in Figure 11.10.

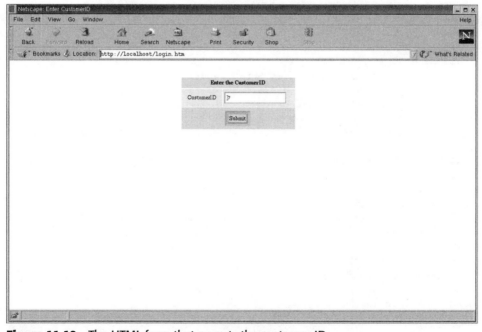

Figure 11.10 The HTML form that accepts the customer ID.

Write the PHP Code That Processes the Customer ID

Next, the development team writes the PHP code that accepts the customer ID from the login page and checks for the existence of a record for the specified customer ID. If this record does not exist, the program exits. Otherwise, the code displays all the fields of the record in an HTML form. Let's name the file that contains the PHP code **display_update_form.php**.

```
<html>
<head>
<title>Update Personal Information</title>
<meta http-equiv="Content-Type" content="text/html; charset=iso-8859-1">
</head>
<body bgcolor="#FFFFFF" text="#000000">
<p> </p><form name="newsmailform" method="post"
action="update_customerinfo.php">
  <table width="250" border="0" align="center" cellpadding="3">
    <tr>
      <td colspan="2" bgcolor="#dddddd">
        <div align="center"><b>Change Information Here</b></div>
      </td>
    </tr>
<?php
$host="";
$uname="root";
$pass="";
$database="megabase";
$tablename="customerinfo";
$connection= mysql_connect($host,$uname,$pass)
   or die("Database connection failed! <br>");
$result=mysql_select_db($database)
   or die("Database could not be selected");
$query = "SELECT * from customerinfo where customerid='" .$customerid
."'";
$result = mysql_query($query);
if($row=mysql_fetch_array($result))
{
echo " <tr bgcolor=\"#eeeeee\"> ";
echo " <td width=\"100\" bgcolor=\"#eeeeee\"> ";
echo " <div align=\"right\">CustomerID</div>";
echo " </td>\n";
echo " <td width=\"150\"> ";
echo $row["customerid"];
echo "      </td>\n";
echo "    </tr>\n";
```

```
echo "<tr bgcolor=\"#eeeeee\"> \n";
echo " <td width=\"100\" bgcolor=\"#eeeeee\"> ";
echo " <div align=\"right\">Name </div>";
echo " </td>\n";
echo " <td width=\"150\"> ";
echo  $row["name"];
echo " </td>\n";
echo " </tr>\n";
echo " <tr bgcolor=\"#eeeeee\"> ";
echo " <td width=\"100\" bgcolor=\"#eeeeee\"> ";
echo " <div align=\"right\">Address</div>";
echo " </td>\n";
echo " <td width=\"150\"> ";
echo " <input type=\"text\" name=\"address\"
value=\"".$row["address"]."\"
>";
echo " </td>\n";
echo " </tr>\n";
echo "<tr bgcolor=\"#eeeeee\"> \n";
echo " <td width=\"100\" bgcolor=\"#eeeeee\"> ";
echo " <div align=\"right\">Date Of Birth </div>";
echo " </td>\n";
echo " <td width=\"150\"> ";
echo  $row["dob"];
echo " </td>\n";
echo " </tr>\n";
echo " <tr bgcolor=\"#eeeeee\"> ";
echo " <td width=\"100\" bgcolor=\"#eeeeee\"> ";
echo " <div align=\"right\">Music Preferences</div>";
echo " </td>";
echo " <td width=\"150\">";
echo " <input type=\"checkbox\" name=\"pop\"";
if($row["pop"]){echo "checked";}
  echo ">Pop<br>\n";
echo " <input type=\"checkbox\" name=\"rock\"";
 if($row["rock"]){echo "checked";}
  echo ">Rock<br>\n";
echo " <input type=\"checkbox\" name=\"jazz\"";
 if($row["jazz"]){echo "checked";}
  echo ">Jazz<br>\n";
echo " <input type=\"checkbox\" name=\"metal\"";
 if($row["metal"]){echo "checked";}
  echo ">Metal<br>\n";
echo " <input type=\"checkbox\" name=\"instrumental\"";
 if($row["instrumental"]){echo "checked";}
  echo ">Instrumental<br>\n";
echo "       </td>";
echo "     </tr>";
```

```
echo "     <tr> ";
echo "        <td colspan=\"2\" bgcolor=\"#dddddd\">\n ";
echo "          <div align=\"center\"> \n";
echo "            <input type=\"hidden\" name=\"customerid\"
value=\"".$customerid."\">\n";
echo "            <input type=\"submit\" name=\"Submit\"
value=\"Submit\">\n";
echo "          </div>\n";
echo "        </td>";
echo "</tr>\n";
}
?>
  </table>
</form>
</body>
</html>
```

Figure 11.11 shows the form on which the user can update personal information.

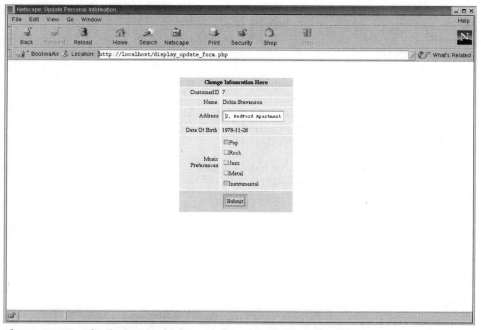

Figure 11.11   The form on which to update personal information.

Write the PHP Code That Updates the Record in the Database

This program accepts the updated information from the update form and corrects the record in the database accordingly. Let's name the file that contains the code **update_customerinfo.php**.

```
<html>
<head>
<title>Updated Record Successfully</title>
<meta http-equiv="Content-Type" content="text/html; charset=iso-8859-1">
</head>
<body bgcolor="#FFFFFF" text="#000000">
<p> </p>
<?php
$host="";
$uname="root";
$pass="";
$database="megabase";
$tablename="newsmail";
$connection= mysql_connect($host,$uname,$pass)
    or die("Database connection failed! <br>");
$result=mysql_select_db($database)
    or die("Database could not be selected");
$query = "UPDATE customerinfo SET address=\"". $address ."\" ,
pop=\"".$pop."\" , rock=\"".$rock."\", jazz=\"".$jazz."\",
metal=\"".$metal."\", instrumental=\"".$instrumental."\"  where
customerid=\"".$customerid."\"";
$result = mysql_query($query);
if (!$result)
{
die(" Query could not be executed.<br>");
}
else
{
echo "<table border=\"0\" align=\"center\" cellspacing=\"1\"
cellpadding=\"5\" width=\"300\">";
echo "  <tr> ";
echo "    <td colspan=\"2\" bgcolor=\"#dddddd\"> ";
echo "      <center><b>".mysql_affected_rows()." record updated
successfully!</b></center>";
echo "    </td>";
echo "  </tr>";
echo "</table>";
}
?>
</body>
</html>
```

Figure 11.12   The output in the browser after the user information is updated.

Figure 11.12 shows the Web page that appears after a user's information is updated.

Summary

In this chapter, you learned to work with MySQL using PHP programming. Then you learned how to create and use a database using PHP programming. Next, you learned to create a table and insert data into the table. Finally, you learned to update the data entered in a table.

Authentication

Getting Started

A Web site is a repository for large amounts of information. However, not all the information on a Web site is accessible to all users because in addition to the regular information, a Web site may contain sensitive data. This data has to be accessible to some users and screened from others. A simple example is email. Email would never have been successful if users could read email messages meant for any others. It is essential for a site to have a feature that creates private areas that are only accessible to authorized users; authentication is used to identify these users.

In the previous chapter, you learned how PHP interacts with MySQL. You also learned to store the information entered by a user in a database. In this chapter, you will learn how to create private areas in a site using PHP.

Authentication

Authentication is a mechanism for allowing an individual to access sensitive or private information or for preventing them from doing so. Accessibility to this information solely depends on the permissions granted to the individual. The most economical and popular way of authenticating users on the Internet is by using a unique combination of a user name and a password. After users enter a valid user name and password, they can gain access to restricted areas. These areas could be either the user's personal settings or the administrative area maintained by the system administrator. An authentication scheme will have the following features:

■ Accepts authorization details from the user at the time of registration

■ Stores the user name and password in a database or a file

■ Has a login page for the private area

■ Uses a PHP script to validate the user name and password

To understand how authentication is implemented in real-life scenarios by using automated registration forms and databases, let's first consider a simple example. We will create a dynamic PHP Web page that does not display its contents until a password, `mypassword`, is supplied. To achieve this, we will have to create the following:

■ An HTML form that accepts the password from the user

■ A page that verifies that the password used is valid

Creating the HTML Form That Accepts User Input

Let's first create the HTML form. This form will have only one text field that accepts the password from the user. Let's name this file **pass.htm**.

```
<html>
<head>
<title>Enter Password</title>
<meta http-equiv="Content-Type" content="text/html; charset=iso-8859-1">
</head>
<body bgcolor="#FFFFFF" text="#000000">
<p> </p>
<p> </p>
<form name="form1" method="post" action="pvtpage.php">
  <table width="310" border="0" align="center" cellpadding="5"
cellspacing="2">
    <tr>
      <td bgcolor="#dddddd">
        <div align="center"><b>Enter the password to see the private
page.</b></div>
      </td>
```

```
      </tr>
      <tr bgcolor="#eeeeee">
        <td height="1"> Password
          <input type="password" name="password">
          <input type="submit" name="Submit" value="Login">
        </td>
      </tr>
    </table>
  </form>
  </body>
  </html>
```

In this code:

- An HTML form is created.
- The form accepts a password from the user.
- The input type for the Password text box is specified as `password`. This is done so that other people cannot view the password when the user enters it.
- The password is forwarded to a PHP file for verification.

Figure 12.1 shows the HTML form that accepts the password from a user.

Figure 12.1 The HTML form that accepts a password.

Let's create the PHP script that verifies this password, and let's name this file **pvtpage.php**:

```php
<?php
if (empty($password))
{
die ("<h1><center>No password mentioned.</center></h1>");
}
if (!($password== "mypassword"))
{
die("<h1><center>Password not valid.</center></h1>");
}
echo "<h1><center>Welcome to the private area!</center></h1>";
?>
```

In this code:

- The program accepts $password and verifies it against a predefined value.

- The predefined value for the password is mypassword. If any other value is specified, access to the private page is denied.

- The program quits if no password is specified, and the message No password mentioned appears.

- The program quits if an incorrect password is specified. The message Password not valid appears.

- If a user enters the correct password, mypassword, the user gains access to the private area. The message Welcome to the private area! appears and the program displays the private page.

Now, you have a fair idea about how a simple authentication mechanism works. However, in a real-life scenario, there is much more to authentication than a single password. Let's examine the set of scripts that the development team at Mega Music Mart must create.

In the preceding example, we saw how a private area can be created, and the private area was accessible only when the password mypassword was specified. However, entry to the private area was allowed without differentiating between individual users, which means that each user was authenticated only on the basis of mypassword. In real life, this isn't enough. To access private areas, each user must have an individual password. To ensure maximum security, it is advisable that you use a combination of the user name and the password.

Problem Statement

Mega Music Mart wants to have a members-only area in its Web site to which only registered visitors can log on. The software development team has decided to perform the following steps to achieve this:

- Create an HTML form to allow the visitor to register by specifying a unique user name and a password

- Define a table called `login` with two fields, `username` and `password`, in the `megabase` database
- Write a PHP script to accept the user name and password from the HTML form and store them in the `login` table
- Create an HTML form that accepts passwords
- Create another HTML form that the customer can use to log on to the private area
- Write a PHP script to validate the user name and password entered by the user

Task List

To accomplish the specified task, the development team at Mega Music Mart will need to perform the following steps:

✓ **Create the HTML form that allows a user to select a password**

✓ **Create the table that stores authorization data**

✓ **Determine a secure way to store passwords**

✓ **Write the PHP code that stores the customer ID and the password in the login table**

✓ **Write the PHP script that validates the customer ID and password**

✓ **Write the PHP code for the second private area**

Create the HTML Form That Allows a User to Select a Password

The development team at Mega Music Mart will first create a simple HTML form and accept the registration details from a customer. Let's name this form **custlogin.htm**.

```
<html>
<head>
<title>Enter Password</title>
<meta http-equiv="Content-Type" content="text/html; charset=iso-8859-1">
</head>
<body bgcolor="#FFFFFF" text="#000000">
<p> </p>
<p> </p>
<form name="form1" method="post" action="addpass.php">
  <table width="330" border="0" align="center" cellpadding="5"
cellspacing="2">
    <tr>
      <td colspan="2" bgcolor="#dddddd">
        <div align="center"><b>Specify a Password for Your
Account</b></div>
      </td>
    </tr>
```

```
        <tr bgcolor="#eeeeee">
          <td>
            <div align="right">CustomerID</div>
          </td>
          <td>
            <input type="text" name="customerid">
          </td>
        </tr>
        <tr bgcolor="#eeeeee">
          <td>
            <div align="right">Password</div>
          </td>
          <td>
            <input type="password" name="password">
          </td>
        </tr>
        <tr bgcolor="#eeeeee">
          <td>
            <div align="right">Confirm Password</div>
          </td>
          <td>
            <input type="password" name="cpassword">
          </td>
        </tr>
        <tr bgcolor="#dddddd">
          <td colspan="2">
            <center>
              <input type="submit" name="Submit" value="Submit">
            </center>
          </td>
        </tr>
      </table>
  </form>
  </body>
  </html>
```

In this code:

- An HTML form is created with three text fields.
- The first field is used to accept the customer ID from the user.
- The second field is used to accept a password from the user.
- The third field is used to confirm the password entered by the user in the second field.
- The second and third fields have an input limit of 15 characters.
- Each of these fields should contain some value. Otherwise, the code will return an error.
- The form submits the information entered in these fields to a PHP script.

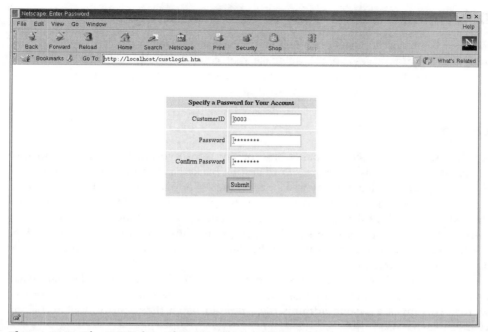

Figure 12.2   The HTML form that accepts user information.

Figure 12.2 shows this form.

Create the Table That Stores Authorization Data

Before creating the PHP script, the development team must create the table that stores this information in the database. This table will contain two fields:

- customerid
- password

Let's create a table named login in the megabase database with these fields:

1. Type the following command at the command prompt to open the MySQL monitor:

   ```
   # mysql
   ```

2. Select the megabase database by typing the following command:

   ```
   mysql>use megabase;
   ```

3. After the database is selected, create the login table by using the following command:

   ```
   mysql> CREATE TABLE IF NOT EXISTS
   login(customerid BIGINT NOT NULL PRIMARY KEY,
   password CHAR(200) NOT NULL);
   ```

Determine a Secure Way to Store Passwords

Passwords are not stored as plain text in databases because if a security breach occurs and hacker gains access to the database that contains the password, all accounts become accessible to the hacker. To avoid such a situation, you can store passwords by using encryption or MD5 hashing algorithm.

Encryption

As discussed earlier, storing passwords or any sensitive information as plain text increases the possibility of the password getting hacked. A solution for this problem is to use *encryption*, which is a way to convert readable, or plain, text to a form that is not readable. Encryption uses an algorithm that changes the coding of the data. To decrypt the text to a meaningful or readable format, the encrypted text must be decrypted. It is difficult to decrypt the text unless the encryption algorithm is known or available. Using encryption, you can ensure that the data is securely transmitted on a network and stored in a database.

If the passwords are stored in an encrypted format, the hacker will need to hack each password individually even after gaining access to the database that contains the passwords. This gives a system administrator time to patch the security hole and even change passwords.

MD5 Hashing Algorithm

Although using encryption is a secure way of storing passwords, using *hashes* ensures maximum security for passwords. A *hash* is a number that is generated using a string of text. A formula that converts plain text to hashes is used to achieve this. A popular mechanism that uses hashes to secure passwords or sensitive information is the MD5 hashing algorithm. The formula is applied to each piece of text and returns a unique value. The main difference between encryption and hashing is that encrypted text can be decrypted, but hashes cannot return the original text under any circumstance. When a user enters a password, this password is converted to a hash, which is compared with the hash value stored in the database. If both values match, the user is able to access the private area on the site.

In PHP, hashes are generated with the md5() function. Therefore, the development team has decided to use hashes to secure the passwords that will be stored in the database.

NOTE In a real-life scenario, encryption and hashing algorithms are used together to ensure maximum security.

Write the PHP Code That Stores the Customer ID and the Password in the login Table

Next, the development team needs to create a PHP script to accept the registration information from the registration form and store it in the `login` table. The following PHP script will produce the required result. Let's name this file **addpass.php**:

```
<html>
<head>
<title>Password Result</title>
</head>
<body bgcolor="#FFFFFF" text="#000000">
<p> </p>
<?php
$host="";
$uname="root";
$pass="";
$database="megabase";
$tablename="login";
$connection= mysql_connect($host,$uname,$pass)
   or die("Database connection failed! <br>");
$result=mysql_select_db($database)
   or die("Database could not be selected");
$query = "INSERT INTO login VALUES('". $customerid ."', '".
md5($password) . "')";
//$result = mysql_query($query);
if (!$query)
{
die(" Query could not be executed.<br>");
}
?>
<table width="330" border="0" align="center" cellpadding="5"
cellspacing="2">
  <tr>
    <td colspan="2" bgcolor="#dddddd">
      <div align="center"><b>New password entered for
        <?php echo $customerid;
          ?>
        as </b></div>
    </td>
  </tr>
  <tr bgcolor="#eeeeee">
```

```
      <td width="50%">
        <div align="right"><b>CustomerID</b></div>
      </td>
      <td>
        <center>
          <?php echo $customerid; ?>
        </center>
      </td>
    </tr>
    <tr bgcolor="#eeeeee">
      <td>
        <div align="right"><b>Password</b></div>
      </td>
      <td>
        <center>
          <?php echo $password; ?>
        </center>
      </td>
    </tr>
    <tr bgcolor="#eeeeee">
      <td colspan="2"><center>Try your new password in the <a
href="login.htm">login page</a></center></td>
    </tr>
</table>
<p> </p>
</body>
</html>
```

In this code:

- The script first verifies the passwords to ensure that:

  - The password field is not empty.

  - The password and confirm password fields contain the same value.

- A connection is established with MySQL.

- The database megabase is selected after establishing a connection with MySQL.

- Authorization details, such as the user name and the password, are written to the login table.

- Password is stored as a MD5 hash using the md5() function.

This completes the registration process. Figure 12.3 illustrates the HTML form that appears when user details are sent to the login table.

Let's now create a login page for the users. Users will use this page to gain access to the personal areas allocated to them on the Web site. Let's name this file **login.htm**.

```
<html>
<head>
<title>Enter Password</title>
```

```
<meta http-equiv="Content-Type" content="text/html; charset=iso-8859-1">
</head>
<body bgcolor="#FFFFFF" text="#000000">
<p> </p>
<p> </p>
<form name="form1" method="post" action="home1.php">
  <table width="330" border="0" align="center" cellpadding="5"
cellspacing="2">
    <tr>
      <td colspan="2" bgcolor="#dddddd">
        <div align="center"><b>Use Your ID and Password to
Login</b></div>
      </td>
    </tr>
    <tr bgcolor="#eeeeee">
      <td>
        <div align="right"><b>CustomerID</b></div>
      </td>
      <td>
        <input type="text" name="customerid">
      </td>
    </tr>
    <tr bgcolor="#eeeeee">
      <td>
        <div align="right"><b>Password</b></div>
      </td>
      <td>
        <input type="password" name="password">
      </td>
    </tr>
    <tr bgcolor="#dddddd">
      <td colspan="2">
        <center>
          <input type="submit" name="Submit" value="Login">
        </center>
      </td>
    </tr>
  </table>
</form>
</body>
</html>
```

In this code:

- An HTML form accepts `customerid` and `password` from the user.
- The accepted input is forwarded to a PHP script that validates the user name and the password.

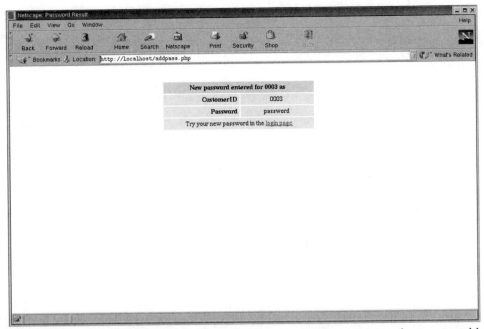

Figure 12.3 The HTML form that appears when user details are sent to the `login` table.

Figure 12.4 shows the registered user login page.

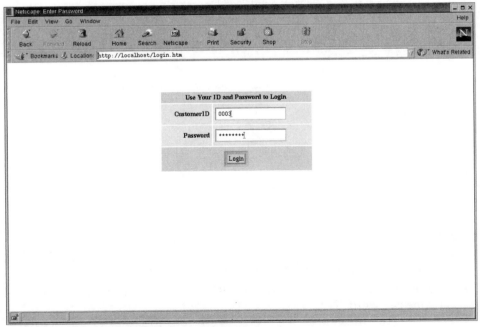

Figure 12.4 The login page for registered users.

After the user name and password are sent to the PHP script, the script validates them with those stored in the database as hashes that were generated using MD5. Therefore, we need to perform the following tasks to validate the password:

- Extract the previously stored hash for the password from the database.
- Compute the hash for the password that was entered by the user in the login page.
- Compare the values.

Write the PHP Script That Validates the Customer ID and Password

In addition to validating the password, this page should display a personalized message to the customer and provide a link to another personalized page within this private area. Let's write the PHP script that includes this, and let's name this file **home1.php**.

```
<html>
<head>
<title>Enter Password</title>
<meta http-equiv="Content-Type" content="text/html; charset=iso-8859-1">
</head>
<body bgcolor="#FFFFFF" text="#000000">
<p> </p>
<?php
if (empty($password)) { die("No Password specified");}
if ((strlen($password) < 5) || (strlen($password) > 15))
{ die("Password too long/short");}
?>
<?php
$host="";
$uname="root";
$pass="";
$database="megabase";
$connection= mysql_connect($host,$uname,$pass)
   or die("Database connection failed! <br>");
$result=mysql_select_db($database)
   or die("Database could not be selected");
$query = "SELECT password from login where customerid='" .$customerid
."'";
$result = mysql_query($query);
if($row=mysql_fetch_array($result))
{
 if(!(md5($password) == $row["password"]))
 {
      die(" Wrong Password!");
 }
}
}
```

```
else
{
die(" User does not exist!!");
}
?>
<table width="330" border="0" align="center" cellpadding="5"
cellspacing="2">
  <tr>
    <td colspan="3" bgcolor="#dddddd">
      <div align="center"><b>Welcome to Your Personal Area
        <?php echo $customerid; ?>
        </b></div>
    </td>
  </tr>
  <tr bgcolor="#eeeeee">
    <td colspan="3"> </td>
  </tr>
  <tr bgcolor="#eeeeee">
    <td colspan="3">
      <div align="center"><b>This is Page 1!</b></div>
    </td>
  </tr>
  <tr bgcolor="#eeeeee">
    <td colspan="3"> </td>
  </tr>
  <tr bgcolor="#eeeeee">
    <td width="33%">
      <center>
        Page 1
      </center>
    </td>
    <td width="33%">
      <center>
<?php
    echo "  <a href=\"home2.php?customerid=". $customerid
."&password=".$password."\">Page 2</a>";
?>
      </center>
    </td>
    <td width="33%">
      <center>
        <a href="login.htm">Logout</a>
      </center>
    </td>
  </tr>
</table>
<p> </p>
</body>
</html>
```

In this code:

- The value specified in the password field is checked for the number of characters entered. Lower and upper limits of 5 and 15 characters, respectively, are specified because shorter passwords are insecure and longer ones take a long time to generate a hash and need a large amount of storage space.

- The corresponding hash value of the password specified by the user is extracted using the unique customer ID of the user. Then, the customer ID entered by the user in the login page is extracted from the database.

- A new hash is generated, using the same MD5 hash algorithm, for the password entered by the user in the login HTML form.

- The two hashes are compared. The private page is displayed if the two hashes match. Otherwise, an appropriate error message is displayed and the program exits.

- If the private area home page is not displayed, a link to another page of the private area is displayed.

- The link for the second page also carries `customerid` and `password` as parameters to the URL of the second page.

- Another link for signing off is present on the Web page. This link directs the user to the login page after logging the user off from the private area.

The method you used to transfer the values in the second page is the same as that used to post these values to the second page. The `POST` method is used to do this. Figure 12.5 displays the Web page that appears after the correct combination of the customer ID and password is specified.

Figure 12.5 The Web page that appears after the password is validated.

Write the PHP Code for the Second Private Area

Next, the development team writes the following code for the second private area Web page. Let's name this file **home2.php**.

```
<html>
<head>
<title>Enter Password</title>
<meta http-equiv="Content-Type" content="text/html; charset=iso-8859-1">
</head>
<body bgcolor="#FFFFFF" text="#000000">
<p> </p>
<?php
if (empty($password)) { die("No Password specified");}
if ((strlen($password) < 5) || (strlen($password) > 15))
{
  die("Password too long/short");
}
?>
<?php
$host="";
$uname="root";
$pass="";
$database="megabase";
$connection= mysql_connect($host,$uname,$pass)
    or die("Database connection failed! <br>");
$result=mysql_select_db($database)
    or die("Database could not be selected");
$query = "SELECT password from login where customerid='" .$customerid
."'";
$result = mysql_query($query);
if($row=mysql_fetch_array($result))
{
 if(!(md5($password) == $row["password"]))
 {
        die(" Wrong Password!");
 }
}
else
{
die(" User does not exist!!");
}
?>
<table width="330" border="0" align="center" cellpadding="5"
cellspacing="2">
  <tr>
    <td colspan="3" bgcolor="#dddddd">
```

```
            <div align="center"><b>Welcome to your personal area
              <?php echo $customerid;
                ?>
              </b></div>
        </td>
    </tr>
    <tr bgcolor="#eeeeee">
      <td colspan="3"> </td>
    </tr>
    <tr bgcolor="#eeeeee">
      <td colspan="3">
        <div align="center"><b>This is Page 2!</b></div>
      </td>
    </tr>
    <tr bgcolor="#eeeeee">
      <td colspan="3"> </td>
    </tr>
    <tr bgcolor="#eeeeee">
      <td width="33%">
        <center>
<?php
      echo "  <a href=\"home1.php?customerid=". $customerid
."&password=".$password."\">Page 1</a>";
?>
        </center>
      </td>
      <td width="33%">
        <center>
          Page 2
        </center>
      </td>
      <td width="33%">
        <center>
          <a href="login.htm">Logout</a>
        </center>
      </td>
    </tr>
</table>
<p> </p>
</body>
</html>
```

In this code:

■ The password was checked and authenticated again by comparing the hashes.

■ The content displayed by the second page is different from the content displayed on the first page (Figure 12.6).

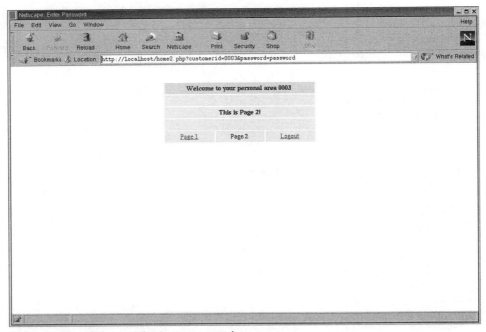

Figure 12.6 The second private area Web page.

Summary

In this chapter, you learned how private areas are created on a Web site. You also learned to store and manage passwords in a database. Finally, you learned about the mechanism for authenticating users on a Web site.

Cookies

Getting Started

The evolution of e-commerce Web sites has resulted in a surge in the use of dynamic Web content. Therefore, it is essential to be able to save state in these applications. However, the HTTP protocol that is used to connect to the Internet is a stateless protocol. That is, after a user's transaction with a server ends, all memory regarding the transaction is lost. It is beneficial for a site that stores dynamic content to have a record of information about when and who accessed the site, but this is possible only by saving state of these dynamic applications. Maintaining or saving state is the ability to retain the values of variables and keep track of the users logged onto a server. When technologies such as CGI scripts were used, it was not possible to maintain state. As a result, when a user sent a request to a server, the server would process the request and respond to it. However, when another request from the same user was sent to the server, the server would not recognize that it was the same user who was placing the request.

Netscape first addressed this problem. With the release of Netscape 3.0, the solution to this problem was initiated: *cookies*. From then on, cookies have been implemented by millions of Web sites across the world to maintain sessions. They help store useful and relevant information about the users in a file on the user's hard disk. This information is sent to the Web server whenever the user tries to connect to the Web site again. When the Web server receives this cookie, it recognizes the user.

In this chapter, you will learn to use cookies to save the state of dynamic Web content on your Web site. First, you will be introduced to the concept of cookies and the built-in functions that can be used to implement cookies on your site. Then, you will learn to use these built-in functions to save state.

Introducing Cookies

Problem Statement

Mega Music Mart wants the users who access its Web site to be able to view information about their earlier visits. In addition, to avoid repetitive logins, user details should be stored in a cookie so that the user need not specify the password repeatedly. This cookie should expire after 24 hours. The development team has been assigned this task, and the following specifications have been laid down:

🗸 **A personalized greeting message should appear when the user logs in.**

🗸 **The last login time should be displayed.**

🗸 **The current date and time should be displayed.**

🗸 **The page view count should be displayed.**

Task List

To successfully perform this task, the development team has decided to implement cookies in its design. To do this, it will need to perform the following tasks:

🗸 **Identify the different ways by which cookies can be used**

🗸 **Implement cookies using PHP**

🗸 **Create the HTML form**

🗸 **Write the PHP code**

Identify the Ways by which Cookies Can Be Used

Cookies are pieces of information that are stored on a client computer by the server computer. Technically speaking, cookies are text strings that a Web server stores on a client computer by using a Web browser. When a user accesses a site, these text strings are stored on the user's computer. Whenever the user accesses the site again, the information stored on the client computer is sent back to the Web server. This helps the Web server identify the user and also keep track of the transactions made by that user. In other words, when a user enters personal information on a Web site, this information is stored on the user's hard drive. Such information can be used to create customized pages for different users. A simple example is of a site that displays a personalized message to a user with the user's name. Cookies are most often used for:

- Tracking a user's path on a Web site
- Storing the items selected by a user in a shopping cart
- Retaining the user's customer ID
- Generating user profiles

As discussed earlier, cookies are a mechanism to store or save sessions on sites that contain dynamic Web applications. Each cookie has a URL associated with it that is used to determine whether a cookie should be sent to the requested server. You can perform several tasks if you have implemented cookies on your Web site, such as:

- Save state of subsequent visits made by a user to a Web page
- Save state of subsequent visits made by a user to different Web pages on a site

To prevent the abuse of cookies, certain restrictions are imposed on the way cookies can be used:

- A browser can store a maximum of 300 cookies.
- One server can store a maximum of 20 cookies on the user's computer.
- The size of a cookie is limited to 4 KB.

NOTE If voluminous data related to user information needs to be maintained, you will need to use PHP 4.0 session support or databases.

Scope of a Cookie

The scope of a cookie is limited to that defined by the Web server that is sending the cookie. The following information can be specified in relation to a cookie:

Expiration information.   Determines the life of a cookie. That is, a cookie is valid only before the specified expiration date, which is specified in Greenwich mean time (GMT). After a cookie expires, it is no longer sent to a Web server. The default value used for this parameter is "Until the browser is closed." This means that a cookie expires as soon as a user closes the browser in use.

Path information.   Specifies path details. That is, it specifies the path to the directories on a Web server for which a cookie is valid. The default value for this parameter is / (all the directories present on a server).

Domain information.   Specifies the domain for which a cookie is valid. A Web server can be limited to a specific host by specifying the hostname as singlehost.com. However, you can also specify an entire domain by specifying the domain name as .domainname.com. The initial dot is used to signify that the Web server is not limited to a specific host and will use all the host computers of the specified domain. The default value for this parameter is the domain name of the server that sets a cookie.

Security parameter.   Can be enabled while using cookies to ensure that they are sent using a secure channel, such as *Secure HyperText Transfer Protocol (HTTPS)*. This guarantees that unauthorized individuals do not access the data present in cookies. If a secure parameter is disabled, data is transmitted over all channels, regardless of whether a channel is secure. The default value for this parameter is Disabled.

Implement Cookies Using PHP

Using cookies in PHP is simple. During the startup of a PHP script, cookies are automatically declared as global variables and can be accessed from anywhere within the PHP script. For example, if you have set a cookie named music that contains the value Rock is great!, the variable $music will be a global variable that contains the specified value.

Cookie support is built into PHP. This section will deal with the following concepts:

- Setting a cookie
- Setting the life span of a cookie
- Creating a test cookie
- Accessing a cookie
- Using multiple value cookies
- Controlling the scope of cookies

Setting a Cookie

In PHP, cookies can be set using the setcookie() function, which sends a cookie to the Web server. However, when using this function, you will need to remember to call it before you use any HTML tag in your script. Otherwise, you may encounter an error message. Even a white space before the starting PHP tag in your script can cause the code to function improperly. Therefore, it is essential to call the setcookie() function before you write other code. The syntax of the setcookie() function is as follows:

```
setcookie (string_name, string_value, expiry_info, string_path,
string_domain, secure_status);
```

In this syntax, six arguments are used with the setcookie() function:

- The string_name argument is used to specify the name of the variable that will contain the value of the cookie. This variable is used as a global variable and is accessible in the subsequent PHP scripts that you create.

- The string_value argument is used to specify the name of the variable that will contain the value of the cookie and is used as a global variable. It is accessible in the subsequent PHP scripts that you create.

- The expiry_info argument is used to specify the time after which the cookie will become unusable; it is specified in GMT. If no value is assigned to this argument, cookies remain valid as long as a browser is open. The expiry_info argument accepts an integer value. The functions time() and mktime() are used to specify a value for this argument.

- The string_path argument is used to specify the directories for which the cookie is valid. By default, cookies are valid for the / directory, which means that the cookie is valid for all the files and directories on a Web server. However, if a directory path is specified, cookies are valid only for the files and directories located in the specified directory.

- The string_domain argument is used to specify the host or the domain for which the cookie is valid. If the domain name is not specified, the hostname of the computer that sent the cookie is set as the default value for this argument.

- The secure_status argument is used to specify whether the cookies should be transmitted using a secure channel. If the value for this parameter is 1, the cookies will be transmitted securely using the HTTPS protocol.

- All arguments except string_name are optional. That is, if you use the single argument string_name with the setcookie() function, the cookie will be set.

- All arguments *except* for expiry_info and secure_status can be skipped by specifying an empty string (" ").

- The expiry_info and the secure_status arguments cannot be skipped because they expect an integer value to be assigned to them. The expiry_info argument is a regular UNIX time integer, and it is returned using time() and mktime().

Setting the Life Span of a Cookie

As discussed earlier, by default, a cookie expires as soon as a user closes a browser. However, this can be avoided by customizing the cookie's life span by setting the expiration time. The expiry time is specified as a timestamp (the number of seconds since January 1, 1970) using the time() and mktime() functions.

The time() Function

The time() function is assigned to the expiry_info argument as follows:

```
$expiry_info = time()+n
```

In this syntax:

- The time() function is passed as a value to the variable $expiry_info.
- The letter n signifies the number of seconds that need to be added to the time() function. If the value of n is 60, the cookie will expire after 60 seconds.

The mktime() Function

The mktime() function is another function that is used within the setcookie() function to specify a cookie's life span. However, the usage of mktime() is different from that of time(). It accepts units of time as parameters and converts them into a timestamp. The syntax of the mktime() function is:

```
$expiry_info = mktime(hour, minute, second, month, year);
```

In this syntax:

- The mktime() function is passed as a value to the variable $expiry_info.
- Five arguments are passed to the mktime() function:
  - The hour parameter accepts an integer value and is used to specify the number of hours.
  - The minute parameter accepts an integer value and is used to specify the number of minutes.
  - The second parameter accepts an integer value and is used to specify the number of seconds.
  - The month parameter accepts an integer value and is used to specify the month.
  - The year parameter accepts an integer value and is used to specify the year.

Creating a Test Cookie

Now that you know the basics of creating a cookie, let's write a simple PHP script to create a test cookie, and let's name this PHP file **testcookie.php**.

```php
<?php
$string_name = "testcookie";
$string_value = "This is a test cookie";
$expiry_info = time()+259200;
$string_domain = "localhost.localdomain";
setcookie($string_name, $string_value, $expiry_info, $string_domain);
?>
<HTML>
<HEAD>
<TITLE> A Test Cookie</TITLE>
</HEAD>
<BODY>
<H1>This is a Cookie!!!</H1>
</BODY>
</HTML>
```

In this code:

- The variable $string_name is assigned the value testcookie, the name of the cookie created.

- The variable $string_value is assigned the value This is a testcookie, the text that will be stored in the cookie.

- The variable $expiry_info is assigned the value test()+259200 (seconds), which indicates that the cookie will be active for three days beginning from the current time.

- The variable $string_domain is assigned the value localhost. This value will differ depending on the host or domain name of the Web server that you are using.

If you have configured your security settings to prompt you before accepting cookies, you might encounter the message box shown in Figure 13.1. The output of the preceding code is shown in Figure 13.2.

NOTE After a Web browser accepts a cookie, it is not possible to extract the value of the cookie unless another HTTP request is sent to the Web server. That is, if the cookie has been set on the first Web page, it can be extracted only when the user reaches the second Web page or any other different page.

Accessing a Cookie

After you set a cookie, you want to access it. When a user sends cookie information with an HTTP request, the cookie is automatically transformed to variables. These are global variables that can be accessed anywhere in your script. There are two ways of accessing cookies. Consider an example in which a cookie named music is sent with an HTTP request. This cookie can be accessed using the following methods:

- The variable $music: A variable with the same name as the cookie is stored.

- $HTTP_COOKIE_VARS["music"]: The variable that is created by the cookie is stored in the global array as $HTTP_COOKIE_VARS["music"]. This helps distinguish between different variables on the basis of the data sources from where they originate.

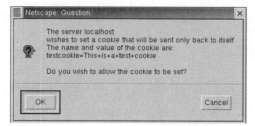

Figure 13.1   The Netscape: Question message box.

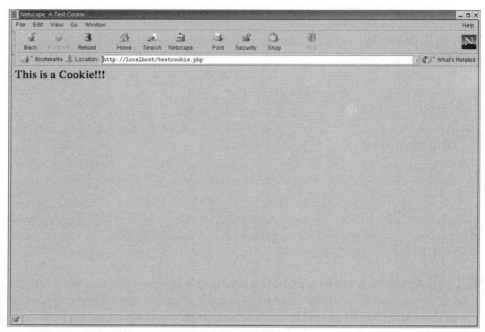

Figure 13.2   The Web page that displays the output of testcookie.php.

NOTE If you happen to set a cookie with an invalid name that cannot be used as a variable name, the cookie name is automatically changed. All invalid characters are replaced by the underscore character. For example, if you use the invalid character % in a cookie name, this character will automatically be replaced by an underscore. Therefore, a cookie named `music%choice` will be converted to `music_choice` when PHP accesses it as a variable.

Using Multiple Values for a Cookie

As discussed earlier, there is a limit to the number of cookies that can be stored on the local computer of a user. However, if you want to store more cookies on a user's computer, you can use multiple values for a cookie. Suppose you want to store the number of times a user has visited your site and the average period of time the user remains on your site and want to display a personalized message for the user. Instead of using three different cookies, you can treat the cookie as an array. Each piece of information that you want to store in the cookie will be stored as an element of the array. Consider the following code:

```php
<?php
if (!isset ($userdetails[0]))
{
```

```
setcookie ("userdetails[0]", $username);
}
$userdetails[1]++;
setcookie ("userdetails[1]", $userdetails[1]);
echo ("Hello $userdetails[0], you've seen this page
".$userdetails[1].($userdetails[1] == 1?" time!": "times!"));
?>
<HTML>
<HEAD>
<TITLE>A Cookie with Multiple Values</TITLE>
</HEAD>
</HTML>
```

In this code:

- A cookie named userdetails is set.

- This cookie is used as an array.

- One of the elements of this array is the name of the user. This name is displayed on the Web page.

- Another element of this array is a cookie that calculates the number of times the user visits the Web page.

NOTE The username will appear in the output of the code only when a value for the username is accepted from the user.

Controlling the Scope of Cookies

It is essential that you control the scope of cookies using the parameters string_path and string_domain with the setcookie() function. The parameter string_path stores the path of the directory whose contents should be accessible to a cookie, and string_domain specifies the host or domain name that will be accessible to a cookie.

Using string_path to Control the Scope of a Cookie

By default, the path specified in a cookie is /, which means that all the directories present on a server are accessible by the cookie. It also means that any script on the server can access the cookie. This, in turn, means that a script belonging to a particular user will be visible to the Web pages of other users, which can result in a security breach. In such a situation, the string_path argument can be set, specifying an exact path to directories. However, a security breach can occur even after you specify the exact path to the directory to be used.

Consider an example in which you have specified the path as /customerinfo/ usernames. All the directories and files under the usernames directory will be accessible to the cookie. If there is a file named **usernames.php** in /customerinfo, this file should not be accessible to the cookie but will be because the filename begins with the word *usernames*. To prevent the cookie from accessing this file, the path will need to be specified with a trailing slash: /customerinfo/usernames/. Now, the usernames. php file will no longer be accessible. This will ensure stringent control on the scope of a cookie. Let's review the right and wrong ways to specify a path. The *incorrect* way is:

```
$string_path = /customerinfo/usernames
```

This will make all the files and directories under customerinfo/usernames accessible to the cookie and will also allow access to other files that begin with the word *usernames*. The *correct* way is:

```
$string_path = /customerinfo/usernames/
```

The trailing slash ensures that only the files and directories in the usernames directory are accessible.

Using `string_domain` to Control the Scope of a Cookie

The variable string_domain can also be used to define the scope of a cookie. Both host and domain names can be specified as values to this argument. However, even when specifying domain or host information, you will need to be careful. It is best to specify a tail match, which can be specified as .musicworld.com. As a result, all host names that end with the text .musicworld.com will be valid host names. Therefore, www.musicworld.com and www1.musicworld.com are valid names. However, .megamusicworld.com will not be a valid name. It is essential to specify domain names with care; otherwise, a security breach is likely to occur.

Deleting a Cookie

When you don't need to use a cookie any longer, you may want to delete it. You do so with the same function that you set it with, setcookie(), using the following syntax:

```
setcookie(music);
```

The argument music is the name of an existing cookie that needs to be deleted.

When you create cookies in PHP, requests are sent to a server in reverse order. Therefore, if you want to create a cookie with a name that already exists, you will need to create the cookie and assign a different value to it and then delete the old cookie. For example, if a cookie named music exists and contains the value rocklovers and you want to delete it, you will need to follow these steps:

1. Create a new cookie and set a new value to it by using the following code:

   ```
   setcookie("music", "poplovers");
   ```

2. Delete the old cookie by using the following code:

   ```
   setcookie("music");
   ```

Create the HTML Form

Let's create the HTML form that accepts the username and the password, and let's name this file **loginscreen.htm**:

```html
<html>
<head>
<title>Enter Password</title>
<meta http-equiv="Content-Type" content="text/html; charset=iso-8859-1">
</head>
<body bgcolor="#FFFFFF" text="#000000">
<p> </p>
<p> </p>
<form name="form1" method="POST" action="cookieimp.php">
  <table width="330" border="0" align="center" cellpadding="5"
cellspacing="2">
    <tr>
      <td colspan="2" bgcolor="#dddddd">
        <div align="center"><b>Please Specify the Password</b></div>
      </td>
    </tr>
    <tr bgcolor="#eeeeee">
      <td>
        <div align="right">Customer ID</div>
      </td>
      <td>
        <input type="text" name="username">
      </td>
    </tr>
    <tr bgcolor="#eeeeee">
      <td>
        <div align="right">Password</div>
      </td>
      <td>
        <input type="password" name="password">
      </td>
    </tr>
    <tr bgcolor="#dddddd">
      <td colspan="2">
        <center>
          <input type="submit" name="Submit" value="Login">
        </center>
      </td>
    </tr>
  </table>
</form>
</body>
</html>
```

Figure 13.3 shows the resulting HTML form.

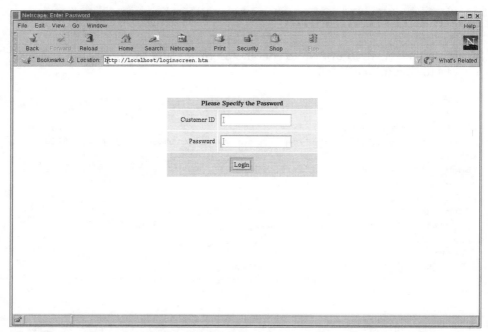

Figure 13.3 The Web page that displays the output of loginscreen.php.

Write the PHP Code

NOTE In this example, it is assumed that the password is superpass. You will need to specify this password at login. After you log in, a cookie will be stored on your computer. Then, you will not need to specify the password for the next 24 hours.

Let's create a file named **cookieimp.php** with the following code:

```php
<?php
  $now = getdate();
  $storetime= $now["weekday"] . " " . $now["mday"] . " " . $now["month"]
. " " . $now["year"] ;

  $storetime.=" Time : ";

  if ($now["hours"] < 10)
  {
   $storetime.= "0" . $now["hours"];
  }
  else
  {
```

```
    $storetime.= $now["hours"];
   }
   $storetime.= ":";
   if ($now["minutes"] < 10)
   {
    $storetime.= "0" . $now["minutes"];
   }
   else
   {
    $storetime.= $now["minutes"];
   }
   $storetime.= ":";
   if ($now["seconds"] < 10)
   {
    $storetime.= "0" . $now["seconds"];
   }
   else
   {
    $storetime.= $now["seconds"];
   }
if (isset($data))
 {
  $counter=++$data[1];

  setcookie("data[0]",$storetime,time() + (60*60*24));
  setcookie("data[1]", $counter,time() + (60*60*24));
  setcookie("data[2]",$username,time() + (60*60*24));
  echo "<b><center>Hi " . $data[2] . " !!</center></b><br>\n";
  echo "<b><center>Last Login Time :" .$data[0]  .
"</center></b><br>\n";
  echo "<b><center>Current Date      :" .$storetime.
"</center></b><br>\n";
  echo "<b><center>Page View Count :" .$data[1]   .
"</center></b><br>\n";
  echo "<b><center>You have successfully logged in!</center></b>";
  die("<b><center>You can access this area without entering a password
for the next 24 hours!</center></b>");
 }
else
{
  if (isset($username) && isset($password))
   {
    if ($password=="superpass")
     {
       $counter=0;
       setcookie("data[0]",$storetime,time() + (60*60*24));
       setcookie("data[1]", $counter,time() + (60*60*24));
       setcookie("data[2]",$username,time() + (60*60*24));
       $url="Location: cookieimp.php";
       header($url);

     }
```

```
            else
              {
                echo "<h1><center>INVALID PASSWORD!!!</center></h1>";
              }
          }
      }
?>
```

Figure 13.4 shows the Web page that appears when the customer ID is specified as Steve and the password superpass is entered.

To validate the cookie, reload the Web page. A Web page appears, indicating that you have accessed the Web page for the second time (Figure 13.5).

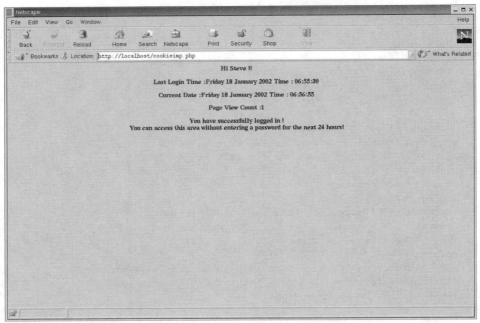

Figure 13.4 The Web page that appears when you enter the correct password.

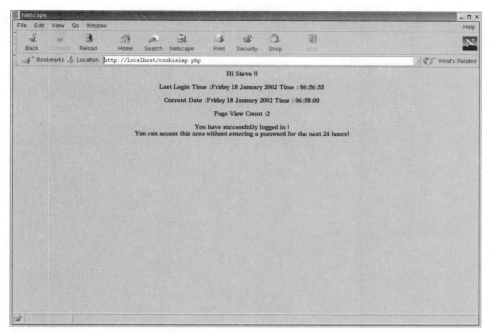

Figure 13.5 The Web page that appears when you reload the Web page.

Summary

In this chapter, you learned to work with cookies. You learned how to use the `setcookie()` function to create a cookie. Next, you learned how to control the life span of a cookie. Then, you learned the procedure for setting multiple values for a cookie. Finally, you learned to delete a cookie.

Handling Sessions in PHP

OBJECTIVES:

In this lesson, you will learn to:

- ✔ **Identify sessions**
- ✔ **Identify session variables**
- ✔ **Set session variables**
- ✔ **Work with sessions**

Getting Started

After reading the chapter on cookies, you have an idea about how sessions are maintained in PHP. However, there is much more to learn about them. Because only a limited number of cookies can be stored on a client computer, it is not always feasible to implement them. A better proposition is to maintain state by using server-side sessions, which enable developers to preserve user preferences over a period of time. This, in turn, helps the developer maintain and create additional customized Web pages for users accessing the site.

Session Handling

This section introduces the session variables that are used in PHP and explains how they are used. The section also discusses session-related functions that can be used in PHP to implement sessions on your Web site.

Problem Statement

The development team at Mega Music Mart has decided to use sessions to maintain state between Web pages that a user accesses. This will prevent the user's password from being transmitted through the URL. Instead, a session ID will be generated and used.

Task List

To implement sessions the following tasks will need to be performed:

✓ **Create the HTML form that accepts the customer ID and password**

✓ **Write the PHP code to store the information in the database**

✓ **Create the HTML form that accepts the already-set password**

✓ **Write the PHP script that validates the password**

✓ **Write the PHP script for the first private page**

✓ **Write the PHP script for the second private page**

✓ **Write the PHP code that helps the user log out**

✓ **Execute the code**

Introducing Sessions

A session can be referred to as the duration for which a user is connected to a site, which is the simplest example of a session. In programming terminology, a session is a block of information that stores all types of variables and values. The features of a session are as follows:

- A session consists of an identification string, which is called the session ID. Each session has a session ID that is stored in either a cookie or the URL.

- This session ID is sent to the user's computer in a cookie called PHPSESSID.

- When the user logs in and a session is initiated, PHPSESSID is the default name for the cookie but can be changed whenever required.

- A similar session ID is stored in the server as a special file that also contains all the data that is stored in a session.

Session Variables

We have discussed the local and global variables that are used in PHP. A local variable has limited scope and can be accessed only within the function in which it is defined. The global variable has an unlimited scope, and it can be accessed outside the function in which it is defined. PHP also uses *session* variables.

Session variables continue to exist if they are not explicitly deleted, and they can be automatically deleted using certain configuration options. Session variables can store:

- Arrays
- String values
- Integer values
- Objects

Session variables and their values are stored in a temporary file in the Web server. A temporary file stores information in the following format:

```
Hello|s:7:"2002";
Bye|s:7:"2001";
```

In this example:

- `Hello` and `Bye` are names of the registered variables.
- The values of these variables are `2002` and `2001`.

Before you access these variables, you need to register them in an active session. First let's examine the procedure for retrieving the value of a registered session variable:

- The PHP parser receives from the user the cookie that contains `PHPSESSID`.
- The PHP parser then searches for a matching session ID stored in a temporary session file.
- The PHP parser then searches for the variable in the session file.
- After the parser finds the variable, its value is extracted.

Creating a Session Variable

The built-in function `session_register()` is used to register a session variable. This function accepts the name of the variable that needs to be registered as an argument, as follows:

```php
<?php
$music = "Hi! The variable is registered!";
session_register('music');
echo $music;
?>
```

In this code:

- A variable named $music is defined.

- The value Hi! The variable is registered! is assigned to the variable $music.

- The session_register() function is used to register the variable $music.

- This variable is specified as an argument to the session_register() function.

The output is:

```
X-Powered-By: PHP/4.0.6
Set-Cookie: PHPSESSID=a0f86f507fb3796183734f0472787d50; path=/
Expires: Thu, 19 Nov 1981 08:52:00 GMT
Cache-Control: no-store, no-cache, must-revalidate, post-check=0, pre-
check=0
Pragma: no-cache
Content-type: text/html
Hi! The variable is registered!
```

In the output:

- The code generates a session ID.

- The session ID is a0f86f507fb3796183734f0472787d50.

- This session ID is stored on the user's local computer, and a duplicate session ID is maintained on the Web server in a temporary file.

- The default path of the cookie is /.

- The expiration date and time of the cookie are also displayed.

Starting a Session

PHP provides a built-in function that is used to start a session: session_start(). This function was first introduced with PHP 4 and is used to create and resume sessions. The function always returns a true value.

NOTE It is advisable to use the session_start() function at the beginning of the PHP script because it performs several tasks, including checking whether a user is currently logged on.

The syntax of the session_start() function is as follows:

```
<?php
session_start();
$music = "Hi! The variable is registered!";
```

```
session_register('music');
echo $music;
?>
<HTML>
<HEAD>
<TITLE>Starting a Session</TITLE>
</HEAD>
</BODY>
```

In this code, the session_start() function is used to start the session. Figure 14.1 shows the Web page that appears when you save the code in a PHP file and view it in the browser.

NOTE You may encounter a message that asks for confirmation before setting cookies. This message will appear only when you have configured your browser to do so. If you encounter this message, simply click the OK button to allow the cookies to be set.

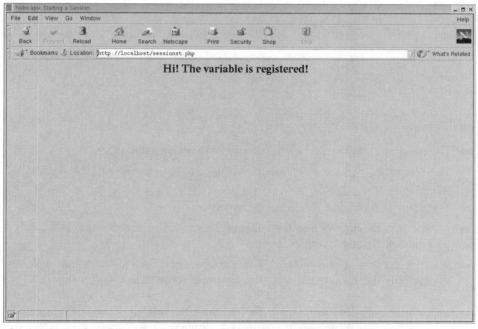

Figure 14.1   The Web page that appears when you start a session.

Modifying Session Variables

You now know how to create sessions. Let's see how session variables are modified. Let's create a simple Web page that calculates the number of times a user accesses it:

```php
<?php
session_start();
session_register('access_count');
$access_count++;
if ($access_count==1)
{
echo "<h1><center>Welcome! You have accessed this page for the first
time!</center></h1>";
}
else
{
$message="<h1><center>You have accessed this page $access_count times.
Thanks!</center></h1>";
}
?>
<html>
<head>
<title>Access Count</title>
</head>
<body>
<?php
echo "$message";
?>
</body>
</html>
```

In this code:

- The `session_start()` function is used to start the session.
- The `session_register()` function is used to register the variable named `access_count`.
- The value of `$access_count` is incremented.
- A condition checks whether the value of the variable `access_count` is 1. If it is, a message is displayed.
- A variable `$message` is defined. This variable contains a message that will appear only if the value of `$access_count` is more than 1.

When the user accesses the page for the first time, the output of the preceding code appears in the browser, as shown in Figure 14.2. When the user accesses the Web page for the sixth time, the output is as shown in Figure 14.3.

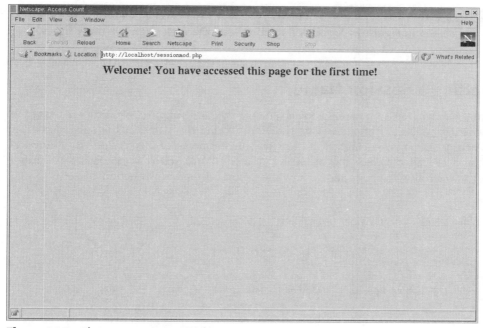

Figure 14.2   The access counter Web page.

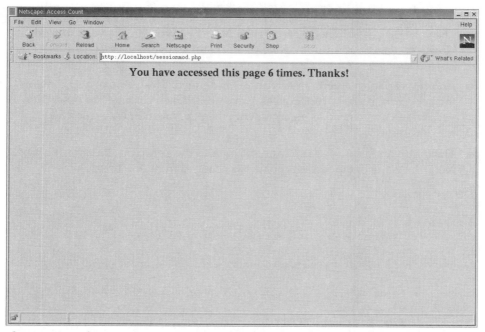

Figure 14.3   The access counter Web page when a user accesses it for the sixth time.

> **NOTE** The session ends as soon as you close the browser. Therefore, to view the screen in Figure 14.3, you will need to load the Web page five more times.

Setting a Session Name

After you set a session name, you can change the name of the session cookie using the session_name() function. This function accepts the name of the session cookie. When no name is specified, it returns the current name of the session. This function should be called before the session_start() and session_register() functions. The following code shows how the session_name() function is used:

```php
<?php
$sessionold = session_name('Pop');
$sessionnew = session_name('Rock');
$sessionlatest = session_name('Heavy Metal');
session_register('Rock');
echo "The old session name was $sessionold.", "\n";
echo "The new session name is $sessionnew!", "\n";
echo "The latest session name is $sessionlatest!!";
?>
```

In this code:

- The variable $sessionold is used to store the function session_name().

- The value Pop is assigned as an argument to the session_name() function. However, the variable $sessionold stores the old value session_name() function, which is PHPSESSID.

- Another variable named $sessionnew is defined. This variable also contains the session_name() function. However, this time it contains the new value Pop, which was passed as an argument when the function was called the previous time.

- The third variable $sessionlatest contains the session_name() function. Now, the value of the session cookie has changed from Pop to Rock.

The output is:

```
X-Powered-By: PHP/4.0.6
Set-Cookie: Heavy Metal=309b6c8a2e72dc4d628dba7d31ff0676; path=/
Expires: Thu, 19 Nov 1981 08:52:00 GMT
Cache-Control: no-store, no-cache, must-revalidate, post-check=0,
pre-check=0
Pragma: no-cache
Content-type: text/html
The old session name was PHPSESSID.
The new session name is Pop!
The latest session name is Rock!!
```

You need to follow a few guidelines when using the `session_name()` function:

- The name assigned for the session should be alphanumeric.

- Special characters, such as tildes (~) and question marks (?), are not allowed.

- The `session_name()` function should always be called before the `session_register()` or `session_start()` function.

Unregistering Variables

You can unregister, or remove, a registered session variable within a PHP script using the `session_unregister()` function. When you use the `session_unregister()` function, the specified variable is removed from the session registry. Therefore, when the session is saved, the session no longer contains that variable. The following code shows how the `session_unregister()` function is used:

```
<?php
session_register('music');
if (session_is_registered('music'))
{
session_unregister('music')
or die ('Could not unregister the session variable');
}
if (session_is_registered('music'))
{
echo "This session is still registered.";
}
else
{
echo "The session has been successfully unregistered!";
}
?>
```

In this code:

- The `session_register()` function is used to register a session named `music`.

- A condition is specified that checks whether the session named `music` is registered. The `session_is_registered()` function is used to do this.

- The `session_unregister()` function is used to unregister the session named `music`.

- The `session_is_registered()` function is called again to check that the specified session variable was successfully unregistered.

The output of this code is:

```
X-Powered-By: PHP/4.0.6
Set-Cookie: PHPSESSID=7b2a5aa26742eb5fd34dc222b8e114f1; path=/
Expires: Thu, 19 Nov 1981 08:52:00 GMT
```

```
Cache-Control: no-store, no-cache, must-revalidate, post-check=0,
pre-check=0
Pragma: no-cache
Content-type: text/html
The session has been successfully unregistered!
```

Deleting Existing Session Variables

To delete a session completely, use the session_destroy() function. It clears all the variables in the current session. The following code shows how the session_destroy() function is used:

NOTE When you use the session_destroy() function, the contents of the session variables are not deleted. To delete them, you need to use the session_unset() function.

```php
<?php
session_start();
session_register("rock");
session_register("pop");
session_register("jazz");
$rock = "I listen to rock!";
$pop = "I listen to pop!";
$jazz = "I listen to jazz!";
$result = session_destroy();
if ($result=1)
{
echo "The session is destroyed!", "\n";
}
else
{
echo "The session could not be destroyed.", "\n";
}
echo $pop;
?>
```

In this code:

- The session_start() function is used to start a session.
- The session_register() function is used three times to register the variables rock, pop, and jazz.
- The variables $rock, $pop, and $jazz are assigned separate values.
- The $result variable is used to store the result of the session_destroy() function.
- The value of the $pop variable is displayed.

The output is:

```
X-Powered-By: PHP/4.0.6
Set-Cookie: PHPSESSID=5f63604c1f1e3adc9962d523f9635f39; path=/
Expires: Thu, 19 Nov 1981 08:52:00 GMT
Cache-Control: no-store, no-cache, must-revalidate, post-check=0,
pre-check=0
Pragma: no-cache
Content-type: text/html
The session is destroyed!
I listen to pop!
```

The output shows that the session was successfully destroyed. However, the value of the variable $pop is still displayed on the screen because the session_destroy() function destroys the session, but the value of the session variable is retained.

Encoding Data

In PHP, it is possible to store all the session variables in the string format and then extract these strings back to the variables. This is done by encoding and decoding data. The session_encode() function is used to encode the current session information to a string. This string can then be decoded to variables using the session_decode() function.

First, let's use the session_encode() function to encode the session information to a text string:

```php
<?php
session_register("rock");
$rock = array("play guitar", "beat drums");
$strrock = session_encode();
$openfile = @fopen("saverock.txt", "w")
            or die ("This operation cannot be performed.");
@fwrite($openfile, $strrock);
@fclose($openfile)
or die ("This operation cannot be performed.");
echo "Success!!";
?>
```

In this code:

- The session_register() function is used to register a session variable named rock.

- The variable $rock is an associative array that has two elements.

- The variable $strrock is used to store the session_encode() function.

- The fopen() function is used to open a file named **saverock.txt** with write permissions.

- The fwrite() function is used to write the session information into **saverock.txt**.

- The fclose() function is used to close the file.

The output   is:

```
X-Powered-By: PHP/4.0.6
Set-Cookie: PHPSESSID=2fff49017853eabad2ece8408ff5a661; path=/
Expires: Thu, 19 Nov 1981 08:52:00 GMT
Cache-Control: no-store, no-cache, must-revalidate, post-check=0,
pre-check=0
Pragma: no-cache
Content-type: text/html
Success!!
```

Let's validate this output by viewing the contents of the file **saverock.txt.** When you open it, it will contain the following:

```
rock|a:2:{i:0;s:11:"play guitar";i:1;s:10:"beat drums";}
```

This shows that the session variable was successfully encoded and the contents were saved in a text file.

Let's now examine how this data can be decoded:

```php
//PART ONE
<?php
session_register("rock");
$rock = array("play guitar", "beat drums");
$strrock = session_encode();
$openfile = @fopen("saverock.txt", "w")
           or die ("This operation cannot be performed.");
@fwrite($openfile, $strrock);
@fclose($openfile)
or die ("This operation cannot be performed.");
echo "Success!!";
//PART TWO
$openfile = @fopen("saverock.txt", "r")
           or die ("Cannot perform the operation.");
$somevar = fread($openfile, filesize($openfile));
fclose ($openfile)
           or die("Cannot perform the operation");
session_decode($somevar);
foreach ($rock as $result)
{
echo "\n", "$result","\n";
}
?>
```

In this code:

■ The first part of the code encodes the data and stores it in the file named **saverock.txt.**

■ In the second part, the fopen() function is used to open the file **saverock.txt** with read permissions.

- The fread() and filesize() functions are used to read the entire contents of the file.

- The fclose() function is used to close the file named **saverock.txt.**

- The session_decode() function is used decode the encoded data.

- The foreach statement is used to loop through the array and display the contents on the screen.

The output is:

```
X-Powered-By: PHP/4.0.6
Set-Cookie: PHPSESSID=96bdd3571c3a41d2a844c08c1c00f8a1; path=/
Expires: Thu, 19 Nov 1981 08:52:00 GMT
Cache-Control: no-store, no-cache, must-revalidate, post-check=0,
pre-check=0
Pragma: no-cache
Content-type: text/html
Success!!
play guitar
beat drums
```

Create the HTML Form That Accepts the Customer ID and Password

Let's write the code for the HTML form that will be used by the user to create an account, and let's name this file **index.htm**:

```html
<html>
<head>
<title>Enter Password</title>
<meta http-equiv="Content-Type" content="text/html; charset=iso-8859-1">
</head>
<body bgcolor="#FFFFFF" text="#000000">
<p> </p>
<p> </p>
<form name="form1" method="post" action="addpass.php">
  <table width="330" border="0" align="center" cellpadding="5"
cellspacing="2">
    <tr>
      <td colspan="2" bgcolor="#dddddd">
        <div align="center"><b>Select a Password</b></div>
      </td>
    </tr>
    <tr bgcolor="#eeeeee">
      <td>
        <div align="right">Customer ID</div>
      </td>
```

```
      <td>
        <input type="text" name="customerid">
      </td>
    </tr>
    <tr bgcolor="#eeeeee">
      <td>
        <div align="right">Password</div>
      </td>
      <td>
        <input type="password" name="password" maxlength="15">
      </td>
    </tr>
    <tr bgcolor="#eeeeee">
      <td>
        <div align="right">Confirm</div>
      </td>
      <td>
        <input type="password" name="cpassword" maxlength="15">
      </td>
    </tr>
    <tr bgcolor="#dddddd">
      <td colspan="2">
        <center>
          <input type="submit" name="Submit" value="Submit">
        </center>
      </td>
    </tr>
  </table>
</form>
</body>
</html>
```

Write the PHP Code to Store the Information in the Database

Now let's write the PHP code that will create the user account and store the customer ID and the password in the database. Let's name this file **addpass.php**.

```
<html>
<head>
<title>Password Result</title>
</head>
<body bgcolor="#FFFFFF" text="#000000">
<p> </p>
<?php
$host="";
$uname="root";
```

```php
$pass="";
$database="megabase";
$tablename="login";
$connection= mysql_connect($host,$uname,$pass)
    or die("Database connection failed! <br>");
$result=mysql_select_db($database)
    or die("Database could not be selected");
$query = "INSERT INTO login VALUES('". $customerid ."', '".
md5($password)
. "')";
$result = mysql_query($query);
if (!query)
{
die(" Query could not be executed.<br>");
}
?>
<table width="330" border="0" align="center" cellpadding="5"
cellspacing="2">
  <tr>
    <td colspan="2" bgcolor="#dddddd">
      <div align="center"><b>New password entered for
        <?php echo $customerid;
          ?>
        as </b></div>
    </td>
  </tr>
  <tr bgcolor="#eeeeee">
    <td width="50%">
      <div align="right">Customer ID</div>
    </td>
    <td>
      <center>
        <?php echo $customerid; ?>
      </center>
    </td>
  </tr>
  <tr bgcolor="#eeeeee">
    <td>
      <div align="right">Password</div>
    </td>
    <td>
      <center>
        <?php echo $password; ?>
      </center>
    </td>
  </tr>
  <tr bgcolor="#eeeeee">
    <td colspan="2"><center>
Try your new password in the <a href="login.htm">
login page</a></center></td>
```

```
    </tr>
  </table>
  <p> </p>
  </body>
  </html>
```

Create the HTML Form That Accepts the Already Set Password

Let's create the HTML form that accepts the password that has already been set by the user, and let's name this file **login.htm**:

```
<html>
<head>
<title>Enter Password</title>
<meta http-equiv="Content-Type" content="text/html; charset=iso-8859-1">
</head>
<body bgcolor="#FFFFFF" text="#000000">
<p> </p>
<p> </p>
<form name="form1" method="GET" action="login.php">
  <table width="330" border="0" align="center" cellpadding="5"
cellspacing="2">
    <tr>
      <td colspan="2" bgcolor="#dddddd">
        <div align="center"><b>Specify your Password</b></div>
      </td>
    </tr>
    <tr bgcolor="#eeeeee">
      <td>
        <div align="right">Customer ID</div>
      </td>
      <td>
        <input type="text" name="customerid">
      </td>
    </tr>
    <tr bgcolor="#eeeeee">
      <td>
        <div align="right">Password</div>
      </td>
      <td>
        <input type="password" name="password">
      </td>
    </tr>
    <tr bgcolor="#dddddd">
      <td colspan="2">
```

```
      <center>
        <input type="submit" name="Submit" value="Login">
      </center>
    </td>
  </tr>
 </table>
</form>
</body>
</html>
```

Write the PHP Script That Validates the Password

Now let's create the PHP script that validates the password specified by the user in the HTML form (login.htm), and let's name this file **login.php**:

```php
<?php
if (empty($password)) { die("No Password specified");}
if ((strlen($password) < 5) || (strlen($password) > 15))
{ die("Password too long/short");}
$host="";
$uname="root";
$pass="";
$database="megabase";
$connection= mysql_connect($host,$uname,$pass)
   or die("Database connection failed! <br>");
$result=mysql_select_db($database)
   or die("Database could not be selected");
$query = "SELECT password from login where customerid='" .$customerid
."'";
$result = mysql_query($query);
if($row=mysql_fetch_array($result))
{
 if(!(md5($password) == $row["password"]))
 {
       die(" Wrong Password!");
 }
}
else
{
die(" User does not exist!!");
}
session_start();
session_register("customerid");
session_encode();
$url= "Location: home1.php?PHPSESSID=".$PHPSESSID;
header($url);
?>
```

Write the PHP Script for the First Private Page

Now let's write the PHP code for the first private Web page of the user, and let's name this file **home1.php**:

```php
<?php
session_start();
if (!(session_is_registered("customerid")))
{
session_unset();
session_destroy();
$url = "Location: login.htm";
header($url);
}
?>
<html>
<head>
<title>First Personal Web Page</title>
<meta http-equiv="Content-Type" content="text/html; charset=iso-8859-1">
</head>
<body bgcolor="#FFFFFF" text="#000000">
<p> </p>
<table width="330" border="0" align="center" cellpadding="5"
cellspacing="2">
  <tr>
    <td colspan="3" bgcolor="#dddddd">
      <div align="center"><b>Welcome to your personal area
        <?php echo $customerid; ?>
        </b></div>
    </td>
  </tr>
  <tr bgcolor="#eeeeee">
    <td colspan="3"> </td>
  </tr>
  <tr bgcolor="#eeeeee">
    <td colspan="3">
      <div align="center"><b>This is Page 1!</b></div>
    </td>
  </tr>
  <tr bgcolor="#eeeeee">
    <td colspan="3"> </td>
  </tr>
  <tr bgcolor="#eeeeee">
    <td width="33%">
      <center>
        Page 1
      </center>
    </td>
    <td width="33%">
```

```
        <center>
<?php
    echo "   <a href=\"home2.php\">Page 2</a>";
?>
        </center>
      </td>
      <td width="33%">
        <center>
          <a href="logout.php">Logout</a>
        </center>
      </td>
   </tr>
</table>
<p> </p>
</body>
</html>
```

Write the PHP Script for the Second Private Page

Now let's write the PHP code for the second private Web page of the user, and let's name this file **home2.php**:

```
<?php
session_start();
if (!(session_is_registered("customerid")))
{
session_unset();
session_destroy();
$url = "Location: login.htm";
header($url);
}
?>
<html>
<head>
<title>Second Personal Web Page</title>
<meta http-equiv="Content-Type" content="text/html; charset=iso-8859-1">
</head>
<body bgcolor="#FFFFFF" text="#000000">
<p> </p>
<table width="330" border="0" align="center" cellpadding="5"
cellspacing="2">
  <tr>
    <td colspan="3" bgcolor="#dddddd">
      <div align="center"><b>Welcome to your personal area
        <?php echo $customerid;
          ?>
        </b></div>
```

```
        </td>
      </tr>
      <tr bgcolor="#eeeeee">
        <td colspan="3"> </td>
      </tr>
      <tr bgcolor="#eeeeee">
        <td colspan="3">
          <div align="center"><b>This is Page 2!</b></div>
        </td>
      </tr>
      <tr bgcolor="#eeeeee">
        <td colspan="3"> </td>
      </tr>
      <tr bgcolor="#eeeeee">
        <td width="33%">
          <center>
<?php
    echo "  <a href=\"home1.php\">Page 1</a>";
?>
          </center>
        </td>
        <td width="33%">
          <center>
            Page 2
          </center>
        </td>
        <td width="33%">
          <center>
            <a href="logout.php">Logout</a>
          </center>
        </td>
      </tr>
    </table>
    <p> </p>
  </body>
</html>
```

Write the PHP Code That Helps the User Log Out

Now let's create the PHP script that will help the user log out, and let's name this file **logout.php**:

```
<?php
session_start();
if (session_is_registered("customerid"))
{
session_unset();
session_destroy();
```

```
$url = "Location: login.htm";
header($url);
}
else
{
 die ("Only logged in users can log out! ");
}
?>
```

Execute the Code

Now let's execute the code using the following steps:

1. Open Netscape Navigator.
2. In the Address box, type http://localhost/index.htm. Figure 14.4 shows the Web page that appears.
3. In the Customer ID box, enter a customer ID.
4. In the Password box, enter a password.
5. In the Confirm box, retype the password.
6. Click the Submit button. Figure 14.5 displays the Web page that appears when you submit the information.

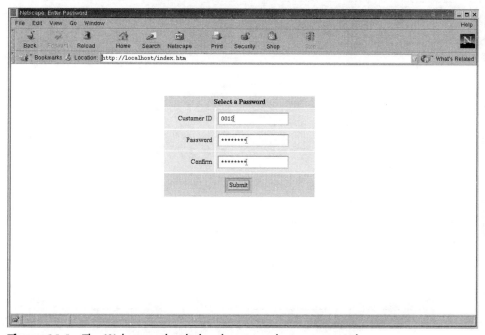

Figure 14.4 The Web page that helps the user select a password.

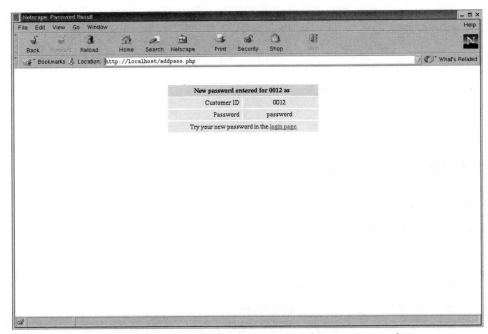

Figure 14.5   The Web page that appears after a user selects a password.

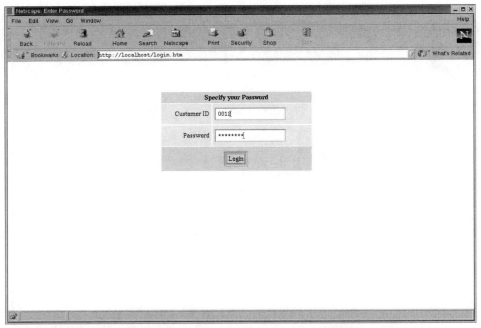

Figure 14.6   The Web page where the user specifies the password to log in.

7. Click the link Page 1 login page to try the new password you have set. Figure 14.6 displays the login page that appears when you click the link.

8. In the Customer ID box, specify your customer ID.

9. In the Password box, type your password.

10. Click the Login button to log in to the first personal Web page. Figure 14.7 shows the Web page that appears when you specify the password.

NOTE Notice that the URL specified in the Address box contains the session ID, which will be used to identify the user in all other Web pages the user accesses.

11. Click the link Page 2 to access the second personal Web page. Figure 14.8 shows the second personal Web page.

12. Click the link Logout to log out of the second personal area.

Figure 14.7   The first personal area Web page.

Figure 14.8   The second personal Web page.

Summary

In this chapter, you learned about the various built-in functions that enable you to maintain sessions. First, you used the `session_register()` function to create a session variable. Then, you used the `session_start()` function to start a PHP session. Next, you learned to set a session name by using the `session_name()` function. Then, you learned to unregister a session variable by using the `session_unregister()` function and delete existing session variables by using the `session_destroy()` function. Finally, you learned to encode and decode data by using the `session_encode()` and `session_decode()` functions.

Sending Email Using PHP

OBJECTIVES:

In this chapter, you will learn to:

- ✔ Send an email using the `mail()` function
- ✔ Create email headers

Getting Started

The age of computers has given birth to the most popular mechanism used for communication, email. It is the most popular and widely used feature of the Internet today. Email has become an inseparable part of daily life, and it is equally as important to a Web site as it is to the end user. In addition to sending and receiving messages, users enjoy benefits such as receiving information and confirmation reports after filling in online forms and gaining access to mailing lists, periodic newsletters, and mass advertisements. For a Web site, email is a way of gaining popularity, which results in multiple users accessing the site on a regular basis.

Sending Email

In this section, you will learn about the procedure for sending email messages using PHP. Now let's examine the case study of Mega Music Mart, where the development team has been assigned an email-related task.

Problem Statement

The marketing team at Mega Music wants to undertake a survey to analyze the satisfaction levels of its customers. To do this, it has planned to accept customer feedback that will be stored in a database. This feedback will then be closely analyzed, and steps will be taken to improve the Web site accordingly. The development team is to accept feedback from the customers and has been given certain specifications for the feedback section. According to the marketing team, the feedback form should include the following fields:

- Name
- Customer ID
- Email address

The marketing team has also specified the questions that should be included in the feedback form:

- How well organized do you find the site?
- How do you rate the collection of music CDs on the site?
- How do you rate the promptness of delivery of CDs?
- How do you rate the services of the customer service department?
- How do you rate the overall effectiveness of the site?

These questions will be analyzed on the basis of the following four parameters:

- Poor
- Satisfactory
- Good
- Excellent

The marketing team wants to include a feature by which a message will be sent immediately to the user who submits the feedback form. To accomplish this, the development team must implement an automated mail system on the Web site. The body of the message should contain a note of thanks to the user. All questions rated as poor should be considered improvement areas, and a note should be sent to the user to confirm that a conscious effort will be made to improve the services. For example, if the CD collection is rated as poor, the user should be sent a message, "We will try to improve our CD collection."

Task List

To accomplish the task assigned to them, the development team will need to perform the following tasks:

- ✔ **Create the customer feedback form**
- ✔ **Create the `feedback` table**
- ✔ **Write the PHP script that sends email messages**
- ✔ **Verify that the mail message is sent**

Understanding Email Basics

Let's first learn to send simple email in the bare minimum format. Later, we will discuss how to use various mail headers to send email. In PHP, the `mail()` function is used to send email. It assumes that you already have a *Simple Mail Transfer Protocol (SMTP)* server set up on your machine. The SMTP server is used to exchange emails on the Internet.

The mail() Function

As discussed earlier, in PHP, mail messages are sent using the built-in `mail()` function, which has several parameters that can be used to send messages. The `mail()` function returns true if the mail is successfully submitted to the local mail system. The syntax of the `mail()` function is:

```
$result = mail($recipient, $subject, $message, $additional_headers);
```

In this syntax:

- The `$recipient` argument accepts a string value and is used to specify the recipient's email address. This attribute can include more than one email address, separated by the comma. You can specify email addresses as follows:

```
//single email address
$result = mail ("musiclover1@megamumart.com");
//multiple email addresses
$result = mail ("musiclover1@megamumart.com,
musiclover2@megamumart.com");
```

- The `$subject` argument accepts a string value and stores the subject of the email message. This argument can be left blank. You can specify a value for this argument as follows:

```
$result = mail ("Thank You For Registering");
```

■ The $message argument accepts a string value and is used to specify the content of the email; it contains the main message body of the email message. It can be left blank. If you wish to store multiple lines in this argument, use \r\n to separate one line from another. You can specify a message as follows:

```
$result = mail ("Hi user!,\r\nThis Is to thank you for the Interest you
have shown In our site.\r\nBye");
```

■ The $additional_headers argument accepts a string value. This argument is optional and is set only when you want to attach text at the end of the email header. You can specify multiple header lines in this argument if you separate each line with \r\n as follows:

```
$result = mail
("From:webm@megamumart.com\r\nReplyTo:admin@megamumart.com");
```

Creating an HTML Form That Accepts Mail-Related Information

Let's create an HTML form that accepts the details and passes them to a PHP script, and let's name this HTML form **mailform.htm:**

```
<html>
<head>
<title>Simple Send Mail Form</title>
</head>
<body bgcolor="#FFFFFF" text="#000000">
<h1 align="center">Mail Form</h1>
<form name="form1" method="post" action="sendmail.php">
  <table width="400" border="1" align="center" bgcolor="cccccc"
bordercolor="#000000" cellpadding="10" cellspacing="0">
    <tr>
      <td>
        <center>
          <b>To</b>
        </center>
      </td>
      <td>
        <input type="text" name="mailto" size="35">
      </td>
    </tr>
    <tr>
      <td>
        <center>
          <b>Subject</b>
        </center>
      </td>
      <td>
        <input type="text" name="mailsubject" size="35">
      </td>
```

```
        </tr>
        <tr>
          <td>
            <center>
              <b>Message</b>
            </center>
          </td>
          <td>
            <textarea name="mailbody" cols="50" rows="7"></textarea>
          </td>
        </tr>
        <tr>
          <td colspan="2">
            <div align="center">
              <input type="submit" name="Submit" value="Send">
            </div>
          </td>
        </tr>
      </table>
  </form>
  <p> </p>
  <p> </p>
  </body>
  </html>
```

In this code:

- An HTML form that accepts user input is created.
- The form has three text fields.
- The first text field To specifies the recipient's email address.
- The second text field Subject specifies a subject for the email.
- The third text field Message specifies the message to be sent.
- The Submit button submits the information.
- The information specified in the form is sent to a PHP script that will process the information and send the mail message to the individual whose email address is specified in the To field.

The HTML form is shown in Figure 15.1.

Writing the PHP Code That Sends Email

Now let's create the PHP script that accepts the form input and sends the email message, and let's name this file **sendmail.php**.

```php
<?php
  if (empty($mailto))
    {
```

```
        die("Recipient is blank!");
  }
 if  (empty($mailsubject))
  {
     $mailsubject="";
  }
 if(empty($mailbody))
  {
     $mailbody="";
  }
 $result = mail($mailto,$mailsubject,$mailbody);
 if ($result)
  {
   echo "<h1><center>Email sent successfully!!</center></h1>";
  }
 else
  {
   echo "<h1><center>Email could not be sent.</center></h1>";
  }
 ?>
```

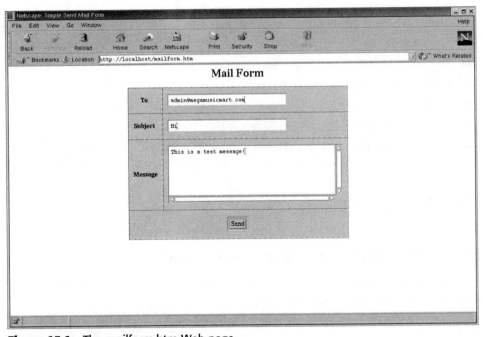

Figure 15.1   The mailform.htm Web page.

In this code:

- The first condition checks the value specified in the To field. If this field is blank, the program closes and the message Recipient is blank! appears.
- The second condition checks the value specified in the Subject field. If it is blank, the mail message is sent without a subject.
- The third condition checks the value specified in the Message field. If no message is specified, a blank email message is sent.
- The variable $result stores the outcome of the mail() function. If the mail is successfully sent to the mail system, the value true is returned. Otherwise, false is returned.
- If the value true is returned, the message Email sent successfully!! appears.
- If the value false is returned, the message Email could not be sent appears.
- The mail() function is used with three arguments.
- The first argument, $mailto, stores the email ID of the recipient.
- The second argument, $mailsubject, contains the subject of the email message.
- The third argument, $mailbody, contains the body of the email message.

The output of the PHP script is shown in Figure 15.2.

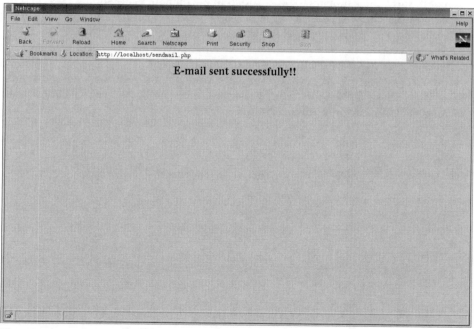

Figure 15.2 The output after the mail is sent successfully.

Creating Mail Headers for the mail() Function

We now know how email messages are sent. Let's learn about some other concepts related to sending email messages by using PHP. As discussed earlier, the `mail()` function allows you to specify various mail headers. Now let's examine the following headers:

From. Displays the email address of the sender.

ReplyTo. Contains the email address to which a reply will be sent when the recipient of the email message clicks the Reply button. This is required only if the ReplyTo address is different from the From address.

Carbon Copies. Specifies the email addresses of those people to whom you want to send a carbon copy of the email. Typically, carbon copies are sent to individuals for information only.

Blind Carbon Copies. Specifies the email address of those individuals whose email ID should not appear when the recipient receives the email message.

Message Priority. Signifies the importance of a message. The values that a client can choose from are:

High. The message is urgent.

Normal. Not urgent and of moderate importance.

Low. Low priority.

Each of the attributes that are to be included in the mail message should be stored in a single variable. This variable can then be passed as a fourth parameter in the mail command as a header. This parameter contains values for various attributes of email. Each attribute is specified in a separate line. This parameter is optional and should be included only if any extra attributes are being defined.

Now, let's create an HTML form that accepts these details from the user and sends an email message in reply. This email message will be sent later using a PHP script. Let's name the HTML form **framemail.htm**.

```
<HTML>
<HEAD>
<TITLE>Mail Form 2</TITLE>
</HEAD>
<BODY bgColor=#ffffff text=#000000>
<DIV align=center><B>Mail Form 2</B></DIV>
<FORM action=sendemail.php method=post name=form1>
<TABLE align=center bgColor=#cccccc border=1 borderColor=#000000
cellPadding=5
```

```
cellSpacing=0 width=400>
  <TBODY>
  <TR>
    <TD>
      <DIV align=right><B>To</B> </DIV></TD>
    <TD>
      <P>Name <INPUT name=mailtoname size=35><BR>E-mail <INPUT
name=mailtomail
      size=35> </P></TD></TR>
  <TR>
    <TD>
      <DIV align=right><B>CC</B></DIV></TD>
    <TD><INPUT name=mailcc size=35> </TD></TR>
  <TR>
    <TD>
      <DIV align=right><B>BCC</B></DIV></TD>
    <TD><INPUT name=mailbcc size=35> </TD></TR>
  <TR>
    <TD>
      <DIV align=right><B>Priority</B></DIV></TD>
    <TD><SELECT name=mailpriority> <OPTION value=1>Highest</OPTION>
<OPTION
      value=2>High</OPTION> <OPTION selected value=3>Normal</OPTION>
<OPTION
      value=4>Low</OPTION> <OPTION value=5>Lowest</OPTION></SELECT>
</TD></TR>
  <TR>
    <TD>
      <DIV align=right><B>Subject </B></DIV></TD>
    <TD><INPUT name=mailsubject size=35> </TD></TR>
  <TR>
    <TD>
      <DIV align=right><B>Message</B> </DIV></TD>
    <TD><TEXTAREA cols=50 name=mailbody rows=7></TEXTAREA> </TD></TR>
  <TR>
<TD colSpan=2>
      <DIV align=center><INPUT name=Submit type=submit value=Submit>
  </DIV></TD></TR></TBODY></TABLE></FORM>
<P> </P>
<P> </P>
</BODY>
</HTML>
```

The HTML page is shown in Figure 15.3.

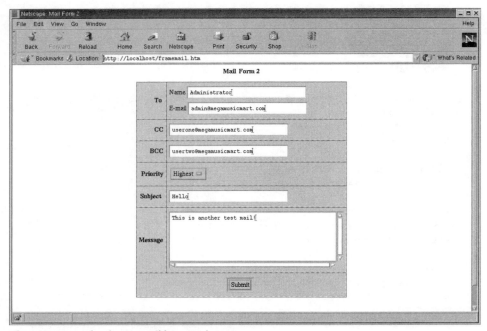

Figure 15.3 The framemail.htm Web page.

Now let's write the PHP script to send the email, and let's name this PHP script **sendemail.php**.

```
<html>
<head>
<title>Mail Sent</title>
</head>
<body bgcolor="#FFFFFF" text="#000000">
<?php
$message="";
  if (empty($mailtoname) || empty($mailtomail))
  {
    die("Recipient is blank!");
  }
  else
  {
    $to = $mailtoname . " <" . $mailtomail . ">";
  }
  if (empty($mailsubject))
  {
```

```php
      $mailsubject="";
    }
  if(($mailpriority>0) && ($mailpriority<6))
  {
    $mailheader = "X-Priority: ". $mailpriority ."\n";
  }
  $mailheader.=  "From: "        . "Sales Team
<sales@megamusicmart.com>\n";
  $mailheader.=  "X-Sender: "    . "support@megamusicmart.com\n";
  $mailheader.=  "Return-Path: " . "steve@megamusicmart.com\n";
  if (!empty($mailcc))
  {
    $mailheader.=  "Cc: "        . $mailcc  ."\n";
  }
  if (!empty($mailbcc))
  {
    $mailheader.=  "Bcc: "       . $mailbcc ."\n";
  }
  if(empty($mailbody))
   {
      $mailbody="";
   }
  $result = mail($to,$mailsubject,$mailbody,$mailheader);
  echo "<center><b>Mail sent to "."$to"."\n<br>";
  echo $mailsubject."\n<br>";
  echo $mailbody."\n<br>";
 // echo $mailheader."\n<br>";
  if ($result)
   {
    echo "<p><b>Email sent successfully!</b></p>";
   }
  else
   {
    echo "<p><b>Email could not be sent.</b></p>";
   }
?>
<div align="center">
  <table width="400" border="1" align="center" bgcolor="cccccc"
bordercolor="#000000" cellpadding="5" cellspacing="0">
    <tr>
      <td width="66">
        <div align="right"><b>To</b> </div>
      </td>
      <td width="308">
<b>
<?php
echo $mailtoname ." [". $mailtomail . "]";
?>
```

```
      </b>
      </td>
        </tr>
        <tr>
          <td width="66">
            <div align="right"><b>CC</b></div>
          </td>
          <td width="308">
<b>
<?php
echo $mailcc;
?>
</b>
 </td>
        </tr>
        <tr>
          <td width="66">
            <div align="right"><b>BCC</b></div>
          </td>
          <td width="308">
<b>
<?php
echo $mailbcc;
?>
</b>
</td>
        </tr>
        <tr>
          <td width="66">
            <div align="right"><b>Priority</b></div>
          </td>
          <td width="308">
<b>
<?php
echo $mailpriority;
?>
</b>
</td>
        </tr>
        <tr>
          <td width="66">
            <div align="right"><b>Subject </b> </div>
          </td>
          <td width="308">
<b>
<?php
echo $mailsubject;
```

```
?>
</b>
 </td>
    </tr>
    <tr>
      <td width="66">
        <div align="right"><b>Message</b> </div>
      </td>
      <td width="308">
<b>
<?php
echo $mailbody;
?>
</b>
 </td>
    </tr>
  </table>
  <p> </p>
</div>
</body>
</html>
```

In this code:

- The information from the mail form is received. PHP automatically creates variables for each form control.

- The $to attribute is formed by combining the name and email address of the recipient.

- The $subject is the subject specified in the mail message. If the subject is not specified, the variable $subject is assigned a blank string value.

- X-Priority: is added to the mail header preceding the $mailpriority value.

- From: followed by an address tells the mail client the email address of the individual who framed the mail.

- Reply-To: followed by an email address is added to the header to specify the reply address.

- The mail() function is called with four parameters; $to, $mailsubject, $mailbody and $mailheader.

- The program closes if the mail is not sent.

- A report of the sent mail in a table format is displayed in the browser.

The output of the PHP script is shown in Figure 15.4.

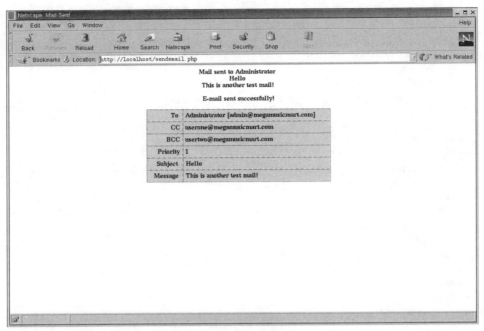

Figure 15.4 The output after sending the email message.

Create the Feedback Form

According to the specifications laid down by the marketing team, the development team creates an HTML form to accept user feedback by writing the following code and saving it in a file named **feedback.htm**:

```
<html>
<head>
<title>Feedback Form</title>
</head>
<body bgcolor="#FFFFFF" text="#000000">
<h1 align="center">Feedback Form</h1>
<form name="form1" method="post" action="feedback.php">
  <table width="573" border="0" align="center" bgcolor="cccccc"
bordercolor="#000000" cellpadding="3" cellspacing="1">
    <tr>
      <td colspan="4"> </td>
    </tr>
    <tr>
      <td width="116"> </td>
```

```html
        <td width="76">
          <div align="left"><b>Name</b> </div>
        </td>
        <td width="258">
          <input type="text" name="name" size="35">
        </td>
        <td width="94"> </td>
      </tr>
      <tr>
        <td width="116"> </td>
        <td width="76">
          <div align="left"><b>Email</b> </div>
        </td>
        <td width="258">
          <input type="text" name="email" size="35">
        </td>
        <td width="94"> </td>
      </tr>
    </table>
    <table width="573" border="0" align="center" cellpadding="3"
cellspacing="1" bgcolor="#CCCCCC">
      <tr bgcolor="cccccc" bordercolor="#000000">
        <td colspan="3"> </td>
      </tr>
      <tr bgcolor="cccccc" bordercolor="#000000">
        <td width="22">
          <div align="center"><b>1</b></div>
        </td>
        <td width="439">How well organized do you find the Web site ?</td>
        <td width="101">
          <select name="organized">
            <option value="0">Select</option>
            <option value="1">Poor</option>
            <option value="2">Satisfactory</option>
            <option value="3">Good</option>
            <option value="4">Excellent</option>
          </select>
        </td>
      </tr>
      <tr bgcolor="cccccc" bordercolor="#000000">
        <td width="22">
          <div align="center"><b>2</b></div>
        </td>
        <td width="439">How do you rate the collection of music CDs on the
site?
          </td>
        <td width="101">
          <select name="collection">
            <option value="0">Select</option>
            <option value="1">Poor</option>
```

```
          <option value="2">Satisfactory</option>
          <option value="3">Good</option>
          <option value="4">Excellent</option>
        </select>
      </td>
    </tr>
    <tr bgcolor="cccccc" bordercolor="#000000">
      <td width="22">
        <div align="center"><b>3</b></div>
      </td>
      <td width="439">How do you rate the promptness of delivery of CDs
?</td>
      <td width="101">
        <select name="promptness">
          <option value="0">Select</option>
          <option value="1">Poor</option>
          <option value="2">Satisfactory</option>
          <option value="3">Good</option>
          <option value="4">Excellent</option>
        </select>
      </td>
    </tr>
    <tr bgcolor="cccccc" bordercolor="#000000">
      <td width="22">
        <div align="center"><b>4</b></div>
      </td>
      <td width="439">How do you rate the services of the Customer Care
department
        ? </td>
      <td width="101">
        <select name="customerservice">
          <option value="0">Select</option>
          <option value="1">Poor</option>
          <option value="2">Satisfactory</option>
          <option value="3">Good</option>
          <option value="4">Excellent</option>
        </select>
      </td>
    </tr>
    <tr bgcolor="cccccc" bordercolor="#000000">
      <td width="22">
        <div align="center"><b>5</b></div>
      </td>
      <td width="439">How do you rate the overall effectiveness of the
site ?</td>
      <td width="101">
        <select name="overall">
          <option value="0">Select</option>
          <option value="1">Poor</option>
          <option value="2">Satisfactory</option>
          <option value="3">Good</option>
```

```
            <option value="4">Excellent</option>
          </select>
        </td>
      </tr>
      <tr>
        <td width="22"> </td>
        <td width="439"> </td>
        <td width="101"> </td>
      </tr>
      <tr>
        <td colspan="3">
          <div align="center">
            <input type="submit" name="Submit" value="Submit">
          </div>
        </td>
      </tr>
    </table>
    <p> </p>
</form>
<p> </p>
<p> </p>
</body>
</html>
```

The HTML form is shown In Figure 15.5.

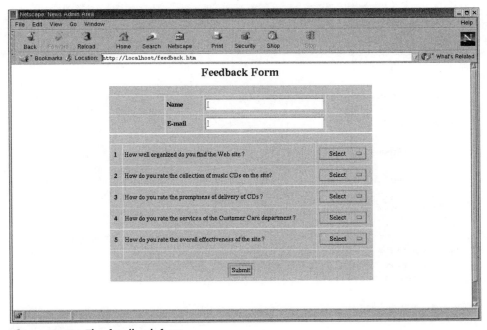

Figure 15.5   The feedback form.

Create the Feedback Table

To store the feedback information, the development team has decided to create a table named `feedback` in the `megabase` database using the following command:

```
mysql> create table feedback (organized varchar(1) not null,
collection varchar(1) not null,
promptness varchar(1) not null,
customerservice varchar(1) not null, overall varchar(1) not null);
```

Write the PHP Script That Sends Email

After creating the HTML form that accepts feedback from the user, the development team needs to create the PHP script that processes the information specified. Let's name this script **feedback.php**.

```
<html>
<head>
<title>Feedback Page</title>
</head>
<body bgcolor="#FFFFFF" text="#000000">
<?php
$message="";
  if (empty($name))
    {
      die("Recipient name is blank!");
    }
  if (empty($email))
    {
      die("Recipient email is blank!");
    }
    else
    {
      $to = $name . " <" . $mailtomail . ">";
    }
  $mailsubject =" Thank You! ";
  $mailheader.=  "From: ". "Mega Music Mart
<feedback@megamusicmart.com>\n";
  $mailheader.=  "Reply-To: "    . "feedback@megamusicmart.com\n";
  $mailheader.=  "Return-Path: " . "feedback@megamusicmart.com\n";
  if (($organized==5) ||
      ($collection==5) ||
      ($promptness==5) ||
      ($customerservice==5) ||
      ($overall==5))
  {
```

```
    die ("Incomplete form! ");
}
    $mailbody = "Thank you for showing interest in filling out our
feedback form.\n";
if ($organized ==1) { $mailbody.= " We will try to improve our site
structure.\n";  }
if ($collection ==1) { $mailbody.= "We will try to improve our CD
collection.\n";  }
if ($promptness ==1) { $mailbody.= "We will try to improve our
promptness.\n";  }
if ($customerservice ==1) {$mailbody.="We will try to improve our
Customer Care department.\n";}
if ($overall ==1) { $mailbody.= "we will try to improve the overall
effectiveness of our site.\n";  }
    $mailbody.=" Mega Music Mart team.";
  $result = mail($email,$mailsubject,$mailbody,$mailheader);
  if ($result)
   {
    echo "<p><h1><center>Email sent successfully!!</center></h1></p>";
   }
  else
   {
    echo "<p><b>Email could not be sent.</b></p>";
   }
  $hostname="";
  $database="megabase";
  $dbusername="root";
  $dbpassword="";
  $result=mysql_connect($hostname,$dbusername,$dbpassword) or die("Could
not connect");
  $result=mysql_select_db($database) or die("Could not select
database");
  $query = "INSERT into feedback VALUES('". $organized."','"
.$collection."','".$promptness. "','". $customerservice. "','".
$overall. "')";
//  echo $query;
  $result=mysql_query($query);
?>
<h1><center>Thank you for your time! </center></h1>
</body>
</html>
```

Verify That the Mail Message Was Sent

After creating the application, the development team wants to find out if the application is working properly. To test the application, perform the following steps:

1. Open Netscape Navigator.
2. In the Address box, type `http://localhost/feedback.htm`.
   A feedback form appears.
3. In the Name section, type the username.
4. In the Email section, specify a valid email ID.
5. Fill out the questionnaire. Figure 15.6 illustrates a filled-in feedback form.
6. Submit the form (Figure 15.7).

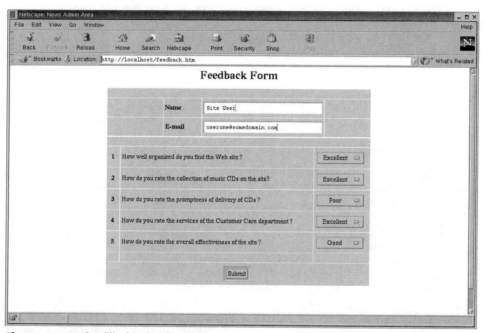

Figure 15.6   The filled in feedback form.

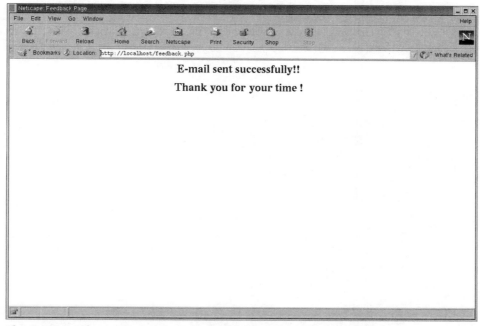

Figure 15.7 The confirmation Web page that appears after the mail is sent.

Summary

In this chapter, you learned to send email messages using PHP. You learned to use the `mail()` built-in function to send email messages. Finally, you learned to use email headers to create a detailed mail format.

Index